# MORE VOICES, NEW STORIES

# MORE VOICES, NEW STORIES
## KING COUNTY, WASHINGTON'S FIRST 150 YEARS

### EDITED BY MARY C. WRIGHT
WITH AN INTRODUCTION BY CHARLES P. LEWARNE

A Project of the Pacific Northwest Historians Guild
Seattle, Washington

King County
Landmarks & Heritage Commission
Hotel/Motel Tax Fund

The Pacific Northwest Historians Guild
Post Office Box 85457
Seattle, Washington 98145-1457

ISBN 0-295-98310-8
Library of Congress Control Number: 2002112815

Distributed by
University of Washington Press
P.O Box 50096
Seattle, WA 98145-5096
www.washington.edu/uwpress

Book design by Amy Allsopp, Divine Design
www.getdivine.com

Front Cover: Franklin Mine Company, 1904, courtesy of the Washington State Historical Society. International District Vietnamese green grocer, courtesy of the *International Examiner*. Back Cover: a Seattle crowd, courtesy of the Museum of History and Industry.

The paper used in this publication meets the minimum requirements of the American National Standard for Information Sciences—Permanence of Paper for Printed Library Materials, ANSI Z39.48-1984.

# CONTENTS

# ILLUSTRATIONS

# PREFACE

Mary C. Wright

Times of reckoning come around with anniversaries and birthdays. It's the perfect time to celebrate but also to think about the past, how we got to where we are today, and what the future might hold. Reflection is an important exercise, especially when it comes to community history and the heritage of our collective past.

Historical insights and images flood us when we look back over the past 150 years of our metropolitan area, King County, Washington. The growth of Seattle and King County rests on the early support and cooperation of the Indian people. Many indigenous people of the area, after living here for thousands of years, welcomed and accepted the newcomers, who brought new wealth and opportunities. In the late 18th and early 19th centuries, European and American explorers and fur traders charted the Northwest, primarily by sea. Beginning in the mid-19th century, Americans arrived to settle. With the Americans' early logging, mining, trade, and other economic activities came the pressing need for workers. Chinese immigrants were among the first to answer the call for labor in the American West, but with the completion of the railroads in the 1880s, the region nearly burst with population growth. Most were American citizens from other parts of the nation, but many were European immigrants. Later, other groups came, including Asians, Latinos and African Americans.

This mosaic of different people, their cultures and contributions is what makes our region unique, interesting, and still growing after 150 years. Curiosity about the lives, ways, and histories of the common people has motivated scholars in the last 30 years to look for innovative ways to recover their history. Often buried or previously ignored, the lives of ordinary people, various ethnic groups, men and women, social and cultural institutions—not just our generals, presidents and other civic, business and political leaders—became subjects for study. The *More Voices, New Stories* project itself is part of this trend in academic history since three of our writers are from the University of Washington. Several others hold doctorates in history.

Scholarly interest in the montage of people in the region has been supplemented by the growth of the heritage community. Recent decades have seen the blossoming of historical societies, museums, websites, local history books, and organizations founded to document and interpret a particular culture. Popular enthusiasm and interest in history is now widespread and goes beyond the purview of the academic historian. Many of the writers from the *More Voices, New Stories* project are from this group of independent scholars, history enthusiasts, and ethnic community activists.

Mixing the two perspectives on local history—academic and community-based—was one of the main purposes of the *More Voices, New Stories* project of the Pacific Northwest Historians Guild. The Historians Guild itself is a diverse group of historians from a wide range of backgrounds and interests, such as archivists, museum professionals, teachers, preservationists, independent scholars, oral historians, and more. Founded in 1981, the Guild's purpose is to preserve, promote, and publish Pacific Northwest history. Although the *More Voices, New Stories* book is the group's most ambitious project to date, each year in March a local history conference is held. It is open to the public and has an interesting array of history talks and presentations. Most of the studies in this book were previously offered at the Historians Guild conference. Visit the organization's web page (www.pnwhistorians.org) to learn more about the conference, Guild activities, functions, and members.

King County's history can be understood in many ways, beyond what we present in this book. Persons interested in historical perspectives such as population increase, institutional growth, and government policies might consult the County's web page (www.metrokc.gov/kc150). Another good framework for local history is the *Seattle and King County Timeline* by Walt Crowley and the HistoryLink staff. Their website (www.historylink.org) covers local history and adds new materials constantly. Charles P. LeWarne's *Washington State* textbook and *Washington: A Centennial History* with Robert E. Ficken are also good starting places. The recent three-volume book series on Seattle history by Richard C. Berner has a wealth of information about the city's past, from 1900 to 1950. *Washington Territory* by Robert E. Ficken has just been released. On-going publications covering local and regional history are the *Pacific Northwest Quarterly*, published by the University of Washington, and *Columbia, The Magazine of Northwest History*, published by the Washington State Historical Society.

Interested in doing historical study? Seattle is fortunate to be the location of the National Archives and Records Administration, Pacific Alaska Region branch that offers wonderful research opportunities (www.nara.gov/regional/seattle). Other government records are available at the King County Archives and the City of Seattle Archives. The University of Washington Libraries (www.lib.washington.edu) also has an extensive collection in local and regional history. The Museum of History and Industry (www.seattlehistory.org) has excellent exhibits and an important archival collection, as does the Washington State Historical Society in Tacoma (www.wshs.org). Smaller museums are well worth seeking out, such as West Seattle's Log Cabin Museum and many others throughout the county. You can begin to explore local history at any of these sites.

I first proposed the idea for this project to the Historians Guild in 1999. Finding the funding, bringing together those interested in researching new aspects of Northwest history, and managing the publication tasks necessary to bring the book to fruition has been a fulfilling challenge. Despite my role, the *More Voices, New Stories* project and book could not have been completed without the help and hard work of many people. First and foremost has been the Board of Trustees of the Pacific Northwest Historians Guild who gave constant support. Thank you to Judy Bentley, Cork Hardinge, Judy Green, Lorraine McConaghy, Peri Muhich, Walter Neary, Paul Spitzer, and 2002 President Chuck Richards.

Knowledge about book publishing and a willingness to share their experience came from Doug Chin, Gail Dubrow, Kim McKaig, and Judy Bentley, and especially Jackie Williams. Karen Blair, Ron Chew, Paul Dorpat, Bruce Hevly, and Carla Rickerson contributed their professional expertise and assistance to the project. Holly Taylor, with the King County Office of Cultural Resources, shepherded us through the process. Making the book better were Merriam Bulhmer, copyeditor, and Amy Allsopp who designed both the book and its cover.

Photographs shared by many institutions help make the book more interesting. Our closest supporters in this regard have been Carolyn Marr from the Museum of History and Industry and Nicolette Bromberg and the staff at the University of Washington Libraries (Manuscripts, Special Collections, and University Archives). Other sources for our photographs have been the Washington State Historical Society, Renton Historical Society, Buddhist Temple Archives, Ellensburg Public Library, Seattle Community College District, the *Seattle Times*, and the *International Examiner*, and many others. Credits are listed with each photograph.

Important funding for this project came from King County's Office of Cultural Resources. All the visitors and business people who come to our area have contributed through the hotel/motel tax, a small portion of which is set aside by the county for cultural development. The Henry M. Jackson Foundation granted us support at a critical time. For their donations, we would also like to thank the Seattle Foundation and the Historians Guild group "Friends of History" (alphabetically): Judith Bentley, Richard Berner, Charles LeWarne, Walter Neary, Carla Rickerson and anonymous donors.

A final thank you is in order to all the historians whose essays make up this collection. The process of editing and publishing was made lighter by their patience and cheerful cooperation. Opinions offered are those of the writers and not of the Pacific Northwest Historians Guild.

The many people who have contributed to the book hope the reader finds it enjoyable, enlightening, and a good appetizer for a more thorough investigation of local history.

Mary C. Wright, Editor
American Indian Studies and the Department of History
University of Washington
Seattle

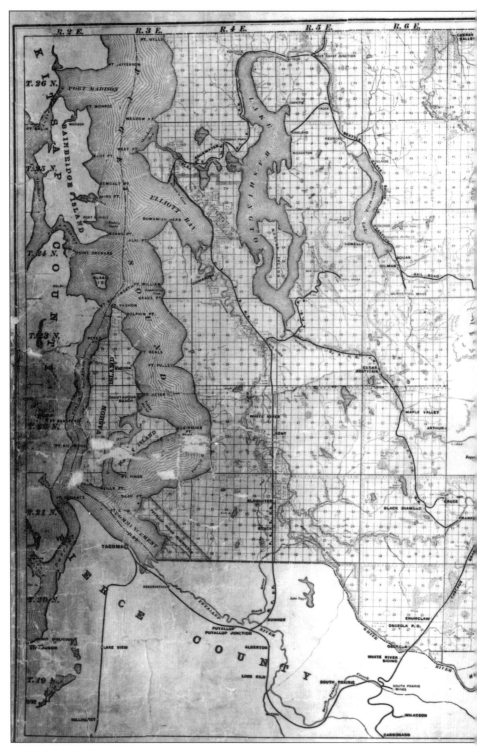

1888 King County map: Courtesy of the Museum of History and Industry.

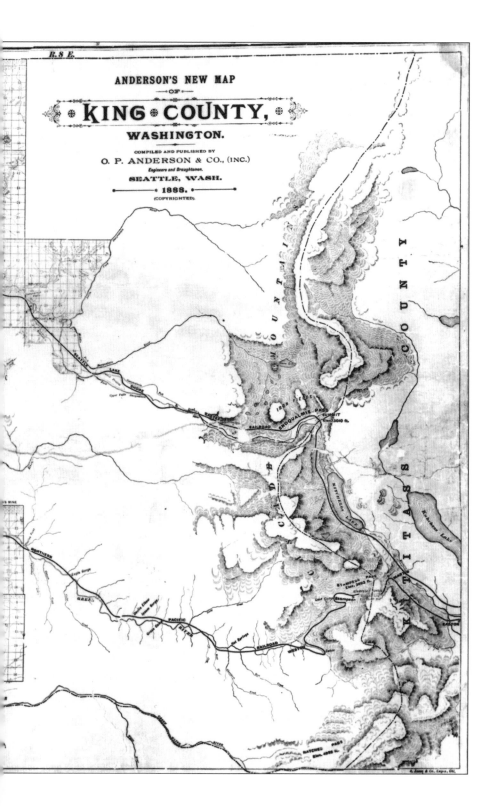

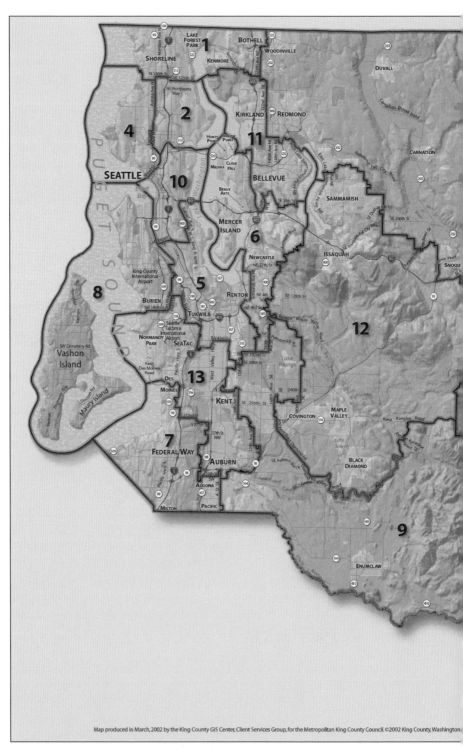

2002 Metropolitan King County Council Districts map. Available for public use, courtesy of King County from their website (www.metrokc.gov/gis).

MT. BAKER-

Tolt Reservoir

SKYKOMISH ②

**3**

ALPINE LAKES

SNOQUALMIE

WILDERNESS AREA

RTH
ND

NATIONAL ⑨⓪

hester Morse
Lake

FOREST

N
W E
S

0 1 2 3 4 5 6 7 8 9 10
MILES

0 1 2 3 4 5 6 7 8 9 10
KILOMETERS

**King County**

# INTRODUCTION

## A BRIEF HISTORY OF SEATTLE AND KING COUNTY

### Charles P. LeWarne

On a drizzly November day in 1851, 10 adults and 12 children came ashore from the schooner *Exact* to a point on Puget Sound they would call Alki. Thus, the Denny Party, so known for its leader, 29-year-old Arthur Denny, stepped onto the beach and into an enduring place in the history of Seattle and King County. Denny's younger brother David and Lee Terry had been there several weeks and were awaiting them with a partly completed cabin. The Denny Party stayed the winter on that point before Arthur Denny, Carson Boren, and William Bell crossed the bay behind them to seek out a site more preferable. They found a sloping hillside instead of the cliffs that blocked growth and hindered logging at Alki. They also found—by dropping at various points a horseshoe attached to a fishing line, according to legend—water deep enough that boats could come close in. And the new site would allow them to avoid the problems of a point buffeted by winds, changing tides, and converging water flow. Shortly, most of the party would move to this new spot, acquire acreage, plat lots, build houses, attract newcomers, start fledgling industries, form a government, and thus create the fabric of a community. Their village would stretch along the shore as these men created the city and the county that were destined to dominate the region.[1]

But wait!

In *More Voices, New Stories*, Kay Reinartz reminds readers that other settlers had arrived that same year—quite likely before the Denny Party—to settle alongside the Duwamish River south and inland from Alki. Centering around the leadership of Luther and Diana Collins, they, too, divided and worked the land, started homes, and played a vital role in the growing political and economic life of the area.

In another essay, Coll-Peter Thrush relates the same event, the Denny Party's arrival, and adds another dimension. He focuses on the landing point itself and its place in the life of Native Americans and of others who also touched that spot. He poses questions about when and how the "creation" of Seattle occurred and how the Denny story took on a local mythic character.

And so it is with the seeking out and the telling and the interpreting of history. The Duwamish settlers were never unknown, and the spot where they landed had other roles, but these facts have rarely been more than an adjunct to the story of the Dennys. History, it has been said, is the story told by the victors—or at least the survivors. The first chroniclers of Seattle's history included members of pioneer families and others who knew those first settlers. The Denny family and others of their group have continued into present generations to contribute in diverse ways to the development of Seattle and King County, while the Duwamish families largely subsided into obscurity and Alki Point became a pleasant outpost apart from the bustling city.

The role of the Denny Party is secure, and deservedly. But the telling of history is flexible enough to entertain new and divergent ideas. As the history of King County became familiar, "more voices" and "new stories" arose to challenge the old. Four decades ago, writers such as Murray Morgan and Bill Speidel poked pleasurable fun at many of the founders, filling in gaps with different interpretations, suggesting new heroes and heroines.[2] Others, including scholars, investigated specific and sometimes obscure aspects of the history. In recent decades small communities and neighborhoods, some initially empowered by the U.S. bicentennial celebrations of 1976, have produced local histories, and such efforts continue to pour forth. Formal historians always grapple with new trends and interpretations that broaden conventional accounts. The authors in this volume belong to that line as they bring to light groups and facets not truly forgotten but never wholly developed—a part of King County history that is as significant as the traditional account.

But what of that traditional account? The Denny group, along with such partners, rivals, and foils as Carson Boren, Henry Yesler, and David Maynard, comprises the first stand in a line of leaders that extends to Dorothy Bullitt, Bill Gates, and Ron Sims today. Their story should never be forgotten or ignored, even as the stories of new groups and elements receive deserved recognition. That is the function of this essay, to remind readers of the familiar and to extend it beyond Seattle and into the county as a backdrop for the thoughtful additions by both well-known and promising new historians that make up this volume.

Arthur Denny, Boren, and Bell secured land on the eastern shore of Elliott Bay and laid the foundation of a village. Maynard, Yesler, Thomas Mercer, Dexter Horton, and others whose names would remain familiar in Seattle arrived in those earliest years. The town took shape around Yesler's steam-powered sawmill, a few stores, a hotel, meeting places, and rough-hewn houses on the hillside. Yesler's wharf became a stopping point for boats plying the Sound. Logs from the hillside and fish from the deep waters could be shipped, largely to California, at a profit. Seattle was not the only such village on Puget Sound, but by the end of 1852 the Oregon Territorial Legislature had made it the seat of a newly created county, and the pioneers passed offices around among themselves. The next spring a post office opened. A pioneer civilization flourished as Seattle got under way.[3]

National events were rapidly affecting the recently acquired northwest corner of the United States. On March 2, 1853, two days before leaving office,

Pictures are rare of the man for whom King County was originally named, William R. D. King, Vice President of the United States when he died in 1853. This drawing was printed in the *Democratic Review* in August 1852.

President Millard Fillmore signed the act establishing the Territory of Washington; it seemed fitting that two of its counties should honor the new president, Franklin Pierce, and his vice president, William R. D. King. Formerly a representative from his native North Carolina, King had enjoyed a distinguished career both as an overseas diplomat and as a senator from Alabama. He was among those who strove to achieve compromise as relations deteriorated between his South and his nation. As president pro tem of the Senate, he was next in line for the presidency after the death of Zachary Taylor propelled Fillmore into the White House. But King died only weeks after being inaugurated as vice president. That he owned slaves in pre–Civil War America did not then offend people. Attitudes change, and in 1986 King County officially altered the person honored by the county's name from William R. D. King to the civil rights leader Dr. Martin Luther King, Jr.[4] Other changes to King County occurred in 1857 when it lost the western portion to newly formed Kitsap County.[5]

Throughout the 1850s Seattle remained small, but it was growing. "Life in the village was serious and strenuous," wrote Clarence C. Bagley, a historian who had known the pioneers. "The friendship of neighbors was the principal source of good cheer, dispelling gloom. Neighbors visited each other, and those occasions were holidays for the visitors and the visited. Evening prayer meetings, spelling schools, and singing schools were means of assembling the community, and occasionally, questions of public concern were debated at meetings of the library associations,

Without having to change its name, the county changed its designated honoree to Dr. Martin Luther King, Jr., in 1986. The Seattle Community Colleges have honored this King with an annual celebration since 1974. Pictured is the 1997 event held at Mt. Zion Baptist Church, Seattle. Courtesy of the Seattle Community Colleges.

which existed without a library or other means of interesting the members."[6] He told of the first wedding and a new two-story building used for dances. The town expanded north along the shoreline during its first decade, but the 1860 census recorded only 275 Euro-Americans as living in the entire county.[7]

Life was both eased and exacerbated by Indian contacts. The immediate neighbors were friendly Suquamish and Duwamish Indians who greatly aided the newcomers. A personal friendship with their chief, Sealth or Seattle, led to the town's name. But wars against Indians throughout the territory in the middle 1850s also left a mark. Two incidents occurred in the White River Valley near present-day Auburn; nine American settlers were killed there late in 1855. A threatened attack on Seattle itself a few weeks later was quelled when a naval ship in the harbor fired a cannon.

Over time additional industries joined logging in Seattle, many also related to forest products. They included a planed lumber mill, sash and door manufacturers, a grist mill, a foundry and metal shop, and ship manufacturing. City fathers learned to work situations to their advantage. In the territorial legislature, Arthur Denny secured a university in the deal that parceled needed institutions around the territory. Its construction brought in workers, many of whom stayed. When the Northern Pacific Railway placed its northwestern terminus in Tacoma, Seattle's city fathers created their own railroad line, the Seattle and Walla Walla, which they intended to cross the mountains to eastern Washington; failing in that, it fortunately connected Seattle with coal mines near Renton. Such early events led booster-historians to promote the concept of a highly vaunted "Seattle spirit."

Even though timber dominated early development, coal was the resource responsible for opening areas southeast of Seattle when veins were found in the 1850s. These discoveries prompted the creation of Renton and Newcastle, and the short and short-lived railroad allowed the transport of the coal to Seattle and farther on by ship. Later in the century, coal was found elsewhere in the foothills, at places such as Black Diamond and Ravensdale. Communities, some of which disappeared after the coal deposits were depleted, sprang up, further opening the area to settlement.

A persisting feature of Seattle's growth involved altering the natural landscape and environment to allow urban growth. Stumps were uprooted and trails graded along the hillsides to facilitate north-south passage. Early on, city fathers realigned an irregular shoreline, and as early as 1876 they regraded a portion of Yesler Way east up the hillside and First Avenue north from Yesler Way to Pike Street. Some of these early efforts went astray amid mudslides and political squabbling. But they foreshadowed massive future endeavors at the turn of the next century. To a considerable extent, the history of Seattle is that of people trying to gain mastery over the geography they found.

City fathers also looked to the nearby hinterland. They saw the potential to benefit their own town. Routes up rivers and across hills and mountains opened places that were valued less for themselves than for their potential to assist Seattle. Crops from new farmlands in fertile valleys and lowlands fed the population, and the excess was shipped out. The Cedar River watershed provided water and later electricity to the city; eventually massive hydroelectric plants reshaped the more distant upper Skagit Valley. When Seattleites sought recreation outside their own limits, lakes, rivers, and mountains beckoned. For the most part, the people of Seattle saw outlying King County as tributary to their own needs.

But the people who began to settle east of Seattle must clearly have viewed their communities as entities in their own right. By the 1870s, when the Alki and Duwamish settlements were two decades old, settlers, usually out of Seattle, began to stake out properties east of Lake Washington. William Casto opened a trading post at Issaquah in 1863, but his Indian workers killed him, his young wife, and a friend a few months later.[8] By 1870 a single voting precinct encompassed the entire east side of Lake Washington.[9]

William Meydenbauer secured land on the eastern shore of Lake Washington and Aaron Mercer claimed the slough a few miles east; both sites are now part of Bellevue. Meydenbauer never lived on his claim, but Aaron and Ann Mercer and their baby occupied a cabin on their property for a short time. By the spring of 1871 Luke McRedmond had found the fertile land fed and drained by streams at the northern end of Lake Sammamish, and the village of Redmond took his name. Nearby, Mr. And Mrs. Warren Wentworth Perrigo established Melrose House, an inn that became a stopping point for travelers and prospective settlers. Soon Perrigo's brother arrived to set up a trading post. According to the Redmond historian Nancy Way, the 60-mile journey from Seattle to Redmond might require two weeks: "They went from the Seattle waterfront up the Duwamish River, into the Black River, then north across Lake Washington and up the Sammamish River."[10] George R. Wilson and Columbus Greenleaf had staked rival claims near present-day Woodinville before Mr. And Mrs. Ira Woodin arrived in 1871. The Woodins had a garden and an orchard and produced milk for sale in Seattle. Homes began appearing all along the Squak (Sammamish) River, many owned by Scandinavians. Within a few years several boats were making runs up the river, a journey hampered by sand bars and sunken logs. By the middle 1880s, Bothell had all the accoutrements of a town, with stores, professional activities, and the means to provide services to mills, homesteads, and logging camps.[11]

The Seattle-based Seattle, Lake Shore & Eastern Railroad Company, which was eventually acquired by the Northern Pacific, began to lay track around the northern side of Lake Washington, hoping to eventually link up with the Canadian Pacific and then along the eastern shore of Lake Sammamish. Thus the area farthest east in the county was opened. Loggers, farmers, and coal miners benefited from the ability to reach closer toward the mountains, affecting settlement there.[12]

From the earliest days some Seattle leaders were eyeing the Cascade Mountains, knowing that a passage through would open Seattle to a vast eastern region and its products. Railroad surveys in the mid-1850s had found two possible passes near Snoqualmie; J. H. Van Bokkelen located the route eventually used by a railroad and then the cross-state highway.[13] In the 1860s a crude wagon road was built. By the end of that decade a herd of cattle had been driven across, the start of a regular source for Seattle meatpackers. And in 1887 Arthur Denny himself was part of a Seattle group that crossed Snoqualmie Pass. Local leaders sought government funds for a mail route and hoped for railroad construction. But the road remained a doubtful proposition until the Milwaukee Road built, in the early 1900s, a line that required a two-mile-long tunnel at the pass. After that, the eastern part of King County was more open to settlement, and goods from the Kittitas and Yakima valleys passed via rail to Seattle and beyond.[14]

When Washington's first official census was taken a year after the territory gained statehood in 1889, almost 43,000 people lived in Seattle, about two-thirds of the county's population of 64,000.[15] Areas outside the city had been growing in the late 1800s. If they seemed to be essentially tributary to their large neighbor on Elliott Bay, individual towns and areas were nevertheless developing in ways that gave each its own clear character and right of being. Although different communities had distinctive features, perhaps one can be used as representative of their general characteristics. "Downtown Redmond circa 1890 was little more than a collection of three or four odd buildings," writes the town's historian. The buildings were spread far apart, and not even wooden sidewalks connected them. The occasional dirt streets "didn't seem to go anywhere important." But the town's first "real store" was among those few structures, as were a saloon and two new hotels; a school, several churches, and a cemetery were under way, along with construction of the later locally famous Red Brick Road. Soon an impressive Northern Pacific depot dominated the town. It was "a thriving hub at the turn of the century . . . bustling with people and shipments of merchandise and shingles."[16]

Small farms and logging and milling operations were commonplace throughout the county, but several communities had unique economic experiences. A group of Seattle investors that included Arthur Denny encouraged the Englishman Peter Kirk to start a steel mill at Kirkland using iron ore from Denny's mines near Snoqualmie Pass. A town got fully established, along with some accessory industries, but the grandiose plans collapsed in the panic of 1893, hindered also by a lack of quality ore and other complications. Yet the town of Kirkland endured, built upon the infrastructure that the venture had engendered. In the first two decades of the new century its population more than tripled.[17] Auburn, originally named Slaughter in honor of the American hero of an Indian skirmish when it was founded in 1886, became a freight terminus for the Northern Pacific Railway in 1913; though that role was modified after a few years, the railroad's importance remained.[18] Meanwhile, Renton had emerged from its coal mining past to retain an industrial base and become home to Pacific Car and Foundry, which manufactured railroad cars and structural steel.[19] Bellevue was a center of truck farms, but it also became the wintering quarters for an Alaska whaling fleet.[20] In 1909 the Carnation Milk Products Company moved the major operations of a large dairy farm and its condensed-milk production from Kent to the area around Tolt, later prompting that city to rename itself for the company.[21]

Small boats were linking Seattle with the towns across Lake Washington. By 1889 a small side-wheeler, the *Kirkland*, was making daily stops at Juanita, Kirkland, Houghton, and Newcastle. Other boats provided occasional transportation between Seattle and the east side of the lake. The building of Leschi Park, a regular stop on the western shore of the lake, and the Yesler cable car line in the next decade assured more consistent transportation across the lake. Passengers debarking the boats at Leschi rode the cable cars across the ridges to downtown Seattle; this would become a common commute for Eastsiders. Eventually, Captain John Anderson acquired the boat line, including auto ferries, and ensured regular transportation across the lake for decades, until the opening of the first Lake Washington floating bridge just before World War II.[22]

As the 19th century became the 20th, Seattle and King County underwent changes from which they never looked back. Again, the Seattle story is familiar. The June 1889 fire that devastated the downtown business district proved a blessing as the city revamped not only its buildings and streets, but also its fire and building codes. In the early 1890s a national depression had local repercussions. But the arrival in 1893 of James J. Hill's Great Northern Railway gave Seattle a new economic importance, and Thomas Burke, the line's local attorney, became a powerful figure. On the heels of this, the *S. S. Portland* docked on June 17, 1897, carrying more than a ton of gold from the Klondike. Many local citizens, the mayor among them, headed north in search of wealth, but their stay-at-home counterparts seemed to derive more enduring affluence by supplying the hopeful gold seekers. An exceptional promotional campaign made Seattle the principal departure point for the north, local entrepreneurs flourished, and new citizens were attracted by the prospect of supplying the prospectors.

Optimistic Seattle leaders reasoned that for the city to realize its destiny as a true metropolis, it must reshape its land on a grand scale. Hills were cut away to expand the business district, with some of the dirt filling in marshlands and other low spots. Remaining slopes were graded; tidelands were reclaimed on the north and south shores of Elliott Bay; a canal was cut to connect Lake Washington and Lake Union with Puget Sound. The canal necessitated a system of locks to allow boat passage from the lakes to the lower saltwater. As a result, Lake Washington was lowered by nine feet, redefining shorelines and draining marshlands to create new land, notably the fertile Mercer Slough in Bellevue, where Aaron Mercer and his family had once lived. The famed Olmsted Brothers firm of Boston was brought in to design a Seattle park system that would take advantage of the city's natural configurations and beauty. Geographically and socially, Seattle was redefining itself. In 1909 the city celebrated its new place in the region and the world with the Alaska-Yukon-Pacific Exposition, which took place on the new University of Washington grounds in the northeastern, still largely rural, corner of the city. Seattle had come of age.[23]

Accounts of these developments commonly emphasize the energetic, aggressive, and politically savvy coterie of city leaders—mostly white men, some of whom had personally known the founders—who made all of this happen. A lawyer, an engineer, and a crusading pastor were in the forefront: the Northern Pacific attorney Thomas Burke, the domineering Reginald H. Thomsen, and First Presbyterian's Mark Matthews. Less obvious to history were their wives and other women who established such amenities as schools, churches, and social organizations. Although the city bore the name of a local Indian, the region's Native Americans were relegated far to the background, although some evidence suggests that they were more essential to the city's well-being than has often been thought. They contributed to the local economy and were an increasing attraction to visitors searching for local color and lore.[24]

Most of the Asians who had come to the area this early were Chinese laborers who arrived after toiling in railroad construction and mining. A few established urban businesses. In the middle 1880s, several Chinese workers in Issaquah hop fields were attacked; then Seattle's Chinese residents, along with others in the region, were driven out in a frenzy of anger and frustration at their "strange" lifestyles and willingness to accept low wages. It has been left to recent historians to uncover the contributions of these groups that played definitive roles as Seattle matured.[25]

Surges of growth in surrounding King County were evident as Seattle swooped up its closest neighbors, including established towns that had their own identities.

The steamboat *May Blossom* is docked on the Sammamish River near Bothell about 1910. Courtesy of the Museum of History and Industry.

By 1910 Seattle had, through annexations, about six times the population and land area it had had in 1890.[26] The mill town of Ballard brought 17,000 new residents into Seattle, Columbia City and Rainier Valley each brought 7,000, and West Seattle and Georgetown added several thousand more. A few less prominent areas joined as well.[27] Thus, early in the 1900s, Seattle's two "birthplaces," the Duwamish Valley and Alki Point, finally become part of the city.

Improved transportation routes and facilities bound King County together and linked it and its principal city with other parts of the state and nation. Early on, small boats scurried around the Sound and the lake connecting the few towns that existed. Some made their way up the Duwamish, White, and Squak rivers with stops at landings along the way. The early Duwamish settlers had been first to build a bridge across that river, thus allowing an overland trail from the south. Other trails extended out from the downtown Seattle shoreline over the ridges to Lake Washington.

Much of the traffic out from Seattle and Lake Washington followed rivers, often a long, arduous journey. Seattle movers and shakers created local short-line roads, usually hoping to connect with larger lines. One such effort led the Seattle, Lake Shore & Eastern Railroad Company to build around the north end of Lake Washington and south to coal mines near Issaquah. Ultimately the track continued east, helping to open that area and creating such towns as North Bend, Snoqualmie, and Fall City. Meanwhile, interurban trains were linking Seattle with

Crossing Lake Washington has always been a factor in the development of King County. An early ferryboat is shown at the Moss Bay landing near Kirkland. Courtesy of MSCUA, University of Washington Libraries, neg. # WA50311.

neighboring towns north to Everett and south to Tacoma. As these transportation lines accessed new areas, stations and communities were built along them.[28]

Seattle's population more than doubled during the first decade of the 20th century. In 1890, 42,837 people lived in the city. By 1900 there were 80,671 and a decade later an astounding 237,194. In the statehood year of 1889, King County was the state's largest county, with 63,989 residents tallied in the following year's census. The number climbed to 110,053 over the next 10 years and doubled to 284,638 by 1910. Four of every 10 county residents lived in its largest city.[29] At the same time, manufacturing increased in Seattle; the number of companies almost tripled during the first decade and a half of the new century to exceed 1,000.[30]

Through 1920 the area's population was still mushrooming, with 315,000 Seattleites and 390,000 in the entire county, but the two entities would gain only 60,000 and 70,000 more residents respectively by 1930.[31] Growth was slowing, and the '20s began with a depressed economy and radical-labor disputes in the Seattle area. Yet Seattle's expanding business district was transformed with modern buildings that would mark the character of downtown for generations to come. Manufacturing increased and spread—especially in the Duwamish flatlands to the south where the Boeing Company grew just outside the city limits. The city itself experienced struggles over public ownership of power production, the streetcar line, the port, which had become one of the West Coast's busiest, and even housing.[32] The suburbs remained essentially small towns with rural underpinnings. Truck farms, many operated by Japanese Americans, were found east of Lake Washington and in the Kent-Auburn Valley, and they provided fresh produce for city people. Also during the '20s, the people of the city became more interested in recreation, and their interests and endeavors spurred them to hike, camp, and ski along the road to Snoqualmie Pass.[33]

The arrival of automobiles created a need for better graded and surfaced roads. By 1929 the county had 1,000 miles of roads, 300 miles of which were paved, with most of the rest graveled.[34] Such improvements were originally seen as local responsibilities until the state began to appropriate funds. The preponderance of automobiles altered the way people lived, across the nation and in King County. Ordinary citizens gained increased mobility, which affected and sometimes determined where they lived, worked, and played. Service stations, sellers of cars and their many accessories, restaurants, motor courts, roadhouses, and other accoutrements of the modern highway sprang up, as did new communities. Built in the early 1920s, Lake Washington Boulevard, its name more grandiose than its reality, was a paved highway circling the lake and bonding Seattle with its lakefront suburbs.[35] Other roads extended out from this one. Seattle became more closely linked to its suburbs, and neighboring towns in turn were connected with one another.

Along with cars, radio, and movies, the extensive use of telephones caused the city and county to be more solidly integrated into the entire national scene. Businesses that processed food, manufactured clothing, and supplied other needs changed daily life. Skyscrapers and department stores became commonplace in cities, and persons in outlying areas had access to them.

During the Great Depression the movement of people into the area slowed to a near stop for the first time in local history. Ironically, these hard times resulted in several cultural institutions appearing in Seattle, new movie theaters and an art museum among them. Other visible effects resulted from the "make-work" programs of Franklin Roosevelt's New Deal, including the construction of bridges and highway facilities and public buildings and parks. Seattle and nearby small communities received permanent benefits.[36]

World War II fostered additional permanent changes. The military's presence became visible to a population highly conscious of its proximity to Japan. Manufacturing took on new importance. Ship building, which had advanced during World War I, continued with Todd and other shipyards in Seattle and a greatly expanded wartime shipyard at Houghton on the east shore of Lake Washington. But the most dramatic and enduring change was in aircraft production. Boeing became the major producer of warplanes and constructed new plants along the Duwamish. Just south of Seattle, B-29s were built alongside the lake at Renton.[37] The eviction and incarceration of almost 10,000 western Washingtonians of Japanese descent, including many American citizens, left the region without one of its most visible and productive ethnic groups. The Nihonmachi district in Seattle and farms near Bellevue, Renton, Kent, and other scattered areas were suddenly vacant. Homes deteriorated and crops went to waste. At the end of the war some families returned, often to unfriendly receptions, but many never did.[38]

On the other hand, the African-American population increased as single men and families poured in to work in war industries. To accommodate them and other newly arrived workers, several entire new housing developments were hastily built. Many blacks remained after the war, predominantly living on the ridges east and south of downtown Seattle, and they permanently altered the ethnic and cultural makeup of the city and county.[39]

War's aftermath demonstrated how significantly the area had changed, economically, socially, and culturally. The Boeing Company, long an important manufacturer, emerged as the dominant industrial giant in an economy no longer based on such extractive undertakings as lumbering, farming, and fishing. Newcomers arrived from all parts of the United States. Many had come to know the Northwest during wartime service and returned to make future lives, and GIs took advantage of postwar benefits for housing and schooling.

The postwar national trend toward suburban living also affected the Seattle area, partially encouraged by two floating bridges that crossed Lake Washington, one completed just before the war and the other in 1963; eastside suburbs were now as close to downtown Seattle as the city's own neighborhoods. Throughout King County, towns that had been small before the war suddenly surged with growth. Rural Bellevue incorporated in 1953 with almost 6,000 residents and eventually spread to cover the seven miles between Lake Washington and Lake Sammamish; by 1970 it was the fourth-largest city in the state.[40] Kirkland, Issaquah, and Mercer Island, the latter popular with the affluent, grew after the bridges opened. Renton held its new population, and farther south former agricultural communities such as Burien, Kent, and Auburn took on suburban characteristics. Along with such established towns suddenly grown big, vast neighborhoods filled previously open spaces, Shoreline and Federal Way notable among them. In 1956 Seattle moved its principal northern border 60 blocks north to 145th Street, absorbing, among other areas, Lake City. Yet, during the 1970s, the city's population declined even as that of the entire county increased.[41]

New business complexes began to appear in the suburbs, and they too attracted people. Such shopping centers as Northgate, Southcenter, and Bellevue Square served the suburban population and attracted persons from Seattle. They were followed by ubiquitous small malls. Commercial companies moved to or were established in the suburbs, and they laid the groundwork for large business parks and then whole new industries. A commercial area appeared upon recently pastoral acreage between Lakes Washington and Sammamish, with the growing Microsoft campus its centerpiece after 1986. The rapid growth of this gigantic software firm had a profound effect upon the whole region and particularly upon its neighboring towns. Redmond, Woodinville, and Issaquah emerged from their small-town roots to become vital and sometimes crowded cities forced to contend with the pressing problems of rapid growth, the need for renewed infrastructure, and a quest for identity in a new set of circumstances.

The construction of interstate highways helped knit the entire region together

Lake Hills, now part of Bellevue, was one of the largest and most spectacular suburban residential developments east of Lake Washington. This aerial photograph of the growing community was taken in the 1950s. Courtesy of the Museum of History and Industry.

and enhance local traffic. Interstate 5 linked Seattle with its northern and southern suburbs; I-405 became an alternate north-south route east of Lake Washington; I-90 crossed the original floating bridge and continued through the county's foothills and across Snoqualmie Pass. Thus Seattle's sphere moved north past the Snohomish County line and south to Pierce County, the latter affected in part by the activities surrounding the Seattle-Tacoma International Airport, which had opened in 1949. The fertile valley that connected Auburn, Kent, and Renton became an asphalt-coated land of commercial centers and malls. A ring of new cities came into being, including Newport and Sammamish, along with Shoreline and Federal Way, both of which ranked among the state's 15 most populous cities immediately upon incorporation. And expansion continued farther east. Not many years earlier, towns such as Enumclaw, North Bend, Fall City, and Duvall had seemed to be rural enclaves dedicated to farming and logging, distant and largely isolated from the city. Well before the 20th century ended, they were within the urban web as well and were often homes to new industries.

The rapid growth introduced problems once unimaginable. As early as the 1960s, once pristine Lake Washington was marked with pollution, evidence that the prized local environment was threatened. The pressures of a bigger population, with more automobiles, boats, and sewage, combined to create concerns, curtailing recreational and other activities around the lake. A band of prominent Seattle and Eastside civic leaders rallied support for a combined effort to clean up the lake. The result was a new government entity that embraced a new concept. The Municipality of Metropolitan Seattle, created in 1958 and commonly called Metro, recognized that problems were not confined to separate cities, towns, and other districts alone, but called for heightened cooperation in order to be dealt with. Originally designed to encompass overall county planning and transportation issues as well as pollution control, Metro was downsized to only the latter.[42] Successful in that endeavor, it took on the transit service in 1972 and in the middle 1990s merged with the county government to become King County Metro. Here was recognition that separate local governments and districts had common needs that transcended traditional boundaries; the move was a portent of future county organization and development.[43]

Another major effort to create and update facilities throughout the county occurred in 1968 when voters considered a package of proposals collectively known as Forward Thrust. Although only seven of the thirteen proposals were approved, those seven included the new multipurpose stadium that became the Kingdome, an aquarium, highways, neighborhood improvements, and sewage facilities. As with the original Metro proposal, a rapid transit system was rejected.[44]

During that same period, King County voters adopted a home-rule charter that changed its government. The governing body of three commissioners was dropped in favor of a council of 13 members, each elected from a district within the county. An elected county executive assumed administrative duties. The first King County executive was the future governor John Spellman; Gary Locke later followed in both positions.[45]

An inevitable part of the growth process that saddened many farmers and nostalgic romantics involved the loss of productive agricultural land. The cost of continuing to farm rose beyond the means of many whose families had done so over several generations. Longtime landowners sold fertile acreage to developers who converted it to residential or commercial uses. In 1979 voters passed an initiative that allowed King County to protect diminishing farmlands by purchasing the development rights.[46] In 1990 the desire to regulate urban sprawl led state legislators to pass the Growth Management Act, which required communities to develop specific plans to handle growth and to coordinate future planning; the intent was to contain density in areas that were already well populated.[47] Such programs angered many landowners who prized their independence and their property rights. Concerns over the power of government heightened, even leading to an abortive attempt to divide the county in the 1990s and create a new Cedar County.[48]

Seattle continued to dominate the entire area and King County, but shifts became evident. By the 1980s morning traffic with the Eastside suburbs was heavy not just from east to west into Seattle, but in both directions. Movement among the suburbs themselves was a feature of daily life as people lived, worked, shopped, and found entertainment without venturing into the larger city.[49] The western portions of King, Snohomish, and Pierce counties blended imperceptibly into one vast megalopolis. During the 1990s almost all of Washington's newly incorporated towns in the state were located in the greater Seattle area.[50]

Seattle and its downtown sought to reassert their traditional role as the social and cultural hub, even as shopping centers and strip malls covered the county's landscape. As early as the late 1950s, leaders considered suburban and rural possibilities when searching for a site for the 1962 Seattle World's Fair, also known as Century 21. The issue was later raised over arenas for new basketball, baseball, and football franchises. But city locations were selected for all. Seattle remained a magnet and effectively revamped much of a downtown that seemed on the verge of declining. New high-rise office buildings and stores, including branches of trendy national chains, gave a new flavor to the downtown area. The Seattle Center— formerly the site of the world's fair—sports stadiums, enhanced waterfront facilities, a new symphony hall, and a new art museum were among the magnets designed to draw suburbanites into the city core by the early 21st century. The annual Seafair festivities, dominated by hydroplane races on Lake Washington and parades, has brought celebrants to Seattle since 1950.

At the same time, other cities adopted their own cultural features. The King County Fair is a traditional event each autumn in Enumclaw, Redmond's Marymoor Park hosts a variety of festivals, and Bellevue's Meydenbauer Center houses small conventions and other events. Theater groups emerged in several towns, with Issaquah's Village Theater attracting an audience from a wide area. The Pacific Northwest Arts and Crafts Fair (now the Bellevue Art Museum Fair) began in postwar Bellevue and eventually spawned an architecturally dramatic art museum. Kirkland became renowned for a unique collection of outdoor sculptures. Most communities also hold local festivals that center around a local feature: salmon in Issaquah, bicycles in Redmond, and the like. Such programs and events draw attendees from well beyond their own communities, usually attracting visitors from Seattle itself.

Of the 1,758,000 people who lived in King County in 2001, 568,100, or about one-third, resided within the city limits of Seattle, a dramatic change from the ratio of several early decades.[51] Caucasians remain the dominant racial group, but the vitality of the Asian- and African-American populations helps to define the regional culture. King County thus has emerged economically, socially, and culturally as an entity in its own right, anchored in but not controlled by the Northwest's largest city.

Building on this somewhat traditional account of local history, the Pacific Northwest Historians Guild presents *More Voices, New Stories*, an offering of essays on the city and the county's past, hoping to engender a further interest in aspects that have often been ignored or slighted.

As noted at the beginning of this essay, Kay Reinartz tweaks the traditional account of the dominance of the Denny Party, whose landing at Alki Point has frequently been accepted as the start of it all. The Duwamish settlers may have come first and surely made contributions that have too commonly been overlooked. Reinartz offers Joseph Foster as being at least the equal of Arthur Denny as a community builder. In assessing Reinartz's comments, and those in the essays that follow, readers might well ponder how history comes to be written and accepted as it is or, perhaps as important, how significantly a revised view alters the familiar story.

As noted earlier, Coll-Peter Thrush takes up the "creation" of Seattle at Alki Point and the Denny Party as part of local folklore and mythology. His essay compels readers to examine varied aspects and to look at that event—and thus others—from a range of differing perspectives.

Several of the authors in this volume deal with ethnic and racial groups and issues that have been underplayed in traditional accounts. The Scandinavian presence has been one of the earliest and most enduring features of King County life. Under the auspices of the Vanishing Generation Oral History Project of Seattle's Nordic Heritage Museum, twelve immigrants and descendants—representing Sweden, Norway, Denmark, Finland, and Iceland—describe what it was like for them to live in Seattle and King County in the 20th century. Their recollections touch on ordinary things as well as those aspects that give a special flavor to their lives. Such word pictures are the stuff upon which later historians draw.

Ed Diaz investigates a labor event that has generally been seen as only a footnote to local history: the recruitment of African Americans who were brought in to break a strike in the coal mines of eastern King County. Again, he raises questions: Is the story, as it has been commonly told, the most accurate interpretation? Were the men inexperienced miners thrust into an unfamiliar situation? Were they even strikebreakers? What have been the contributions of these persons and their descendants?

The stories of King County's Jewish and Japanese populations are not altogether unfamiliar. More than a few Jews have been significant leaders in Seattle's past, and accounts of Japanese Americans, especially their wartime expulsion, ring through the area's history. But Jackie Williams and Ron Magden highlight specific aspects of these groups. Williams looks not at male Jewish leaders but at the part played by Jewish women and the philanthropic organizations and benefits they bestowed upon the community. And Magden considers the establishment and growth of Japanese Buddhists in King County, and how the religion has endured.

Nhien Nguyen relates a hauntingly personal story of people who arrived within the memory of many readers. She draws upon the often painful recollections of several Vietnamese immigrants who came to start new lives in a culture that was not only unfamiliar but often less refined that what they had been accustomed to.

As the number of Hispanic residents in the area increases, a few Hispanic women have assumed prominence in the political sphere. Elizabeth Salas introduces readers to three remarkable Mexican American women from Seattle, two of them state legislators and the third an activist candidate for the city council. Education, opportunities for all and farm worker rights are issues that link their cultural background to their political activities.

Michael Reese's essay also concerns women, but women who are perhaps those most likely to be overlooked in conventional histories: mothers on pensions. Reese describes the national and state context, the policies and legislation, and the various, diverse attitudes that professionals and others had toward these hidden women. This account has sociological overtones and a continuing relevance.

Robert Fisher and Eric Flom lead readers through aspects of social history that are a familiar part of many local lives: dinner and a show. Often the "big" events of the past, the development of an economy and a method of governance, overshadow the personal reality of how people truly lived and enjoyed themselves. Fisher tells of Seattle's restaurant industry. Readers can learn about influences upon the industry, see how tastes have changed, and get glimmerings of an evolving Northwest cuisine. Gourmets and casual diners may well recognize some familiar names and find their memories aroused. Flom, meanwhile, guides readers through the history of the area's theater from crude pioneer days to more recent glitter. Changing aspects of local theatrics have included community performances, road shows, vaudeville, and other forms of stage entertainment. Flom also describes the evolving architectural patterns of theater buildings.

In honor of King County's 150th anniversary, the Pacific Northwest Historians Guild, an organization made up of people who research and write and teach about–and love–the history of this corner of America, invites you to read about some of its less heralded aspects.

Enjoy!

## NOTES

[1]This story, frequently told, is derived from written recollections of the pioneers themselves. A good account is in Roger Sale, *Seattle Past to Present* (Seattle and London: University of Washington Press, 1976), 7–8. The general account of Seattle's early history as recounted in this essay is based largely upon Sale as well as the Clarence C. Bagley and Cornelius Hanford volumes cited below. Also useful is Walt Crowley and the staff of HistoryLink's, *Seattle and King County Timeline* (Seattle: HistoryInk, 2001). See also James R. Warren, *King County and its Queen City: Seattle, an Illustrated History* (Woodland Hills, Calif.: Windsor Publications, Inc., 1981).

[2] Murray Morgan, *Skid Road: An Informal Portrait of Seattle*, revised edition (New York: The Viking Press, 1960); William C. Speidel, *Sons of the Profits; or, There's No Business Like Grow Business! The Seattle Story, 1851-1901* (Seattle: Nettle Creek Publishing Company, 1967).

[3] Clarence C. Bagley, *History of King County Washington*, 3 vols. (Chicago and Seattle: The S. J. Clarke Publishing Company, 1929), 1:356.

[4] Lewis O. Saum, "'Who Steals My Purse': The Denigration of William R. King, the Man for Whom King County Was Named," *Pacific Northwest Quarterly*, 92:181–89 (Fall 2001).

[5] Bagley, 187.

[6] C[ornelius]. H. Hanford, editor, *Seattle and Environs* (Chicago and Seattle: Pioneer History Publishing Co., 1924), I:128.

[7] Bagley, 104.

[8] Amy Eunice Stickney and Lucile McDonald, *Squak Slough, 1870–1920: Early Days on the Sammamish River, Woodinville-Bothell-Kenmore* (Bothell: Friends of the Bothell Library, 1977), 1; Bagley, 360–61.

[9] Lucile McDonald, *Bellevue: Its First 100 Years*, revised edition (Bellevue, Wash.: Bellevue Historical Society, 2000), 39.

[10] Nancy Way, *Our Town Redmond* (Redmond, Wash.: Marymoor Museum, 1989), 2–3.

[11] Stickney and McDonald, 3–7, 15, 39, 74.

[12] Bagley, 310–14.

[13] Yvonne Prater, *Snoqualmie Pass from Indian Trail to Interstate* (Seattle: The Mountaineers, 1981), 25–27; Judith Bentley, "McClellan & Tinkham: Naming Features in the 'Heroic Man' Tradition," *Columbia: The Magazine of Northwest History*, 16:21 (September 2002).

[14] Prater, 32–33, 95–105.

[15] Calvin F. Schmid and Stanton E. Schmid, *Growth of Cities and Towns, State of Washington* (Olympia, Wash.: Washington State Planning and Community Affairs Agency, 1969), 25, 62.

[16] Way, 65.

[17] Bagley, 838–43.

[18] Bagley, 712–22.

[19] Bagley, 759–60.

[20] McDonald, 107–108.

[21] Bagley, 811–12.

[22] McDonald, 73–79.

[23] Richard C. Berner, *Seattle 1900–1920: From Boomtown, Urban Turbulence, to Restoration* (Seattle: Charles Press, 1991), 83–84, 103–106, 127–32.

[24] Unpublished talk by Christopher Friday, Seattle, 9 February 2002.

[25] Doug Chin, Seattle's *International District: The Making of a Pan-Asian Community* (Seattle, Wash.: International Examiner Press, 2001). Gail M. Nomura, "Washington's Asian/Pacific American Communities," *Peoples of Washington: Perspectives on Cultural Diversity* (Pullman, Wash.: Washington State University Press, 1989), 113-55. Robert Edward Wynne, "Reaction to the Chinese in the Pacific Northwest and British Columbia, 1850 to 1910," Ph.D. dissertation, University of Washington, 1964.

[26] Schmid and Schmid, 154.

[27] Berner, 63.

[28] Bagley, 310–14, 786–93.

[29] Schmid and Schmid, 25, 62.

[30] Berner, 28.

[31] Schmid and Schmid, 25, 62.

[32] Richard C. Berner, *Seattle in the 20th Century, Volume 2: Seattle 1921-1940, From Boom to Bust* (Seattle: Charles Press, 1992), 11–33, 43–77, 168–77.

[33] Prater, 82–92, 129–42.

[34] Bagley, 480–81.

[35] McDonald, 101, 122.

[36] Berner, *Seattle in the 20th Century, Volume 2*, 247–78.

[37] Richard C. Berner, *Seattle in the 20th Century, Volume 3: Seattle Transformed, World War II to Cold War* (Seattle: Charles Press, 1999), 44–46.

[38] Berner, *Seattle in the 20th Century, Volume 3*, 18–42, 124–30.

[39] Quintard Taylor, *The Forging of a Black Community: Seattle's Central District from 1870 through the Civil Rights Era* (Seattle and London: University of Washington Press), 159–89.

[40] Charles P. LeWarne, "Bellevues I Have Known," *Columbia Magazine*, 11:7–8 (Summer 1997).

[41] *1980 Census of Population . . . Number of Inhabitants . . . Washington State* (Washington, D. C.: U.S. Department of Commerce, 1982), 49:8, 49:17.

[42] Robert E. Ficken and Charles P. LeWarne, *Washington: A Centennial History* (Seattle and London: University of Washington Press, 1988), 151-152.

[43] Crowley, 88.

[44] HistoryLink, www.historylink.org; Warren, 167–68.

[45] Crowley, 79; www.metrokc.gov.

[46] http://dnr.metrokc.gov/wlr/LANDS/farmpp.htm.

[47] Charles P. LeWarne, *Washington State*, revised edition (Seattle and London: University of Washington Press, 1986), 255.

[48] See, for example *Seattle Times*, 27 November 1995 (Snohomish County edition). B-1; 4 February 1997 (Snohomish County edition). B-1. *Herald* (Everett, Wash.) 23 February 1994, B-3.

[49] Charles P. LeWarne, "Introduction to the 2000 Revision," in McDonald, 18–19.

[50] Office of Financial Management, State of Washington, Forecasting Division, *2001 Population Trends*, (Olympia, Wash.: [State of Washington], 2001), 13.

[51] Office of Financial Management, 8, 9.

# CREATION STORIES

## RETHINKING THE FOUNDING OF SEATTLE

Coll-Peter Thrush

In a 1991 essay about the mythic origins of baseball, the natural historian Stephen Jay Gould argued that stories about beginnings

> come in only two basic modes. An entity either has an explicit point of origin, a specific time and place of creation, or else it evolves and has no definable moment of entry into the world . . . we seem to prefer the . . . model of origin by a moment of creation—for then we can have heroes and sacred places.[1]

In Seattle, the specific time of creation is November 13, 1851, the sacred place is a promontory jutting out into Puget Sound known as Alki Point, and the heroes are the Denny Party: men, women, and children who came to establish a settlement called New York on a wilderness shore, and who became the founders of Seattle.[2]

The story usually goes like this: On a cold, rainy morning in November 1851, the schooner *Exact* dropped anchor in Elliott Bay after a harrowing passage from Portland in Oregon Territory. For the next couple of hours, 23 settlers led by Arthur Armstrong Denny—women, children, and infants among them—shuttled themselves and their belongings between the schooner and the cobbled shore, where they were met by Arthur's brother David, who had come ahead to find a place to settle. Upon learning that this windswept beach with a half-built cabin was to be their new home, the women in the Denny Party began to cry, the misting rain causing their bonnets to sag. The little group's anxiety only heightened, so the story goes, when several Indians, including one who called himself something like "See-athl," appeared on the scene. After some hesitant communication between the settlers and the Natives, the group set to work finishing the cabin. They christened this new settlement New York-Alki, meaning "New York eventually" in the Chinook Jargon, the local lingua franca. And so, on that day, the settlement that would become the Pacific Northwest's dominant city was born. Seattle's history had begun.

For more than a century, this version of Seattle's founding has been told again and again through memoirs, histories, and reenactments, profoundly shaping the way Seattleites think about their city and its past.[3] According to the Alki mythology, the members of the Denny Party were the selfless vanguards of civilization on Puget Sound. Emphasizing the character of the founders, one historical article from 1906 cast them as altruistic visionaries:

> Call it what you will, call it the instinctive desire of man for exploration, call it the "wanderlust," if you will, that moved them. These men would never have sought these inhospitable shores and here remained to found a city and a state, if a sordid thought for their own welfare had been their only impulse. I am not idealist enough to believe that these men were actuated only by the grand idea of erecting an empire for those who came after to enjoy. Perhaps they were not even consciously moved by this idea, but that spirit nevertheless they had and it sufficed to make them heroes.[4]

Likewise, the landing has been portrayed as the birth of something called the "Seattle Spirit," a combination of moral rectitude and physical fortitude that led inevitably to the building of a great metropolis. Many observers, concerned about the "softness" and immorality of modern urban life, made much of this Seattle Spirit and called for its renaissance.[5] However, at its core, the Seattle Spirit stood on a foundation of racial conflict; in one typical recounting of the story, Seattle's founders had "braved a wilderness peopled only by Indians, many of them hostile, and they accepted the most severe hardships as a matter of course. In them was born the Seattle Spirit."[6] The urban promise of Seattle, then, was born in the meeting place between "savagery" and "civilization."

Beyond its racial undertones, the story of the Denny Party has been seen as not just one city's particular origin, but as a metaphor for something much larger. In 1893, for example, just a few months after Frederick Jackson Turner gave his seminal address on the role of the frontier in American history at the Columbian Exposition in Chicago—itself a powerful articulation of the alleged encounter between "savagery" and "civilization"—the *Seattle Post-Intelligencer* outlined a similar role for the landing at Alki:

> It is an oft-told story, but it is one of those which can never grow wearisome, for it is a type of hundreds of others which form in the mass the greatest wonder of the nineteenth century—the transformation of a wilderness into a populous republic, surpassing in wealth, prosperity and high civilization any empire of olden or modern times, and of hundreds of little parties of two dozen adventurers dwelling in log cabins into great cities of lofty palaces which defy comparison with the great cities of the old world.[7]

The events of November 13, 1851, represented not just the local past, but the entire sweep of American history. Ten years later, during celebrations that included a visit from President Theodore Roosevelt, the local jurist and historian Cornelius Hanford proclaimed that those looking for the city's beginnings

> [M]ust recognize God in every stupendous undertaking, and in order to find the real origin of a city, and understand the reasons for its being, we must go away back to the time when the waters were divided from the land, and the lines of its shores were drawn to make heavens in which ships may find protection from storms . . . it was not a mere blunder or chance which led the pioneers to Seattle.[8]

For Hanford and many others, the Alki landing was not only divinely ordained, but represented the march of the nation across the continent and exemplified the arrival of the United States on the world stage. From 24 men, women, and children, the story went, a city was born that would rival those of the Old World and glorify America's achievements.

But if the Denny Party's arrival at Alki symbolized the "greatest wonders" of the 19th century to many observers, it also represented a much broader sweep of American history. As early as the 1890s, local writers linked the events at Alki to other myths of American founding. More than city builders, the founders were also, in the words of one commentator, the "new pilgrim fathers."[9] The connection between the Denny Party and the Plymouth Pilgrims was a common one. In 1941, another historian wrote that Seattle's development "acted out the building of America accurately, but with the growing momentum of more than two centuries. At the far end of telescoped time, Seattle's beginning was the same as the beginning of the nation."[10] In these interpretations, Seattle's founding was an altruistic bequest to the urban future, sped forward by the inertia of the American past. A direct line connected the religious hard-liners of early New England to that band of Midwestern settlers at Alki Point. In both cases, what the author John Seelye has called "a boat, a ship, some people" came to stand for something much larger: American predestination.[11]

One local artifact articulates this alluring vision of Seattle's origins in ways that no text can. Housed at Seattle's Museum of History & Industry is Lillian Smart's diorama version of Seattle's creation. Comprising wax figures, handmade miniature clothing, shellacked greenery, and a painted beachscape, the diorama shows the members of the Denny Party coming ashore at Alki. All the elements of the story are there: the *Exact* lying offshore, the half-finished cabin, the crying women in sagging bonnets, the children gazing warily at two Indian observers, including Chief Seattle. Within just a few months of the diorama's completion, in 1953, its sponsors, the Alki Women's Improvement Club and the West Seattle Business Association, claimed "thousands of Seattle residents, tourists, and school children have stood in front of it, admiring its beauty and realism, and paying silent homage to Seattle's founders."[12] And indeed, the diorama has been a kind of pilgrimage site, a link to the past for generations of Seattleites. Still on display at the beginning of the 21st century, Smart's diorama is the image that most likely comes to many local residents' minds when they think of the city's founding. It is a powerful distillation of Seattle's founding myth.

That a diorama has become the most familiar image of Seattle's founding seems only appropriate, in that it reflects the nature of the city's creation story. Like the wax figures that have not moved since Smart installed them in that wooden case, November 13, 1851 is a moment frozen in time, obscuring the complexity of what had gone before and what would come after. And like any good mythology, the story of the landing at Alki emphasizes some elements of the past while obscuring or erasing others. As a corrective to the Denny Party mythology, then, we might imagine other Alki Point moments, each playing its own role in the founding of Seattle. What follows are a collection of these "alternative dioramas," emphasizing the larger context in which that rainy November morning took place. Each tells a different kind of story about the place that would become Seattle, as well as about the shortcomings of the mythic image we have come to know as Seattle's creation story. To begin this collection of alternative creation stories, we must first travel to Alki Point before it was Alki, when it carried another name: Prairie Point.[13]

*Creation Story Number 1*

## WAHALCHU AND THE UNDERSEA LONGHOUSE: THE NATIVE WORLD

In Lushootseed, the indigenous language of Puget Sound, Alki Point was known as Prairie Point after the grassy openings between wind-stunted trees on the shelf above the beach. Although the nearest permanent winter towns were some distance away, on the Duwamish River, Prairie Point was a place well known to and well used by generations of Native people. All around Prairie Point, other place names attested to ways in which indigenous communities knew and used their landscape. The narrow strand where Arthur Denny and the party made landfall, for example, rested at the foot of Waterfall Point, a brooding headland that would later be renamed Duwamish Head. Between Prairie Point and Waterfall Point, back from the beach, lay a marsh called Place of Disease. South of Prairie Point, a creek called Capsizing, came pouring out of the forest near Crowded Head, named for the thick brush that covered it (and now Lincoln Park's Point Williams). Just beyond Crowded Head lay a shallow cove known as Scorched Face, describing dark stains on the exposed bluffs. Like many Lushootseed place names throughout Puget Sound, those around Alki Point illustrated the deep practical knowledge of place held by local indigenous communities.

Native landscapes in Puget Sound were also inhabited by forces Western taxonomy would classify as supernatural, and the vicinity of Prairie Point was no exception. Just south of the point was a small creek called Cold Weather House, possibly a reference to a primordial battle between North Wind and South Wind, since no human houses were ever said to have been located there. Farther along the shoreline, near today's Fauntleroy ferry terminal, was Has a Horned Snake, where an odd red boulder stood (and still stands) at the waterline. Catching sight of the boulder, inhabited or guarded by a huge serpent with the head, antlers, and forelegs of an elk, could either twist an unwary observer's body into knots or bestow some of the strongest doctoring powers.[14]

It is tempting to think of these Native places, and the knowledge and practices that took place in them, as somehow separate from the settler history that would take place among them in the years to come. Indeed, many histories of Seattle portray the landing of the Denny Party at Alki Point as simultaneously the beginning of Seattle's urban history and the end of local Indian inhabitancy. However, these indigenous connections to place continued after white settlement, as one Native man's experience with the landscape—or, more correctly, the seascape—around Prairie Point shows.

Sometime well before the arrival of the *Exact*, perhaps in the late 1830s, a young man named Wahalchu was hunting ducks in the waters off Prairie Point. However, ducks were not his only quarry; he was also in search of spirit power. And he found it there near Prairie Point, if only briefly: as he was retrieving spent arrows from his duck hunt, he saw a longhouse deep in the green waters of Puget Sound, surrounded by herds of elk and with schools of salmon swimming over its cedar-plank roof. This, Wahalchu knew, was the home of a spirit power that brought great wealth and respected leadership to those who had it. Without help, however, he could not pursue the power then and there, and so he returned home. In later years, though, Wahalchu who would place his mark under the Christianized version of his name, Jacob Wahalchu, on the 1855 Point Elliott Treaty—would still remember his encounter in the waters off Prairie Point.[15] Similarly, Native memories—and in some cases, use—of these places would continue well after white settlement and the development of Seattle's urban landscape. Despite the dramatic changes to come, including eventual dispossession and dislocation, Alki Point would remain Prairie Point in the minds and hearts of many local indigenous people.

*Creation Story Number 2*

## GEOPOLITICS COME TO PRAIRIE POINT:
## WILLIAM TOLMIE'S SURVEY, 1833

By the time that the man who would become Jacob Wahalchu went looking for ducks and power in the waters off Prairie Point, a new kind of people were already setting their sights on the inland sea they had named Puget Sound. Captain George Vancouver had come and gone in the summer of 1792, and four decades later both the British and the Americans held competing claims to the region. The Hudson's Bay Company established a fort on the Nisqually Plains in 1832, which quickly became a locus of Native-white interaction on Puget Sound as indigenous people from throughout the region came there to trade.[16] Meanwhile, Fort Nisqually established satellite trading posts throughout Puget Sound, capitalizing on and reshaping long-standing indigenous trade networks.

For a short time, Prairie Point was considered for one of these satellites. An 1833 survey by the physician and Fort Nisqually factor William Tolmie provides the first written description of what would someday be known as Alki Point:

> It was about one mile in length and from 100 to 150 yards in width, and raised about 30 feet above the sea level, toward which it presented a steep clay bank. The surface was flat and dotted with small pines, and the soil was mostly sand.
>
> At its northern extremity the coast is indented with a bay five or six miles wide and perhaps three miles long into which flows Ouvrie's river . . .
>
> The south side of the bay and the river is inhabited by the Tuomish Indians, of whom we saw several parties along the shore, miserably poor and destitute of firearms. The opposite coast of the sound is possessed by the warlike Suquamish, with whose chief we are on friendly terms.
>
> A fort well garrisoned would answer well as a trading post on the prairie where we stood. It would have the advantage of a fine prospect down the sound and of proximity to the Indians, but these advantages could not compensate for an unproductive soil and the inconvenience of going at least half a mile for a supply of water.[17]

Tolmie's is the first Western account of many of the places and peoples who would play central roles in the story of Seattle: Elliott Bay, the Duwamish River—here called "Ouvrie's river" after a company employee—and the Suquamish and "Tuomish" (Duwamish) Indians.

Ultimately, Tolmie decided not to locate a post at Prairie Point, a decision rendered moot in 1846 with the signing of a treaty between Britain and the United States. Puget Sound became solely American territory, and the British influence at Fort Nisqually began to fade as the settlement became increasingly American and Indian. Trade based at the fort continued to have far-reaching impacts on Native communities; during an outbreak of dysentery and measles in the winter of 1847 and 1848, for example, indigenous people from all over Puget Sound were trading there and likely took the diseases home with them to places such as Prairie Point.[18] Although only fleeting, Tolmie's visit to the future Alki Point was an example of the growing European and American presence in Puget Sound that would eventually lead to the founding of cities there.

*Creation Story Number 3*

## AMERICAN NAMING AND CLAIMING: THE WILKES EXPEDITION, 1841

Soon after the Hudson's Bay Company began exploiting indigenous trade networks in Puget Sound, the Americans came to pursue their own ambitions. The first official Americans came in 1841, when the United States Exploring Expedition, led by Lieutenant Charles Wilkes, sailed up the Sound. Authorized by the Jacksonian Congress, the naval expedition sought to strengthen American claims to lands north of the Columbia River. As the men on Wilkes's small but poetically named fleet—the sloops of war *Vincennes* and *Peacock*, the ship *Relief*, the brig *Porpoise*, and the tenders *Sea-Gull* and *Flying Fish*—carefully mapped and measured the bays and inlets, they created a new geography that overlaid the indigenous one. Just as Vancouver had nearly half a century earlier, Wilkes named places as a way of staking an American claim on the landscape he explored. But where Vancouver had overlooked Prairie Point, Wilkes did not. That summer, Prairie Point obtained its first colonial name, when Wilkes christened it Point Roberts after the expedition's physician.[19]

The landscapes of Puget Sound "savoured of civilization" for Wilkes, but the Native residents seemed little more than placeless, harmless annoyances:

> All these Indians may be termed Nomadic for they seldom occupy the same spot over a few months together but change their residence in order to approximate the places where they are supplied with food.
>
> These Indians suffer little inconvenience in their changes of residence; for, having but few chattels, they can remove at a few moments' notice; and after landing at an entirely strange place, they are at home the moment their fires are lighted.[20]

The nomadic movements Wilkes saw reflected well-established patterns of summer migration to and from resource sites; had the expedition come in the winter, it would have found indigenous people living in large permanent winter towns. To Wilkes, however, Native movement also implied that the Indians of Puget Sound were unlikely to stand in the way of white settlement, having little connection to particular places. Of course, he would be proven wrong in the coming decades, as Native people resisted attempts to remove them from what would come to be known as their "usual and accustomed places."

On another point, though, Wilkes was right. A second reason he expected little resistance to white settlement among Indian people was the series of diseases that were, in his words, "rapidly thinning them off."[21] Indeed, throughout the 1830s and 1840s, epidemics such as smallpox, measles, and influenza ravaged Native societies across Puget Sound country and beyond. In some communities, the mortality could have been as high as 60 percent, seeming evidence that the land was making itself ready for new owners.[22] But as other newcomers would soon learn, even the horror of plague would not sever indigenous connections to places like Prairie Point.

*Creation Story Number 4*

## INDIGENOUS ALKI: SAMUEL HANCOCK VISITS THE POINT, 1846

It is easy to imagine Native people disappearing in the wake of disease and colonial encroachment, but in the middle of the 19th century they remained the dominant presence in Puget Sound. The low-lying point where the Denny Party would eventually land was still very much an Indian place, even after the epidemics of the 1830s and 1840s. When Samuel Hancock, one of the first American settlers in Puget Sound, came to Prairie Point in 1849, he was made well aware that Native people were still in charge of Puget Sound:

> [W]e reached Alki Point, an excellent harbor against the prevailing winds in Winter, without accident. A great many Indians came from their houses to the beach here, to ascertain where we came from. All the Indians I have met with in this region have a great deal of curiosity, and they are certain to know very soon after your arrival amongst them, all that the Indians who are with you are in possession of in relation to you; so they were soon pretty posted in regard to me; indeed such was the nature of my business, that I desired they should know as I expected to derive considerable information from them about the soil. As they seemed well disposed, I opened my valise and gave them all presents, to the men pipes and tobacco, to the women small looking-glasses and brass rings. These seemed to please them very much, and by way of reciprocity, or to obtain more presents they gave me as many clams and salmon as I wanted.[23]

Turned into a diorama of its own, Hancock's visit—described several years after the founding of Seattle, hence the premature use of the name "Alki Point"—would be the near inverse of Lillian Smart's Denny Party scene. Instead of two Indian men among 24 white men and women, a single white man would stand alone among scores of Native men and women, testament to the continuing vital presence of indigenous society in Puget Sound on the eve of 1851.

These first four creation stories highlight histories well under way by the time the Denny Party arrived: the deeply inhabited indigenous landscape; the backdrop of epidemic disease; British and American imperial ambitions in the region; and the first glimmers of permanent non-Indian settlement. Together, these histories helped clear the way for the sailing of the *Exact*. A second group of creation stories, all from the year of the Denny Party's landing, complicates Seattle's origins further by showing just how contingent that landing was. In short, they illustrate just how easily Seattle's much-beloved creation story might never have happened in the first place.

*Creation Story Number 5*

## THE MYSTERIOUS MR. BROCK, 1851

While Arthur Denny is unanimously credited with being the "Father of Seattle," that title might just as easily go to an enigmatic figure named Brock. A resident of the Willamette Valley, the burgeoning settler paradise at the western end of the Oregon Trail, Brock appears only briefly, not unlike one of Shakespeare's plot-driving apparitions. When the Denny and Boren families, exhausted from the overland passage, arrived at the confluence of the Burnt and Snake rivers on the current border of Idaho and Oregon, Brock was there. In the shadow of bunchgrass-covered hills blackened by summer wildfires, Arthur Denny and Brock discussed the prospects of settlement in the Willamette Valley. The Oregon man warned that the best land in the Willamette was already spoken for, but that another prime area for settlement lay just to the north.

In his memoirs, Arthur Denny recalled that "[m]y attention was thus turned to the Sound, and I formed the purpose of looking in that direction." Just as Brock's Christian name remains a mystery, so do his motives: he might have been driven by altruism, or perhaps he simply wanted to dam or turn away the flow of Willamette Valley immigration. Regardless of the reason, his bit of rumor and speculation—he apparently had never seen Puget Sound—effectively and suddenly diverted the Dennys from a path they had decided on long before. As they labored up the difficult Burnt River Canyon, heading overland to the Columbia River, they were now on their way not to the open prairies of the Willamette but to the densely wooded shores of Puget Sound.[24]

The mysterious Mr. Brock highlights the contingency of Seattle's founding. While it is portrayed as inevitable in many of its retellings, the arrival of the Denny Party might never have taken place. Had the fateful encounter with Brock never happened, the Dennys and their compatriots would have been unremarkable latecomers to a thriving Willamette Valley, and the title of "founding father" would have gone not to Arthur Denny, but perhaps to an aging whaling captain from New England.

Si?al [Chief Seattle], a local headman, was critical in helping establish white settlements and commercial ventures in the 1850s. MSCUA University of Washington, neg. # NA 1511.

*Creation Story Number 6*

## THE WHALER AND THE HEADMEN: CAPTAIN FAY AND CHIEF SEATTLE, 1851

After decades of success in the New England whaling industry, Captain Robert Fay turned his attention west and by 1851 was looking for new business opportunities in Puget Sound. The wealth of the inland sea, in particular its bounty of salmon, seemed the piscine equivalent of a gold mine. From a base of operations in the mudflat settlement of Olympia at the head of the Sound, Fay set out in search of workers who could help him in his venture. He found them at Waterfall Point, in the form of Native families under the leadership of a man named Seattle. Fay and Seattle began negotiating a contract under which the Indians would catch and preserve salmon that would then be shipped in barrels to markets in San Francisco. On one of his trips to Seattle's encampment at Waterfall Point, Fay offered passage to David Denny, John Low, and Charles Terry, and on the 25th of September the four men came ashore just inside the headland of Waterfall Point. Fay returned to Olympia, leaving Denny, Low, and Terry to search for a site for the rest of their party. [25]

It is Fay, then, who bears some responsibility for the founding of Seattle; had he not offered seats in his scow to the three Midwesterners, the Denny Party might never have come to Prairie Point. And had Brock never told Arthur Denny about Puget Sound in the first place, Fay himself might have become a founding father in his own right as the mastermind behind the first American commercial venture on Elliott Bay. Rather than weeping women in sagging bonnets and a half-built log cabin, Lillian Smart might have spent months creating wax figures of indigenous men and women frozen in the act of drying fish for consumption on the Barbary Coast, a radically different image of Seattle's origins.

### Creation Story Number 7

## A SEPARATE GENESIS: THE DUWAMISH VALLEY, 1851

Fay, Denny, Low, and Terry were not the only white men with ambition on the shores of Elliott Bay in 1851. A short distance up the twisting estuary of the Duwamish River from Seattle's fish-processing station, several settlers had begun scratching homesteads out of the forested landscape. Recounted in detail by Kay Reinartz elsewhere in this volume, the story of these other "founding fathers"— Luther M. Collins, Henry Van Asselt, and Jacob and Samuel Maple highlights the fact that the members of the Denny Party were not alone in seeking a permanent home in what would eventually become Seattle, nor were they the first.[26]

So why, then, don't Collins, Van Asselt, and the Maples hold the title of first white settlers in the land that became Seattle? Historians of the city have routinely dismissed claims that the Duwamish Valley claims were the beginning of Seattle for several reasons. Writing in 1916, for example, the historian and pioneer Clarence Bagley argued that, unlike the commercial ambitions of the Denny Party, the Duwamish venture was "only a farming enterprise, and their claims were beyond Seattle's boundaries for thirty years or more."[27] And, in fact, the Duwamish settlers seem to have had little interest in establishing urban institutions such as the stores, schools, and churches that other settlers, including the Denny Party, would be known for.

Similarly, none of these men—Fay or the Duwamish settlers—arrived with women and children in tow (although the Duwamish group sent for their families soon after arriving). This meant that their story had little of the pioneer family melodrama attributed to the Alki landing: no sagging bonnets or Indian-fearing children in these dioramas. Finally, a third reason for the symbolic weight of the Denny Party likely stems from differences between the groups' relationships with Indians. While the Denny Party enjoyed remarkably peaceful interactions with local Native people, the settlers on the Duwamish had more complicated and less amicable relations, including several violent conflicts, with their Indian neighbors.[28] Meanwhile, Fay's employer-employee relationship with Chief Seattle does not carry the emotional power of the Denny landing.

According to Welford Beaton, an early-20th-century Seattle booster, "Seattle started deliberately."[29] In most histories of the city and its founders, the notion of Seattle as a predetermined outcome is a central component of the Alki mythology. The very titles of local histories attest to the city's destiny: one, titled *Westward to Alki*, casts the early life of Arthur Denny's brother David as little more than prologue to the inevitable 1851 landing, while former mayor George Cotterill's *Climax of a World Quest* traces Seattle's 20th-century commercial dominance back to the voyages of Wilkes, Vancouver, and even Magellan.[30] In these and other accounts, the arrival of "Seattle's Pilgrims" seems preordained. However, as these three 1851 creation stories attest, rather than an event sprung like Athena from the forehead of Arthur Denny, the founding of Seattle was a tentative process and could have happened differently. The vagaries of chance and the agency of Indians had everything to do with getting to New York-Alki. And once the Denny Party had arrived, getting along at Alki proved to be more complicated than the mythology lets on.

*Creation Story Number 8*

## INDIAN TOWN: NEW YORK-ALKI, 1852

Within a few short weeks of the arrival of the Denny Party at Prairie Point, at last christened Alki, the little settlement had taken on a surprising character. Instead of a small settlement of two dozen white Midwesterners, New York-Alki had become a new Indian settlement. Arthur Denny himself described the transition:

> [S]oon after we landed and began clearing the ground for our buildings they commenced to congregate, and continued coming until we had over a thousand in our midst, and most of them remained all winter. Some of them built their houses very near to ours, even on the ground we had cleared, and although they seemed very friendly toward us we did not feel safe in objecting to their building thus near to us for fear of offending them, and it was very noticeable that they regarded their proximity to us as a protection against other Indians.[31]

Denny's own words paint a radically different picture than that ensconced in Seattle's founding mythology. Instead of a 12-to-1 white-to-Indian ratio, we see the reverse, and then some: a 40-to-1 Indian-to-white ratio. Together with Samuel Hancock's account of the point in 1849, Denny's memoir suggests that Prairie Point, as local Native people surely would have still called it, could be both an Indian place and a white place.

Although named New York for the nation's commercial and cultural hub and

Local Native peoples, like these men in front of Henry Yesler's cookhouse, played important roles in Seattle's early years. Their labor–in construction, domestic service, subsistence activities, and other arenas–made urban founding possible. The date of the photograph is unknown, but likely occurred before the cookhouse was dismantled in 1866. University of Washington Libraries, neg. # NA 1389.

inspired by the tidy towns of Denny's Illinois frontier, this new urban settlement, like others in the Pacific Northwest, would by necessity include Indians. At Alki, in the settlement of Seattle that would be founded across Elliott Bay the next spring, and elsewhere in Puget Sound, Native people participated in the process of urban settlement. They provided knowledge of local resources that were critical to settler survival, they served as the dominant labor force, and Indian women often married settler men. Although often portrayed as the beginning of the end for Native people in and around Seattle, the landing at Alki was instead the beginning of a shared history, in which Indians would continue to play a central role.[32]

Nearly half a century has passed since Lillian Smart created the diorama that so accurately captured the mythic vision of Seattle's founding. In those five decades, much has changed: our understanding of Seattle's past, the visibility of Native people in politics and public discourse, and the very practice of history itself. Whereas in the 1950s practitioners of American history emphasized consensus, conformity, and triumph, historians today are more willing to place conflict, diversity, and consequences (unforeseen and otherwise) at the center of the story. Meanwhile, new fields of history—Native American history, women's history, and environmental history, for example—have brought new stories to the table. In the case of Seattle, King County, and the Pacific Northwest, this means that the local past is acquiring a new richness and complexity. In isolation, none of the alternative creation stories offered here can replace the story of the Denny Party, just as focusing solely on the events of November 13, 1851, leaves out crucial elements of Seattle's urban and indigenous origins. Perhaps the lesson here is that the diorama approach to history is now obsolete, with Lillian Smart's labor of love best understood as an artifact of its time and place, when history seemed simpler.

Deciding which creation stories to tell is not just a matter of academic predilection. During the 2001 sesquicentennial of Seattle's founding, for example, conflict over the legacy of Seattle's history challenged the celebratory tone of many of the events and reminded participants that the human and environmental costs of the Alki landing remain. At several sesquicentennial events, for example, representatives from the Duwamish tribe reminded celebrants that the indigenous people of what is now Seattle—indeed, many of the descendants of the communities most closely associated with the city's namesake, Chief Seattle, remain unrecognized by the federal government.[33] Long overshadowed by the romance of the Denny Party mythology, these stories of conflict challenge us all to forge new creation stories that incorporate a diversity of perspectives. Stephen Jay Gould wrote that we prefer creation stories with heroes and sacred places; he also suggests that we prefer creation stories that are simplistic. Perhaps it is now time to allow for creation stories that are more complicated and to include lost places as well as sacred ones. Perhaps it is time to rethink the diorama approach to local history and to create a more humane, inclusive story of Seattle's creation.

## NOTES

A version of this essay was presented at the 2001 Pacific Northwest Historians Guild conference at the Museum of History & Industry in Seattle. The author wishes to thank John Findlay, Richard White, Lorraine McConaghy, and Mary Wright for their insights and encouragement.

[1] Stephen Jay Gould, "The Creation Myths of Cooperstown," in *Bully for Brontosaurus: Reflections in Natural History* (New York: W. W. Norton & Company, 1991), 48.

[2] One of the more strident points made by local historians and descendants of the Denny Party is that Alki should be pronounced "al-kee," not "al-kigh." The former is indeed the Chinook Jargon pronunciation; the latter was established during the years of Prohibition, when "al-kee" took on unsavory connotations.

[3] For familiar examples of Seattle's creation story, see Sophie Frye Bass, *When Seattle Was a Village* (Seattle: Lowman & Hanford Company, 1947); Murray Morgan, *Skid Road: An Informal Portrait of Seattle* (New York: Viking Press, 1951); and Roger Sale, *Seattle, Past to Present* (Seattle: University of Washington Press, 1976).

[4] W. T. Dovell, "The Pathfinders," *Washington Historical Quarterly* 1:1 (1906), 48–49.

[5] For a collection of writings about this "Seattle Spirit," see Christian Rohrabacher, *The*

*Seattle Spirit: A Chronological History of Seattle, U.S.A., with Chronological Illustrations* (Seattle, 1907).

[6] "The City's Birthday," *Seattle Post-Intelligencer*, 12 November 1945, 12.

[7] "The City's Birthday," *Seattle Post-Intelligencer*, 13 November 1893.

[8] Rohrabacher, 77.

[9] "The City's Birthday," *Seattle Post-Intelligencer*, 13 November 1890, 6.

[10] Archie Binns, *Northwest Gateway: The Story of the Port of Seattle* (Garden City, N.Y.: Doubleday, Doran, & Company, Inc., 1941).

[11] John Seelye, *Memory's Nation: The Place of Plymouth Rock* (Chapel Hill: University of North Carolina Press, 1998), 6.

[12] Dodie Badcon, "Diorama Gets New Guide," press release circa 1955, Badcon Collection, Museum of History & Industry.

[13] Because of technical considerations — most importantly, the printing of characters that do not appear in English — actual Lushootseed spellings of people and places are not included in this essay. For Lushootseed spellings, see the sources cited below. For more on the Lushootseed language, including pronunciation, see Dawn Bates, Thom Hess, and Vi Hilbert, *Lushootseed Dictionary* (Seattle: University of Washington Press, 1994).

[14] These placenames were recorded by Thomas Talbot Waterman, and were published in his article "The Geographical Names Used by the Indians of the Pacific Coast," *The Geographical Review* 12 (1922), 175–94. The remainder of his work, simply titled "Puget Sound Geography," can be found in manuscript form in the Smithsonian Institution Archives and the University of Washington Libraries' Special Collections division. Recently, Waterman's manuscript was updated into the current Lushootseed orthography in Vi Hilbert, Jay Miller, and Zalmai Zahir, eds., *Puget Sound Geography* (Seattle: Lushootseed Press, 2001). Collecting these placenames in the 1910s, Waterman claimed that about half of the Native place names in Puget Sound had been forgotten. How he would have known that is unclear, but it is likely that the names included here only partially reflect the depth and density of local Indian geography.

[15] Jacob Wahalchu's story is recounted in Jay Miller, *Lushootseed Culture and the Shamanic Odyssey: An Anchored Radiance* (Lincoln: University of Nebraska Press, 1999), 12.

[16] For primary sources on Fort Nisqually, see Cecelia Svinth Carpenter, *Fort Nisqually: A Documented History of Indian and British Interaction* (Tacoma, Wash.: Tahoma Research Services, 1986).

[17] Quoted in C. T. Conover, "Just Cogitating: Hudson's Bay Company Rejected Alki Point as Post Site," *Seattle Times*, 29 March 1959, 6.

[18] Robert Boyd, *The Coming of the Spirit of Pestilence: Introduced Infectious Diseases and Population Decline among Northwest Coast Indians, 1774–1874* (Vancouver: University of British Columbia Press, 1999), 155.

[19] Charles Wilkes, *Narrative of the United States Exploring Expedition during the Years 1838, 1839, 1840, 1841, and 1842*, vol. 4 (New York: G. P. Putnam, 1844), 483; and Edmond S. Meany, ed., "Diary of Wilkes in the Northwest," *Washington Historical Quarterly*, vol. 17 (1923), 139.

[20] Wilkes, 4:483 and Meany,139.

[21] Meany, 140.

[22] Boyd, 267.

[23] Samuel Hancock, *The Narrative of Samuel Hancock, 1845–1860* (New York: R. M. McBride

& Company, 1927), 94–95.

[24] Arthur Armstrong Denny, *Pioneer Days on Puget Sound* (Seattle: C. B. Bagley, Printer, 1888), 9–10.

[25] See Thomas W. Prosch, *Chronological History of Seattle from 1850 to 1897* (Seattle: n.p., 1900), 24; Roberta Frye Watt, *Four Wagons West: The Story of Seattle* (Portland, Ore.: Metropolitan Press, 1931), 28–29; Frank Carlson, "Chief Sealth" (master's thesis, University of Washington, 1903), 26; and Emily Inez Denny, *Blazing the Way; or, True Stories, Songs, and Sketches of Puget Sound and Other Pioneers* (Seattle: Rainier Printing Company, 1909), 43.

[26] Prosch, 22–24; Watt, 30–32.

[27] Clarence Bagley, *History of Seattle from the Earliest Settlement to the Present Time* (Chicago: The S. J. Clarke Publishing Company, 1916), 17.

[28] Prosch, 22–24.

[29] Welford Beaton, *The City That Made Itself: A Literary and Pictorial Record of the Building of Seattle* (Seattle: Terminal Publishing Company, 1914), 19.

[30] Gordon R. Newell, *Westward to Alki: The Story of David and Louisa Denny* (Seattle: Superior Publishing Company, 1977) and George F. Cotterill, *Climax of a World Quest: The Story of Puget Sound, the Modern Mediterranean of the Pacific* (Seattle: Olympic Publishing Company, 1928).

[31] Denny, *Pioneer Days on Puget Sound*, 13-14.

[32] For a history of Indian-white relations during the period of urbanization and settlement in Puget Sound, see Alexandra Harmon, *Indians in the Making: Ethnic Relations and Indian Identities around Puget Sound* (Berkeley: University of California Press, 1998).

[33] For accounts of sesquicentennial events, see both the *Seattle Times* and the *Seattle Post-Intelligencer* for the week of November 13, 2001.

# The Duwamish Valley Pioneers' Place in Early King County History

## Kay F. Reinartz

The first Euro-Americans to settle in the area that came to be known as King County, Washington, arrived in 1851. There were, in fact, two separate settling parties: the Collins Party and the Denny Party. Because the people in the Denny Party founded the Seattle community, historians focusing on the history of Seattle have generally overlooked the story of the Collins Party. This settling party reached Elliott Bay more than three months before the Denny Party and homesteaded in the Duwamish Valley. One goal of this essay is to begin to correct this historical oversight by relating the "first comer" settling story of the Collins Party. In addition, active leadership from the Duwamish Valley pioneer community in King County government throughout the 1850s and 1860s will be discussed.

Among the early Duwamish settlers two men, Luther M. Collins and Joseph Foster, stand out for the significant roles they played in forming King County and Washington Territory. Their contributions are undeniable, although they have been largely left out of the history books. A brief summary of the highlights of their contributions as leaders in the first decades of King County and Washington Territory is included in this essay.

Undoubtedly a major reason the Collins Party is ignored as the "first comers" to King County is that the Duwamish Valley remained unincorporated King County until the 20th century. As the Elliott Bay area evolved from wilderness to an urbanized environment, the northern section of the Duwamish Valley was incorporated as Georgetown in 1904 and then annexed to the city of Seattle in 1909. By the 1990s, the city of Tukwila, located south of Seattle and incorporated in 1908, had annexed all of the valley south of Georgetown.[1]

In the interest of keeping the historical record of the first Euro-American settling activities in King County straight, it is necessary to pause to acknowledge John Holgate, who predated both the Collins Party and the Denny Party in electing to settle in the Elliott Bay area. Holgate was the son of a couple from the eastern seaboard who had pioneered first in Ohio and then Iowa, where John grew up. Adventurous and self-confident, in 1847 the 18-year-old youth traveled from Iowa to Oregon with a Quaker wagon train. He eventually made his way to Olympia. Interested in finding land to claim under the Oregon Donation Land Act, in

August of 1849 he hired Indian guides to paddle him up Puget Sound from Tumwater. After exploring the environs of Elliott Bay, Holgate selected land on the lower Duwamish River. Unfortunately, the land he chose was not to be his. He was called home to Iowa by the death of his father late in 1849, before he had time to file his land claim. By the time Holgate returned to the Duwamish, Luther and Diana Borst Collins had filed a claim on the land he had selected and were living on the land. Holgate subsequently filed a claim on land in what became the Georgetown area. In 1868 he joined the gold rush to Boise Idaho, where he died.[2]

## THE HISTORIC DEBATE:
## THE COLLINS PARTY VERSUS THE DENNY PARTY

The crux of the historical debate regarding the first settling parties in King County is the arrival dates of the two groups. This historical point became an issue following Arthur Denny's 1888 publication of his *Pioneer Days on Puget Sound*, in which he laid out a chronological order of events for the Collins Party's Duwamish Valley settlement. According to Denny, on September 14, 1851, the Collins exploring party arrived in Elliott Bay and selected their land the next day. On September 26, 1851, they moved onto their claims.[3]

Regarding his own Alki settling party, Denny reported, "On the 25th or 26th of September, 1851, John N. Low, Lee Terry and David T. Denny arrived at Alki Point, where Low and Terry located a claim, and on the 28th of September Terry and Denny laid the foundation for the first house on the claim."[4]

Denny's published chronology of the pioneer settling activities on Elliott Bay, as well as his public statements asserting that the Collins Party had arrived in September of 1851, elicited strong objections from surviving members of the original Collins Party and their descendants, who denounced Denny's dates as flat-out wrong. Samuel Maple, a member of both the Collins June scouting party and the settling group, and Eli Maple, who joined his father and brother in the Duwamish Valley in the spring of 1852, were particularly outspoken in their challenges to Denny's published chronology. Clarence Bagley, who wrote the first history of King County, diplomatically acknowledged the controversy regarding the settling dates by stating, "Mr. Denny said their [Collins Party] permanent location was made September 14, 1851; but E. B. Maple claimed that it was made June 22, 1851, on the day of their first arrival."[5]

## THE DUWAMISH SETTLERS' ACCOUNT OF THE SUMMER OF 1851

While those with firsthand knowledge of the Duwamish settlers' experience objected to Arthur Denny's inaccurate chronology, no one wrote and published an account of the Collins Party's settling activities. It was not until the third decade of

the 20th century that professional historians actively questioned Arthur Denny's
dates and his version of the Collins Party's initial settling activities.

A highly credible challenge to Arthur Denny's dates came in the late 1930s
from Professor Hillman F. Jones, curator for the Washington Historical Society
Museum, and Judge August Toellner. Both men were specialists in the history of
the Duwamish Valley. Toellner had come to the Duwamish Valley in 1875 and was
a teacher at the Duwamish Primary School. He went on to become a lawyer, then
a judge. He maintained a practice in Seattle for many years. His interest in the
history of the Duwamish Valley settlers began when he was living and teaching in
the valley, during which time he became personally acquainted with the surviving
original settlers—Samuel Maple, Henry Van Asselt, and Lucinda Collins—as well
as Eli Maple. He also knew the descendants of other settlers who had come to the
Duwamish Valley in the 1850s and 1860s and found that they vouched for the June
arrival date. While conversing with the pioneers and their descendants, he often
heard the story of the Collins Party's arrival in the summer of 1851.[6]

Toellner provides the following account of the Collins Party's activities in the
summer of 1851, based on oral testimony he collected. On June 21, 1851, the
exploration party traveled by Indian canoe from the Collins homestead on the
Nisqually River to Pigeon Point at the mouth of the Duwamish River. They made
their way up the river, camping that night in an area known in the 19th century as
the Meadows, now the site of the King County International Airport. The party
was impressed with the fine tidal stream and the extensive areas of open meadow
with rich, fertile bottom soil, which they called "little prairies." These prairies
were free of large trees and lacked the dense vegetation that grew almost everywhere else. They had been created by the combination of ancient beaver dams and
silt brought down by periodic floods. In addition, a serious forest fire in recent
history had destroyed many trees. Not having to spend long, precious days clearing the land before a crop could be put in had much appeal, since it meant the
settlers could realize a harvest that very season. What they had been told about the
large Indian population was quite evident, and they estimated that approximately
700 Indians were living at Duwamish Head and another 300 along the riverbank.[7]
On June 23 they selected their claims, Collins planted a crop of potatoes with seed
potatoes he had brought with him, and they returned to the Nisqually homestead.[8]

Knowing it would be almost impossible to move the livestock and household
goods through the dense forest, Collins searched up and down the Sound for a
suitable boat. He located and bought an old scow that he "sided up" to confine the
animals. Once the scow was ready, the party's goods were loaded along with the
animals and people, and they headed down the Sound to Elliott Bay with Collins at
the rudder. It was soon evident that the vessel was both overloaded and un-seawor-
thy; it sank shortly after they set out, but not before the animals were brought
ashore.[9]

The scow was unloaded, hitched to the horses who pulled it ashore, repaired,
and reloaded with the group's goods. There were no passengers this time. Now

Jacob Maple navigated the scow, keeping it close to shore. Everyone else, including the children, walked down the Sound, driving the animals along the tide flats. It was a slow trip with many stops to pull the animals out of the gullies and wash ways that they fell into on the rough beach. Thus did the party make its way to Alki Point, where, like Noah's Ark, the scow was reloaded with men, women, children and animals. Now Collins was at the rudder. With utmost caution he maneuvered the awkward vessel to the mouth of the Duwamish and they rode the inflowing tide up to their claim sites.[10]

That summer on the Duwamish was busy with settling-in work, including tending the vegetables planted in June, and building cabins, barns and fences to confine the animals. Around September 23rd, Luther and Diana Collins and a couple of others took the scow back to the Nisqually to pick up additional belongings and a load of nursery stock that Diana had been cultivating on the homestead for four years. Collins had sold the land to a man named Ballard, a friend of the group who had come west with Van Asselt in 1850.[11] The loaded scow was guided back to Elliott Bay, rounding Alki Point close to shore. Bagley reports that David Denny, who was camped at Alki along with others on September 27th said that the Collins group rounded Alki Point in the early evening. He noted that "the two women, the wife and daughter of Collins, conversed in Chinook, the trade jargon of the Northwest, with Captain Fay," who was at the Alki camp. David Denny also reported that on September 28 Luther Collins and an Indian passed the beach driving oxen before them.[12]

## A PROFILE OF THE COLLINS SETTLING PARTY

The historic record yields enough information for a simple sketch of the Duwamish settlers. It is not clear exactly who was with Collins on the June scouting party to Elliott Bay. Some accounts mention Jacob and Samuel Maple and Henry Van Asselt. Eli Maple, Jacob Maple's younger son, who joined his father and brother in April 1852, reported that his father and brother and a man named Thompson went with Collins on the initial scouting trip. Eli was probably referring to John Thornton, a friend of Van Asselt's who had come to Puget Sound with Collins that spring. Thornton eventually homesteaded near Port Townsend. It is likely that Van Asselt did not go on the scouting party since he was recovering from an injury sustained when he accidentally shot himself in the shoulder while cleaning his gun.[13]

There is no confusion regarding who was in the actual settling party that moved into the Duwamish Valley a few weeks after the scouting party made their visit. This group consisted of Luther Collins, 34; his wife, Diana Borst Collins, about 32; and their children, Lucinda, 13, and Stephen, 7. The others were Jacob Maple, 58; his son Samuel Maple, 22; and Henry Van Asselt, 31. As is so often the case in life, a series of coincidences led to these people meeting, settling together, and becoming lifelong friends. The Maples and Van Asselt eventually became relatives by marriage when the Dutchman married Jacob Maple's daughter Catherine in 1867.[14, 15]

At the center of the group were Luther and Diana Borst Collins. Married in 1838, the adventurous young couple homesteaded first in Illinois and then in Iowa. In 1847, they joined a wagon train bound for Oregon Territory. Luther herded their livestock while Diana drove the wagon the 2,000 miles over the Great Plains and across the Rocky Mountains. The livestock was part of their business plan. They intended to breed and sell livestock to other settlers, many of whom would lack draft animals because they had traveled to the Northwest by sea. They also planned to sell nursery stock to the homesteaders, and tins filled with a variety of fruit tree cuttings were nailed to both sides of the wagon. In the fall of 1847, the couple staked a claim on the Nisqually River in the south Puget Sound area, built a homestead, and set about building their breeding herds of domestic livestock, including horses and oxen. In addition, they cleared land and planted the fruit tree cuttings carefully kept alive on the long overland journey.[16, 17]

In spite of his occasionally abrasive manner, he had a good deal of charisma.[18] Luther Collins was tall, fair and apparently handsome. He was an intelligent and dynamic person. Clarence Bagley describes Collins as "a rough, boistering [sic] sort of a fellow; bold and venturesome; impatient of legal, moral or social restraint; strong, determined and willful; a leader among men with whom he usually cast his lot."[19]

Diana Borst Collins holds the distinction of being the first Euro-American woman in King County. While the written record does not yield a vivid image of her, one gains a sense of her character from the things she did. It is obvious that she was both adventurous and stable. She thrived in the frontier environment. Intelligent and creative, as well as physically strong, she adapted quickly to frontier conditions and became skilled at whatever was needed. By nature and necessity she was independent and highly self-reliant, as her restless impatient husband frequently left her in charge of their numerous enterprises for months on end. After they staked their first claim on the Nisqually River she remained constantly on the land, looking after the growing livestock herd, delivering the new calves and colts, dealing with an array of human and animal illnesses, and cultivating the crops, which included extensive propagation of the nursery fruit tree stock. Daughter Lucinda reported years later that they lived side-by-side with the Indians, and when her father was gone her mother was totally dependent on the Indians for help with the farming and other heavy work.[20]

## THE CALIFORNIA GOLD RUSH BRINGS THE DUWAMISH SETTLERS

The California gold rush was responsible for bringing together the people who became the first settling party in King County. In 1850 Luther Collins left Diana to look after the children and the Nisqually homestead, and took off for the California goldfields, where he enjoyed early success in accumulating a small fortune. About to return to Puget Sound country, Collins met Jacob and Samuel Maple, father and son, most recently from Iowa. They too had "struck it rich" and were intent on finding a good place to homestead.[21, 22]

The Maples came from a long line of people who had sought their fortunes on the ever-moving western frontier. The elder Maple, a widower of 58, was already an old man by the standards of the day, when life expectancy was around 60. Short of stature, he was a man of remarkable vitality, stamina, strength, and wilderness lore. He was a seasoned frontiersman with a real sense of adventure who had literally grown up on the frontier. Born in 1793, Maple was 7 when his parents moved the family from the Monongahela River Valley in Pennsylvania to the Ohio frontier. In 1840 he moved his own family from the now-settled Ohio region to the Iowa Territory frontier. His son Samuel, 23, was tall, and farm-bred.[23]

The Maples and Hill Harmon, another successful gold prospector, agreed to go north with Collins to look over the Puget Sound country in the late spring of 1851. On the journey they met five men, each of whom had acquired about $1,000 in gold dust. Among them was Henry Van Asselt, who had immigrated from Armela, Gelderland, Holland, in 1847 at the age of 23. Short with a wiry, powerful build and remarkably broad, muscular hands, Van Asselt liked to say that he had arrived in America with no assets but his hands and head. Within three years he had worked his way to Iowa. Determined to take a look at the Oregon Territory, he joined four other men to travel west on the Oregon Trail in 1850. The men walked much of the way, hauling their gear in two ox-drawn wagons. Reaching the Willamette Valley in the autumn, they spent the winter working in a shingle mill. As winter ended they headed south to the California goldfields, where their dreams of amassing the means to acquire land and homestead were accomplished in five and one-half weeks of panning.[24]

When Collins brought the gang of men up from California, Luther and Diana Collins had been homesteading four years in isolation from other settlers and they wanted to form a community on Puget Sound. Luther Collins looked at the five men he met traveling north with hunger for land in their eyes and fat pouches of gold dust on their belts, and saw excellent candidates for his community. A charismatic promoter, Collins convinced the men that they would find good land on Puget Sound. Arriving at the Nisqually basin, Henry Van Asselt was not satisfied. He felt that the thin, sandy soil would not support the kind of community that he wanted to help build, with schools, churches, and the refinements of civilization. By this time the congenial, serious-minded Dutchman had achieved a position of great respect in the group, the consensus was they did not want to stay on the Nisqually. Diana and Luther Collins agreed that they would move to a different location if the group could find a place they all liked.[25]

In the course of four years of living on Puget Sound, Collins had extensively explored the Sound and its environs. He told the men that about 40 miles farther

north there was a beautiful river that flowed into a bay that would make an excellent harbor. The river valley had good land that would support a large community.
The main drawback, in Collins' opinion, was the large number of Indians living in
the area. The men agreed to take a look at the area and paid Collins to take them
there. Indians were hired to paddle their canoes. After a two-day journey they
reached Elliott Bay, where they investigated the river system that came to be known
as the Duwamish, Black, and White rivers.[26]

## SEASONED FRONTIERSPEOPLE

The absence of good printed records regarding the date of the Collins Party's
arrival in King County compels historians to consider what would be logical behavior for a group of men and women with substantial experience surviving in a
wilderness environment. Unlike the Denny Party, largely a group of people with
little frontier experience, the Collins Party was composed of people who had years
of experience living in harsh frontier conditions, including the Pacific Northwest.
While exact dates are not known, there is much evidence indicating that it was
June when Collins brought the men he had met in the California goldfields to
Puget Sound Country. It is illogical that the group would have been seriously exploring for homestead sites in late September, which was far too late in the season
to get the basic settling-in activities completed before the autumn rains. The
Collinses were aware of the seriousness of the rainy winters and the need for good
shelter. In addition to themselves, they had two children and livestock that they
needed to protect from the weather and feed through the winter.

The Duwamish settlers' first season on the river included finding and repair-
ing a scow, moving the Collins family's belongings and livestock from the Nisqually
homestead, clearing land, building cabins, planting and harvesting potatoes, planting more than 1,000 fruit trees, cutting firewood for the winter, and gathering and
preserving food for the winter. There simply was not enough time to get it all done
after September 27, Arthur Denny's date for the commencement of the Duwamish
Valley settlement. Undoubtedly Arthur Denny brought his settling party to Elliott
Bay in November because he did not realize that the rainy season could be deadly
without watertight shelter. When his brother David let fall the remark that "he
wished they had not come," Arthur was furious. Inez Denny, David's daughter,
recorded in her book *Blazing the Way* that her father hastened to explain to his
brother that, lacking even a single cabin with a roof, the entire party was in danger
of not surviving.[27]

## THOSE IN POWER WRITE THE HISTORY

In comparing the chronologies of the initial settling activities on Elliott Bay in the summer of 1851, according to the Collins and Denny parties, there is more than a three-month discrepancy in the date set for the arrival of the Collins Party. Denny's version has his party and the Collins settling party arriving and beginning settling activities at essentially the same time. Indeed, Denny places his Alki settlement only two days behind the Duwamish settlement. Consideration of the contradictory accounts brings up some questions: a) Why the discrepancy? b) Why did Arthur Denny feel compelled to "officially" record the arrival dates of the Collins Party in his book, which is mainly about his accomplishments. Was Arthur Denny intent upon establishing a historical "myth" that enhanced the prestige of his Alki settlement as essentially the first settlement in King County, which, in fact, has been believed by most people throughout the 20th and into the 21st centuries? Arthur Denny rose to be a major power in Seattle—politically, economically, and socially. Historical memory has carried the image of him as a proud, domineering person who often took credit for the accomplishments of others. Of course, this is conjecture and cannot be verified.

A final element in this historical puzzle arises from the fact that Henry Van Asselt's signature appears at the end of Denny's chronology, along with the signatures of a number of the Denny Party members. If it is indeed Van Asselt's signature, he is contradicting the testimonial of other members of the Collins Party. By 1888 Van Asselt had become a part of the Seattle Pioneer Association and played a central role in that group. He was also a personal friend of Arthur Denny. Van Asselt was an elderly man in 1888 and the soundness of his mind is unknown. Van Asselt's motivations are obscured by the clouds of time; however, further research may uncover some explanation. One might speculate that Van Asselts' close friendship with Arthur Denny as well as long association with the Denny Party pioneers and membership in the Seattle Pioneers Association might have prompted him to support Arthur Denny's version of the "first comers" story. Perhaps some as-yet undiscovered documents will further illuminate this historical mystery.

Examination of histories written after Arthur Denny's *Pioneering on Puget Sound* verifies that once Denny published his version of the order of events, historians generally have accepted the story as conclusive. In the "classic" King County histories published over the past 100 years, including those by Clarence Bagley,[28] Frederic J. Grant,[29] and Ezra Meeker,[30] the Collins Party's scouting arrival date varies from September 12 to September 21, 1851. In spite of this, other historians, such as Lowell Beaver, author of *Memories from Historic Markers and Plaques*, published in 1963, acknowledge that the September arrival is suspect and mention the Collins Party's account of their settling activities in June of 1851.[31]

The premier early historian of King County, Clarence Bagley, begins his discussion of the "first comer" settling activities in the first volume of his *History of King County* with the following statement:

The date of the first settlements at Alki and Seattle were accurately recorded, but there has been much confusion about the first settlement in

King County . . . The actual settlement at [the Duwamish River] by L. M.
Collins, Henry Van Asselt, [and] Jacob and Samuel Maple was for many
years understood to have been about September 15, 1851.[32]

In the first volume of his earlier book, *History of Seattle*, published in 1916, Bagley
had expressed ambivalence about the arrival date of the Collins Party. He dealt
with the issue with the following statement: "Mr. Denny said their permanent
location was made September 14, 1851; but E.B. [Eli] Maple claimed that it was
made June 22, 1851, on the day of their first arrival." In several other places in his
narrative he reports that the descendants of the Collins settling party, Eli Maple
among them, testified that Denny's dates were wrong and the original Collins Party
arrived on June 21, 1851, and staked their claims on June 22, 1851.[33]

Further indications of Bagley's ambivalence regarding the reliability of Denny's
chronology are found in his inclusion of newspaper accounts supporting an early
June arrival date for the Collins Party. For example, in October 1855, the editor of
the *Puget Sound Courier* of Steilacoom reported that L. M. Collins had brought in
samples of his harvest of more than 300 bushels of "fine, luscious peaches raised on
his farm . . . The second year's bearing." The editor went on to report that "Collins
has a large nursery and orchard with over 1,000 trees . . . The trees were planted
the fall of 1851."[34]

Frederic J. Grant includes a somewhat detailed account of the Duwamish settlers in his *History of Seattle*. Grant acknowledges the Collins Party as the first
settlers and says that their settlement took precedence over the Denny group "by
only a few days." However, he also states that the Collins group was in the Puget
Sound region in June of 1851.[35]

Over the decades, as professional and casual researchers alike have relied on
the classic histories and reiterated Arthur Denny's report of the settlement dates of
the first comers, that version has become more firmly entrenched. One could speculate that the objectivity of late-19th- and early-20th century King County historians was overshadowed by their desire to avoid challenging Denny's chronology of
the pioneer history. After all, he was a personal friend of most of those historians.
In addition, the Denny family had achieved high status in Seattle and the region,
and it would not have been politic to caste a shadow on its glory. The motivations
of later historians are less obvious. However, the history books published in the
20th century, with few exceptions, have aggrandized those who achieved prominence and position in Seattle, while generally ignoring the rest of King County.

## The Collins Family

The Collins pioneer family members did not live long lives. In 1862 Luther Collins joined the Boise gold rush and drowned while crossing the Snake River. Diana Borst Collins remained on their homestead until she died in 1874. Diana's brother G. M. "Jerry" Borst came to Puget Sound in the 1860s and opened up the Snoqualmie Valley to settlement. His niece Lucinda Collins, the daughter of Luther and Diana, and her second husband, John Fares, joined him. Lucinda had the distinction of being the first Euro-American woman in the valley. Lucinda had no children but adopted a boy from a wagon train passing through Snoqualmie Pass whose parents had died during the journey. There is no record of this adopted son and his activities. Lucinda died in 1884. Stephen Collins, Luther and Diana's son, married an Indian woman whose name is unknown, with whom he had a child, but there is no known record of the line of descent. The commonly held assumption is that there were no survivors. Stephen's life ended in suicide in the 1870s. Diana and Lucinda were both buried in the old Pioneer Cemetery in Seattle, later the site of Denny Park. Their graves were moved to Lakeview Cemetery on Capital Hill when Denny Hill was razed. Stephen's burial place is unknown.

Sources: Clarence Bagley, *History of King County*, vol. 1 (Seattle, Wash.: S. J. Clarke Publishing Co., 1929), 358; Kay F. Reinartz, *Tukwila, Community at the Crossroads* (Tukwila, Wash.: City of Tukwila, 1991), 5–8; August Toellner, "Pioneers Fete 89th Year of Landing on Duwamish," *Seattle Times*, 21 June 1940.

## The Duwamish Community Growth And Participation In King County Government

The 1850 U.S. Census for Oregon Territory showed a total population of 13,294, with 457 living in the Puget Sound district. By the end of 1852 approximately 20,000 settlers lived in the territory, and there was a growing interest in dividing the huge territory for administrative purposes. Washington Territory was created in response to this need. A census taken in the summer of 1853 reported 3,965 settlers in the newly created Washington Territory, with 170 in King County.[36] The Duwamish Valley was home to 13 settlers in 1853. This was almost 8 percent of the population of King County at that time. By 31 December 1855, 20 settlers had filed donation claims in the Duwamish Valley, and most of the land bordering the river was taken. In the next decade the remaining valley bottomland was claimed, including most of the future Duwamish-Allentown area, the area east of the river at Foster Point, and the Southcenter district.[37]

By 1856 a close-knit, strongly supportive community had formed along the Duwamish River in spite of the distance between homesteads resulting from the large size of the claims, up to 640 acres. Including settlers in the northern section of the White River, the community in 1856 consisted of 26 adults: five married couples, one single woman, and 15 single men, three of whom were widowers. With the 17 children, the total community was 42 people. As in all frontier communities, single young men predominated; however, the community had a notably larger proportion of older people than was typical. The average age of the 11 bachelors was 25, while the average age of the married men was 53.[38]

While the Duwamish pioneers have been generally thought of as farmers, a notable number were not from farm backgrounds. Trades and professions in the community in 1856 included tailor, plasterer/mason, cooper (barrel maker), carpenter, furniture maker, blacksmith, lawyer, physician and engineer. As the Puget Sound area became more populated, many of the men left farming in favor of pursuing their original occupations.[39]

Clarence Bagley announced in his massive *History of King County* that the Duwamish settlers, being farmers, occupied themselves with farm work and took "but a small part in the political activities of King County."[40] Careful study of the King County commissioner's records and other governmental documents, beginning in 1852, shows that Bagley's quick dismissal of the Duwamish pioneers from early King County history is erroneous. Bagley, faced with an overwhelming amount of historical information on the founders and developers of Seattle, most of whom he knew personally, simply chose not to look into the active role of the Duwamish pioneers. The records show that in the formative years of King County, people living in the Duwamish area were regularly involved in King County and Washington territorial politics and government. Luther Collins and Joseph Foster, who homesteaded in the valley in 1852, stand out as significant regional leaders in this historic period (Foster is discussed later in this essay).

## FORMATION OF KING COUNTY, OREGON TERRITORY
### FIRST RESOLUTION: A NEW COUNTY, 1853

Be it remembered that on this 5th day of March, A.D. 1853, the County Commissioners Court of King County was convened in the house of D. S. Maynard in the Town of Seattle, and duly organized in accordance with an act of the Legislative Assembly of Oregon.

Present: L. M. Collins* and A. A. Denny, Commissioners, and H. L. Yesler, Clerk, the following business was transacted:

Ordered that the following named persons be summoned to serve as grand jurors-to-wit: George Holt,* Jacob Maple,* Samuel Maple,* Henry Price, Henry Smith, Edward A. Clark, and James Wilson. And as petit jurors: David F. Denny, Wm. N. Bell, John Sampson, John Moss, Wm. Carr, David Maurer, John Strobel, and Henry Van Asselt.*
Ordered that the court adjourn to meet on the first Monday.

Signed, L. M. Collins,* A. A. Denny, Commissioners

* Asterisks added to indicate Duwamish Valley settlers.
Source: King County Commission Record, 5 March 1853.

On 22 December 1852, Thurston County, which encompassed all of Oregon Territory north of the Columbia River to the Canadian border, was divided into Thurston, King, Pierce, Island, and Jefferson counties. King County was thus established while the land was still part of Oregon Territory. Luther M. Collins was appointed to represent King County in the Oregon Territorial Legislature in 1853, along with John N. Low and Arthur A. Denny.

Everyone agreed that the distance between the counties north of the Columbia River and the Oregon Territory's capital in Salem was too great to function efficiently. Soon after the creation of the new counties, agitation began for a separate territorial government to be created for the region north of the Columbia River. A convention was held at Monticello, near the mouth of the Cowlitz River on the Columbia, to petition Congress for the creation of a new territory to be called Columbia. The seven delegates from King County were Luther M. Collins, Charles C. Terry, George N. McConahan, William Bell, John Low, Arthur Denny and Dr. David Maynard. The memorial was adopted on March 2, 1853, with the name changed from Columbia to Washington, because it was felt that Columbia would be confused with Washington, District of Columbia.[41]

On 5 March 1853, King County was established as a political entity located in Washington Territory. Five of the 17 men making up the historic body which created King County were from the Duwamish River settlement. In the first two decades after its formation, Duwamish Valley settlers figured prominently among those appointed to fill county offices.

### Duwamish Settlers Holding King County Offices, 1853-1868

• King County Commissioners: Luther M. Collins, first commission appointee (1853–54); Luther M. Collins, Cyrus Lewis, G. W. Loomis (1855–56); Francis McNatt (1857–58); John Thomas, (1858–60); Henry Adams (1860–62)
• King County Sheriff: Louis Wyckoff (1860)
• Deputy Sheriff: Stephen Foster, first deputy appointee, served under Carson Boren (first sheriff) (1853–54)
• King County Constable: Bennett L. Johns, first appointee (1853–54)
• King County Assessor: John Holgate, first appointee (1853–54)
• King County Postmaster: William Gilliam (1867)
• King County Road District Supervisor: Luther M. Collins (first appointee), (1854); Cyrus Lewis (1855–56, 1866–68)
• King County Grand Jury: Jacob Maple, John Buckley, Henry Van Asselt, Louis V. Wyckoff, Timothy Grow (1853–54); Henry Adams, Henry Holt (1860).
• King County Petit Jury: Joseph Foster, Stephen Foster, Charles Brownell, William Gilliam (1853–54), Henry Adams, Samuel Russell (1859–62).

Source: King County Commission Record, vol. 1, 5 December 1853, 31 December 1868; King County Commission Record, March 1851–December 1869.

### Joseph Foster, a Man for the Times

On April 4, 1853, at 4 a.m., Joseph and Stephen Foster arrived at Alki Point on Elliott Bay aboard the brig *Carib*. Two hours later Charles Terry took them off the ship in a hand-carved cedar canoe paddled by Indians. Flora Fleming Foster, Joseph Foster's daughter-in-law, recorded the story from Joseph's account. In the summer of 1852 the brothers had traveled on the Oregon Trail to Portland, where they worked for a few months before taking off for the California goldfields. They were unsuccessful in their gold panning efforts in the Northern California gold-fields. By March of 1853 they had made their way to San Francisco. Looking for adventures and opportunity, they booked passage on a ship for Australia. A few hours before sailing they changed their minds, sold the tickets, and caught the *Carib* for Puget Sound Country.[43]

After arriving in April, the Foster brothers explored the Elliott Bay area and selected land in the Duwamish Valley. Joseph Foster decided to stake his claim right at the confluence of the Duwamish, Black, and White rivers, a place the Indians called Mox la Push. He predicted that a great city would one day arise at this point. This place is in the vicinity of today's Southcenter, developed in the 1960s. Stephen picked land a little farther north on the Duwamish, where the river made a long, narrow loop. This place came to be known as Foster Point. Years later Joseph bought his brother's land and his principal residence was located at Foster Point. The place is still marked by a grand oak tree, which Joseph planted as a seedling in the 1870s.[44]

When Joseph Foster came to King County in 1853, it was an almost unbroken wilderness with a few tiny settlements. He lived to see a great commonwealth built in that wilderness and played a conspicuous part in its formation through his active leadership as the representative from King County in the Territorial Legislature for more than two decades.

Washington Territory was established the year Foster arrived in the Puget Sound region, and he soon became interested in territorial government and politics. In 1858, at age 31, Foster was elected as King County's Representative to the Territorial Legislature, a step that marked the beginning of his outstanding career in public service, which continued to 1886. He was elected to 11 terms, serving in the upper and lower houses a total of 22 years. Although he was an ardent Democrat, his outstanding ability and objective nonpartisan public spirit won him votes from many Republicans, and he was often the only Democrat to be elected from the Republican King County.[45]

The legislative session was held in the winter, when there was a pause in the all-consuming work of homesteading. The severe winter of 1860 did not keep Foster from getting to Olympia to take his seat as the representative from King County. Now in his second term, he had experience and confidence, and demonstrated the progressive vision and effective leadership that were to mark his long political career. In that single session Foster sponsored and saw through the Legislature two bills that had major impacts on regional history down to the present: the bills creating the road over Snoqualmie Pass and locating the University of Washington in Seattle.[46]

Early in the session he sponsored H.M. 1, which provided for the construction of the Military Road from Seattle via Snoqualmie Pass to Fort Colville. Through Foster's personal efforts this bill passed both houses that session. At this time Foster also presented a request for incorporation of the Seattle Library Association. Twenty percent of the charter members of the association were from the

Joseph Foster, 1828-1911, Duwamish Valley pioneer and Washington Territory leader. Foster was elected to the Territorial Legislature for 11 terms representing King County in both the upper and lower houses. He was offered the office of Governor of Washington Territory in 1887, but declined. Courtesy of the Museum of History and Industry.

Duwamish Valley and included William Gilliam, John Holgate, George Holt, and Henry Van Asselt, in addition to Foster and his wife, Martha Steele Foster.[47]

Having assured the construction of the road through Snoqualmie Pass and a library for Seattle, Foster spent the winter of 1860 debating in his own mind and with others the best locations for the territorial capital and the new territorial university. Foster initially had concluded that it was better for the future of King County to have the territorial capital rather than the university located in Seattle. But after a conversation about the long-term implications with the Reverend Daniel Bagley in the winter of 1860, Foster changed his mind and shepherded through the Legislature the passage of a bill locating the university in Seattle, leaving the capital in Olympia.[48]

Later, in the 1890s, as the original Elliott Bay pioneers looked back over the years since the beginning of settlement, a debate raged over who was "the father of the University of Washington." Arthur Denny said he was, but others gave

Joseph Foster the credit since he had sponsored the bill to locate the university in Seattle and made sure it passed. Foster made the following public statement, which reflects his characteristically confident yet modest approach to issues of his day:

> I think I should be in position to know all about the question as to who has the right to be called the 'Father of the University of Washington.' I introduced the bill in the Legislature locating the university at Seattle. I got the billed passed and signed. Who then knows more about it than I do? Before the Legislature adjourned I came home on a visit and talked to everybody interested. I remember two men out of the lot. I met Arthur A. Denny and he and I agreed that my bill was a good thing, because we could trade that university off in one or two years and thereby get the territorial capitol for Seattle.
>
> When I met Daniel Bagley I told him of the nice little plan that Mr. Denny and I had in view—Bagley knocked that plan into a cocked hat in about two minutes. He said to me, "Nonsense, Joe, don't do anything of the kind. You've got something far better than a capitol. You go back to Olympia and get John Webster, Edmund Carr and me appointed regents or commissioners and I will show you that a university is better than a capitol.
>
> He talked to me more on that line and got me convinced, so I went to Olympia and did what he asked me to. Bagley worked like a Turk on that job and built the University of Washington in a year. He handled the whole business, and if the University has a father, his name is Daniel Bagley.[49]

Throughout the 1870s and 1880s, Foster continued to represent King County in the Legislature. He became well known and beloved across Washington Territory for his fair and even-handed approach to issues. He was also recognized as a formidable power in the political realm, for he had good friends everywhere and was famous for his ability to convince the most determined opponent to come over to his side through logical reasoning. Among the numerous significant bills he successfully sponsored in the Legislature, the Washington Territory Woman Suffrage Bill, 1883, was the one that he reported gave him the most satisfaction and sense of major accomplishment.[50]

Joseph Foster was astute in business matters and made numerous wise investments after coming to the Duwamish Valley. By the 1880s he had accumulated 440 acres of land in the Duwamish Valley, and his many successful enterprises supported the family. His farm land was rented out, and Foster divided his time between managing his business interests and civic service.[51]

## CHIEF SEATTLE, FRIEND OF THE DUWAMISH SETTLERS

Chief Seattle grew up in the area called Mox la Push, at the confluence of the Duwamish, Black, and White rivers. He gained a position of prominence with his people as a result of his success in vanquishing a raiding party of "mountain people" in the vicinity of what is now Fort Dent Park. Chief Seattle was very well acquainted with the settlers in the Duwamish and White river valleys, and was a welcome guest at their gatherings from the 1850s to the 1870s. Legend has it that in honor of the marriage of Henry Van Asselt and Catherine Maple, Jacob Maple's daughter, in December 1862 at the Maple homestead, Chief Seattle and his people celebrated one of the grandest potlatches ever witnessed by the settlers. Joseph Foster and Chief Seattle formed a close friendship that lasted throughout their lifetimes. Chief Seattle's high regard for Foster is reflected in his daughter Angeline's decision to name her son Joe Foster, as a namesake for Foster. It was a practice among some of the Indians to name their children after prominent white men they respected and admired.[42]

Joseph Foster loved rural life and was devoted to maintaining the homestead, which remained the main family home. Whenever Joseph was there he worked regularly in the fields and garden, and while he was frequently urged to move to Seattle, where he would be closer to the hub of political and business activity, he never seriously considered leaving the Duwamish Valley. The community of Foster grew up around his homestead. In 1893 he established the original public school district in the Duwamish Valley, School District 144, and helped build the first school on land that he donated.[52] Foster High School, a secondary school in the South Central School District, is a direct descendant of Foster's school.

Foster was well known throughout Washington Territory and respected for his abilities, honesty, and wise decisions led to his being offered the governorship of Washington Territory in 1887. He declined this high honor in favor of dedicating his energies to King County, his local community, and his family.[53]

Joseph Foster died on January 17, 1911, at age 82. His estate was estimated to be worth more than $500,000 and included 300 acres in his homestead, his businesses, and residence lands in Seattle, Georgetown and Foster. There was widespread mourning, and tributes to this foremost citizen of Washington poured in from across the Northwest commending his ethical character and accomplishments for the public good.

The day of Foster's funeral and burial in the family plot at Lake View Cemetery in Seattle a special Interurban funeral train came to Foster Station, where

Joseph Foster's casket was put aboard a car draped in black crepe. Many additional cars followed, carrying almost everyone who lived in the valley. At every stop, all the way to Capitol Hill, more mourners boarded the train. The casket was taken off the train and hundreds of people silently walked behind the casket to witness Foster's burial. Frederic J. Grant, a contemporary biographer of Joseph Foster, said,

> His talents and integrity profoundly impressed his associates in the Legislature and throughout his tenure of office his opinions were always received with the greatest respect. He declined to grant any favors for which a consideration was offered to him and so great was his sense of honor that he declined to use even the passes commonly provided by railroads for legislative members.[54]

As the city of Seattle steadily grew, incorporating in 1869, it became the unquestioned power center of King County. The Duwamish homesteader Joseph Foster stands as a remarkable example of a non-Seattle resident who maintained strong regional influence because of his long tenure in the Legislature representing King County.

## Sesquicentennial Reflections on King County History

The brief look at the small Duwamish pioneer community demonstrates that from the earliest days people and places outside of Seattle proper have played significant roles in shaping the course of events in King County, Washington. There is considerable evidence in the historic record that others who lived in the county rather than in Seattle were, like Foster, major leaders. For the most part their story has not been adequately told. Further research is needed to bring forth the contributions of King County communities and leaders to balance a history that currently overemphasizes Seattle.

At the time of the state's centennial, 1989, a number of King County communities published community history books. Yet numerous other communities lack even a basic chronology of the local history. In the more than 80 years since Clarence Bagley produced his *History of King County*, there has been no substantial effort to either update or revise the county history. Moreover, there have been no attempts to synthesize the history of King County as a region. In contrast to the noticeable lack of regional history books, new histories of Seattle appear regularly. The logic of looking at the county as a region becomes more obvious each decade as Seattle becomes less important as an urban center than as a dynamic element in the greater megalopolis of western Washington that extends from Everett to Olympia.

## NOTES

[1] Kay F. Reinartz, *Tukwila, Community at the Crossroads* (Tukwila, Wash.: City of Tukwila, 1991), 77.

[2] Abbie Holgate Hanford, "Narrative of the Indian Up Rising, 1855–1856," University of Washington Allen Library, MSCUA, (typewritten manuscript).

[3] Arthur A. Denny, *Pioneer Days on Puget Sound* (Fairfield, Wash.: Ye Galleon Press, 1965), 85.

[4] Denny, 85.

[5] Clarence Bagley, *History of Seattle*, vol. 1 (Chicago, Ill.: S. J. Clarke Publishing Co., 1916), 20.

[6] August Toellner, "June 21, 1851 Set as Date of First Settlers in Seattle [King County]," *Duwamish Valley News*, 18 May 1934, 1; August Toellner, "First Settlers Chose the Duwamish," *Duwamish Valley News*, 2 July 1937, 1–2; August Toellner, "Pioneers Fete 89th Year of Landing on Duwamish," *Seattle Times*, 21 June 1940, 4.

[7] Frederic James Grant, *History of Seattle* (New York: American Publishing and Engraving, 1891), 24–25, 46–47.

[8] August Toellner, "June 21, 1851 Set as Date of First Settlers in Seattle [King County]," *Duwamish Valley News*, 18 May 1934, 1; August Toellner, "First Settlers Chose the Duwamish," *Duwamish Valley News*, 2 July 1937, 1–2; August Toellner, "Pioneers Fete 89th Year of Landing on Duwamish," *Seattle Times*, 21 June 1940, 4.

[9] *Ibid.*

[10] *Ibid.*

[11] *Ibid.*

[12] Bagley, *History of Seattle*, vol. 1, 17–18.

[13] Grant, 46–49.

[14] Grant, 46–49.

[15] August Toellner, "June 21, 1851 Set as Date of First Settlers in Seattle [King County]," *Duwamish Valley News*, 18 May 1934, 1; August Toellner, "First Settlers Chose the Duwamish," *Duwamish Valley News*, 2 July 1937, 1–2; August Toellner, "Pioneers Fete 89th Year of Landing on Duwamish," *Seattle Times*, 21 June 1940, 4.

[16] Grant, 24–25, 46–49.

[17] August Toellner, "June 21, 1851 Set as Date of First Settlers in Seattle [King County]," *Duwamish Valley News*, 18 May 1934, 1; August Toellner, "First Settlers Chose the Duwamish," *Duwamish Valley News*, 2 July 1937, 1–2; August Toellner, "Pioneers Fete 89th Year of Landing on Duwamish," *Seattle Times*, 21 June 1940, 4.

[18] Grant, 24–25, 46–47.

[19] Clarence Bagley, *History of King County*, vol. 1 (Seattle, Wash.: S. J. Clarke Publishing Co., 1929), 358.

[20] August Toellner, "June 21, 1851 set as Date of First Settlers in Seattle [King County]," *Duwamish Valley News*, 18 May 1934, 1; August Toellner, "Pioneers Fete 89th Year of Landing on Duwamish," *Seattle Times*, 21 June 1940, 4.

[21] Grant, 24–26, 46–49.

[22] August Toellner, "June 21, 1851 Set as Date of First Settlers in Seattle [King County]," *Duwamish Valley News*, 18 May 1934, 1; August Toellner, "First Settlers Chose the Duwamish," *Duwamish Valley News*, 2 July 1937, 1–2; August Toellner, "Pioneers Fete 89th Year of Land-

ing on Duwamish," *Seattle Times*, 21 June 1940, 4.

[23] Grant, 24–26.

[24] August Toellner, "June 21, 1851 Set as Date of First Settlers in Seattle [King County]," *Duwamish Valley News*, 18 May 1934, 1; August Toellner, "First Settlers Chose the Duwamish," *Duwamish Valley News*, 2 July 1937, 1–2; August Toellner, "Pioneers Fete 89th Year of Landing on Duwamish," *The Seattle Times*, 21 June 1940, 4.

[25] *Ibid.*

[26] *Ibid.*

[27] Emily Inez Denny, *Blazing the Way* (Seattle, Wash.: Rainier Printing Co. Inc., 1909), 51.

[28] Bagley, *History of Seattle*, vol. 1, 17–20.

[29] Grant, 24–26, 46–49.

[30] Ezra Meeker, *Pioneer Reminiscences of Puget Sound* (Seattle, Wash.: Lohman & Hanford, 1905; reprinted 1980).

[31] Lowell Beaver, *Memories from Historic Markers & Plaques* (Puyallup, Wash.: privately printed, 1963) 164–65.

[32] Bagley, *History of King County*, vol. 1, 35.

[33] Bagley, *History of Seattle*, vol. 1, 20.

[34] Bagley, *History of King County*, vol. 1, 100–101.

[35] Grant, 46.

[36] King County Road Engineer, *Fifth Annual Report* (Seattle, Wash.: King County Roads Division, 1939), 14–16.

[37] Donation Claim Land Records, King County, Washington Territory.

[38] Donation Claim Land Records, King County, Washington Territory.

[39] Donation Claim Land Records, King County, Washington Territory.

[40] Bagley, *History of King County*, vol. 1, 35.

[41] King County Road Engineer, *Fifth Annual Report*, 14–16.

[42] Reinartz, *Tukwila*, 26.

[43] Flora Fleming Foster, "The Honorable Joseph Foster, Life Sketch" (typewritten manuscript, circa 1930), 1–5. University of Washington Libraries, MSCUA.

[44] Reinartz, *Tukwila, Community at the Crossroads*, vii–ix.

[45] Foster, 28–30.

[46] Reinartz, *Tukwila*, vii-ix.

[47] Bagley, *History of Seattle*, vol. 1, 281–82.

[48] Bagley, *History of King County*, vol. 1, 202.

[49] Bagley, *History of King County*, vol. 1, 202.

[50] Foster, 29–32.

[51] Foster, 29–32.

[52] Reinartz, *Tukwila*, 126, 224–28.

[53] Reinartz, *Tukwila*, vii-ix.

[54] Grant, 499–501.

# REEXAMINING THE PAST

## A DIFFERENT PERSPECTIVE OF BLACK STRIKEBREAKERS IN KING COUNTY'S COAL MINING INDUSTRY

### Ed Diaz

"Strikebreaker" by definition is "a person who is active in trying to break up a strike, as by working as a scab, supplying scabs for the employer, intimidating strikers, etc." One definition of a "scab" is "a worker who refuses to join a union, or who works for lower wages or under different conditions than those accepted by the union."[1]

Strikebreakers are not only held in contempt in the eyes of labor unions, but many times risk serious injury or even death by crossing picket lines. Yet throughout America's labor history, workers—white and black—have been willing to risk the consequences involved in becoming strikebreakers. Until fairly recently in this nation's history, black men and women were unsympathetic to the unions' calls for a collective stand against capital since most unions made a determined effort to exclude men and women of color. Booker T. Washington, who had considerable influence during his life and was the founder of the National Business League, felt that the opportunity for African Americans to work as free men was assisted by the actions of strikebreakers. Furthermore, he believed the only benefit that unions provided for blacks was making some of them think about becoming capitalists.[2]

In Seattle, as in other places around the country, labor disputes were sometimes opportunities for black labor to find jobs. For instance, the butchers' strike of 1917 and the dockworkers' strike of 1919 were two of several strikes that provided African Americans with work in Seattle, at least on a temporary basis. One woman, whose husband was looking for work without any success at the time of the 1919 dockworkers' strike, remembered her husband going to Tacoma as a strikebreaker for a one week period. The money he made during that period, she enthusiastically said, was "very good, because he made more money that week than he ever made one week in his life . . . and we'd eat good . . . It was very good, very good."[3]

During the 1919 butchers' strike, Horace Cayton, who at the time was publishing *Cayton's Weekly*, a Seattle newspaper, expressed the views of most black workers when he wrote, "Organized labor must unqualifiedly cut out this colorphobia if it hopes to ever enlist the sympathies and support of [colored] working men."[4]

The black men (and women, in the case of the butchers' strike) who replaced the striking white workers were residents of the Seattle area, but more than a quarter of a century earlier, labor troubles in some of Washington's coal mines led to the *importation* of black workers, first to Roslyn in 1888, then to King County in 1891. The men who were brought in were usually referred to as scabs, slaves, and pawns, and in one later publication ("Spawn of Coal Dust: History of Roslyn, 1886–1955") were described as "a corrupt lot."[5]

The history of Washington's mines has been amply documented, as has the history and foibles of the labor organizations involved in the numerous strikes against the mining industry, so this essay does not delve into those subjects. Rather, its purpose is to shed some light on what is generally missing in King County's historical accounts: specific material concerning the black strikebreakers, of whom little is recorded.

The public's primary source of historical information concerning mining communities such as Newcastle and Franklin—the public library—has little to offer in information concerning black coal miners. What are presented in the historical accounts are usually derogatory statements that have been accepted as fact without any evidence to substantiate them. For example, "Spawn of Coal Dust: History of Roslyn 1886–1955," a 350 page type written manuscript, has only two minute references to black miners. One is found in relation to the town's cemeteries (22 listed), where it is noted that the Colored Cemetery had (as of 1955) 315 graves, second in number only to the Foresters Cemetery. The other brief mention is in a section titled "The First Mine Strike," which, unlike most of the other sections of the publication, has no source listed. This is what the general public "learns":

> The Company filled the places of the strikers with Negroes who were brought from Illinois. Two shipments of them were brought to Roslyn and Ronald by special trains that were well guarded by deputies. For two years after this the black population was greater than the white, but the first Negroes imported were *such a corrupt lot* [emphasis added] that they were replaced by white workers, by the Company, as soon as it was possible.[6]

Corrupt lot? In what way? There's no explanation, just the statement. One may also ask why, if the blacks were so corrupt and were replaced as soon as possible, so many of their dead were buried in Roslyn. While this may seem like a small point to some, it is significant in that the author of the statement makes no apparent effort to seek the truth, but wants to "prove" that the character of black miners was beneath that of the whites.

W. E. B. DuBois, in his essay "The Propaganda of History," complained, "The historian has no right, posing as a scientist, to conceal or distort facts."[7] DuBois might have added: Or to make statements purporting to be fact without any supporting data.

For another example of the sparse coverage of the early black miners, one need look no further than *The Coals of Newcastle: A Hundred Years of Hidden History*. The 120 page publication has but one short paragraph concerning black miners:

> While Newcastle had its problems, the company's mine at Franklin gained the reputation of being the most unlucky. In 1891, when it was closed more than six months due to a fire, the management experimented with importing cheap black laborers. Six hundred and fifty black miners were recruited in Missouri, purportedly for Newcastle, but actually for Franklin.[8]

So what is the truth about the "black strikebreakers"? Who were these men, some with wives and young children, who left their homes, traveled more than 1,500 miles by train, and dared to replace white workers? What factors induced them to take a trip into the unknown? Once here, did they become part of the Washington community or were they forever outsiders traveling from place to place looking for strikes to break? This study strives to answer these questions. However, in order to learn why certain events took place in King County, one must be some-what familiar with other aspects of American history, particularly Southern his-tory. Only when this is considered can the reasoning, expectations, and actions of the "strikebreakers" be better understood.

No claim is being made that all of the reader's questions will be answered, but it is hoped that anyone with unanswered questions will be thirsty enough for addi-tional information to conduct further research on this topic, which up to this point has been no more than a historical footnote. At the very least, the reader should walk away with a different perspective of King County's black "strikebreakers."

## Slavery, Southern "Justice," and the Mining Experience

Many, if not most, black miners who came to the Northwest to work in the state's coalmines during the late 19th century were from the South, which raises an inter-esting question. How could these men, whose work experience must surely have been in agriculture, believe they could work in and survive the hardships of the mining industry? It's a fair question, but based on a false premise—that mining was a field unfamiliar to African Americans. In fact, as early as 1760, slave labor was used to dig for coal in Virginia, a state where many of Washington's imported miners had lived.[9] During the ensuing years, the use of slave labor to dig for coal increased as more mines became operational in other Southern states, including Tennessee, the birthplace of John Hale, one of the original black miners imported to work at the Franklin mines.[10]

When the Civil War started, the Confederate government took no chances with coal production. To ensure that sufficient coal was available for its needs, legislation was enacted that exempted anyone who operated a coal mine with 20 or more slaves from having to serve in the field. So black men, albeit involuntarily, had gotten plenty of experience in the mines, and had been doing so since before the Declaration of Independence.[11]

After the Civil War the South had to find ways of revitalizing a devastated economy, and with the end of slave labor another form of cheap labor was sought. One answer was convict leasing, which had two major benefits for the South: cheap labor and a reassertion of slavelike control over these newly "freed" men and women. Under post–Civil War convict leasing arrangements, state and local governments agreed, under contract, to provide prison labor to businesses and planters. In return, government officials would be paid a certain sum for "leasing" the prisoners.[12]

Of course, in order to make the arrangement worthwhile for the parties concerned, prison labor had to be supplied on a consistent basis. This was not a problem, since Southern "justice" ensured that a supply of prisoners was always available.

Convict leasing became a valuable source of income for many Southern states, and for many years it was "one of Alabama's largest source of funding," according to the *New York Times*.[13] During one two year period (1901 through 1902), for instance, 3,000 misdemeanor cases were brought before local courts in just *one* Alabama county. Records show that in Jefferson County, Alabama, during that period, black men were imprisoned for "obscene language," "vagrancy," and "disrespectful language" toward whites, and most of the men charged found themselves working in the Sloss Sheffield coal mines.[14]

A safe assumption would be that at least some of the black men who emigrated from the South got their mining apprenticeship by having the misfortune of being trapped by the convict leasing system. Of course, an untold number of black men had worked as miners for wages in the South and at mining camps in the Midwest. Some people may be surprised to learn that even such historic notables as Booker T. Washington and Carter G. Woodson, at one time during their lives, earned their wages in the mines. In any case, the perception that African Americans were unfamiliar with coal mining is clearly wrong, and it's fair to say that many, if not most, of the men who arrived on the trains in 1888 to work at Roslyn and in 1891 to work in King County had some sort of mining experience.

## CRIMES AGAINST HUMANITY

Land ownership means stability, a certain amount of wealth, and something to pass on to future generations. Owning farmland also means there is a way of feeding a family if all else fails. Before, during, and after the Civil War, African Americans managed to acquire land. For Southern blacks, who were denied the benefits of citizenship in so many ways, land ownership alleviated some of the pain of the social afflictions that were heaped upon them. But even in the dawn to dusk, back breaking work of dirt farming, the Southern black family found no peace. White mobs throughout the South and in many border states such as Missouri and Kentucky forced numerous blacks from their homes and land, ordering them to leave the area.[15]

Carter G. Woodson, recognized as the father of African American history and originator of what has now become Black History Month, described some of the barbarism that Southern blacks faced on a daily basis. Anyone with a black skin was a candidate for a rope and a limb, and, according to Woodson, "[t]he lynching of the blacks . . . has rapidly developed as an institution." But it wasn't enough to hang African Americans: the "sport" became so popular in many communities that many victims were "burned in the daytime to attract crowds that usually enjoy[ed] such feats as the tourney of the Middle Ages."[16]

## AVOIDANCE, EMIGRATION, AND MIGRATION FROM THE SOUTH

To avoid the insufferable conditions that blacks faced in many communities, some tried to avoid contact with whites altogether by forming all black communities within the South. One such settlement, the all black refuge of Mound Bayou, Mississippi, met with some level of success for a period of time, but permanent avoidance was an impossible dream.

"Return to Africa" movements, although appearing from time to time, had few serious advocates among the masses. After all, they were born in the United States, had little knowledge of Africa other than what might have been passed on by earlier generations, and, as they pointed out, the United States was their country too.

The Reverend Hesekiah C. Rice, a Baptist preacher who met the black immigrant miners in King County when they arrived in 1891, spoke out in a loud, clear voice against emigration to Africa. Directing his statement to the Knights of Labor concerning African Americans' right to work, his annoyance toward those who advanced the idea that blacks should leave the United States and live in Africa was clearly evident when he said, "America is our country. We were born here and we don't know anything about Africa."[17]

Since avoidance within the South and emigration to Africa met with little success, many felt the only viable option was to migrate from the South to other areas of the country.

The story of the Great Migration of African Americans during World War I is familiar to many people, but not so well known, spoken of, or written about is the migration that started with the end of Reconstruction. With new anti black laws in the South, "bulldozing," and the apparent abandonment of blacks by the federal government, Southern blacks were justified in their fear of re-enslavement. Black men and women with their children started fleeing from Southern hostility to any part of the country that their meager resources would allow.[18]

In *A Century of Negro Migration*, Carter G. Woodson stated his belief that migration would prove to be the most "significant event" in the lives of black Americans since the Civil War. Migration, according to Woodson, was a major part of the African American struggle to "flee from bondage and oppression in quest of a land offering asylum to the oppressed and opportunity to the unfortunate."[19]

In his study of Nicodemus, Kansas, an all black town, Van B. Shaw wrote, "Migration from areas of extreme discrimination to more favorable social environments has . . . been used by the Negro as a means of escape from the frustration of his subordinate role."[20]

One of many calls for migration from the South to other sections of the country came from Richard T. Greener, a prominent African American, who had absolutely no confidence that Southern blacks would receive any type of federal protection from Southern violence. Greener encouraged black men and women to travel west. "West" at the time usually meant Kansas and the territory of Oklahoma, but Carter G. Woodson found in his study of black migration that there was no limit to where blacks would migrate to find a better life.[21]

Many black families migrated to the Oklahoma Territory thinking that they had finally found peace and freedom. However, when Oklahoma became a state and more whites settled there, blacks again found themselves facing strong anti black sentiment. Irene Henderson Grayson, whose family migrated from Alabama to Oklahoma, and finally to the Northwest, explained that after statehood things changed considerably. Oklahoma state laws, she said "were Arkansas law, and, if you know anything about Arkansas at all, you would know what a great change it would be. That's why my husband didn't like [it], he didn't like prejudices. We'd go try to find some place where we would, you know, have our freedom."[22]

One group of families traveled beyond America's Northwest borders, migrated to Canada, and founded an all black town known as Amber Valley in British Columbia. Gail Davis, a Seattle resident who was born in Canada, indicated how desperate blacks were to find a place where they could live in peace no matter how far they had to go.

> My folks were originally from the South . . . I'm not sure what the numerical breakdown was on those that went on. But I know Amber Valley itself was settled by 160 blacks, my grandfather was amongst that number, and they came up from Oklahoma and went as far north as they could go until the cold winter—as my dad used to say—[caused] the animals to start dying on them.[23]

There's no question that many of the black miners who came to King County's mines were from the South, but not all of them were fleeing the conditions described above. Indeed, even blacks who weren't from the South usually had compelling reasons to leave their home states. Even in Northern states, blacks generally faced hostility and discrimination. And after the Civil War, an increasing num-

ber of Northern whites, fearing an influx of freedmen, made life even more un-
bearable for African Americans, especially when it came to labor.

Condemned by American society because of color, barred from working in
most industries, locked out of unions, unable to support their families, African
Americans looked for any method possible to earn an honest living, even if it meant
breaking a strike. Horace Cayton comments in the *Seattle Republican*:

> Then all kind of industrial works were closed against them owning to the
> hostility of the labor unions of working by the side of black men, but soon
> strikes began to be common and the Negro, not having been permitted to
> join the labor unions and work in such places, became willing subjects to
> take the strikers' places.[24]

So, in addition to migrating because of hostility toward them, black Americans
were looking for a place to work on a regular basis, to earn a decent living, to
provide for themselves and their families. It should be no surprise, then, that when
offered steady work and given the opportunity to migrate to the Northwest, where,
it was believed, "a land offering asylum" was to be found, many black Americans
jumped at the opportunity to do so. Harriet Joyce Craven Greenwood, a Roslyn
resident who can trace her family back to Washington's pioneer black coal miners,
explained that the men who came West really had no idea what to expect, but each
had hopes and expectations for a better life than the one being left. Those miners
were willing to travel to a place they knew little or nothing about because they saw
an opportunity for a better life. "All they knew was that they had a good job awaiting them, a better life, and that's what they were looking for, you know—and a
place to take care of their families."[25]

## JAMES SHEPPERSON, THE RECRUITER

At the entrance to Roslyn's Mount Olivet Cemetery there is a dedication to James
Shepperson that reads: "James Shepperson founded the first Free Masons Lodge
in Roslyn, The Knights of Taber Lodge, and 2 Black American Churches located
in Roslyn." The inscription indicates that Shepperson was very active in civic affairs, but his most important contribution as far as the black miners were concerned isn't revealed. James E. Shepperson, according to descendants of the original miners and the newspaper publisher Horace Cayton, is the man who actually
recruited them.

While the mining companies planned and nurtured the idea and sent officials
to oversee the operation, someone had to go into the areas where black candidates
were most likely to be found, post handbills, knock on doors, talk to the potential
miners, sign them up, and act as their spokesperson. James Shepperson was that
person, according to Mrs. Greenwood and others. While working for Mr. Ronald,

James Shepperson (circa 1915) recruited African American miners to work in Washington's coal mining industry. Courtesy of Ellensburg Public Library, Local History Collection, Ellensburg, Washington.

a mine official at Roslyn, Shepperson learned of the mining company's plan to recruit black men to work at the mines and became the company's recruiter. Traveling to the Midwest and the South, he came back with a trainload of men ready to work in 1888. "No one knew what was out in Washington. Jim Shepperson's the one who brought the black pioneer miners here . . . He just had handbills that they put on different places, you know, poles, trees, meeting places, anywhere, that there were job opportunities out in Washington," stated Mrs. Greenwood.[26]

Sandy Moss, who came with his parents to Seattle in 1900, when he was about 5 years of age, remembers hearing stories about Shepperson. During a 1975 interview he described some details of what he had heard:

Oh yes, yes there was a fellow up there named Jim Shepperson and he was a big burly fellow, very likeable fellow about six feet two and weighing about 250 pounds . . . They hired him to go and recruit miners to come there. So he says what kind of miners do you want? They say we want blue, black, gray, grizzly, anything except white. And we'll put them to work.[27]

Irene Grayson, who personally knew James Shepperson, credited him with not only recruiting black miners, but with paving the way for other black Americans to come to Washington State.

> I was able to visit with the man that went around the different states, able to visit, and became well acquainted with Mr. James Shepperson, the man that imported black people to the state of Washington for coal mining . . . Yes, many other black people came after Mr. Shepperson broke the ground or opened the way for the blacks to come to the State of Washington.[28]

In his 1896 "Special New Year's Edition" of the *Seattle Republican*, Horace Cayton profiled a dozen Washington African American pioneers and old timers. Shepperson's profile was the most detailed and contained excellent background information on him, including his mining and recruiting experience. Cayton pointed out that despite the danger from union men—some of whom threatened to kill him when—"Shepperson was sent to look for colored men to work the mines . . . he never returned without his men."[29]

James Shepperson's role in King County history should not be overlooked. It was the success in 1888—in the view of the mining operators—of importing black miners to work at Roslyn that led the way for the recruitment of additional black miners to work at Franklin and their use at Newcastle.


## ARRIVAL, PROBLEMS, AND WORK

It was Sunday morning, May 17, 1891, when the "Black Train," as the *Seattle Post Intelligencer* called the trainload of black men, women, and children, along with armed guards, arrived at Palmer, Washington, close to Franklin. The men disembarked from the train, were met by additional armed guards, and together marched to Franklin. The women and children stayed on the train and headed for Seattle. After the men were settled in Franklin, the women and children joined them. The entire operation was pulled off with such secrecy and military precision that it caught the residents of Franklin by complete surprise.

"Black strikebreakers" were words of contempt to white workers, and, in some, aroused extreme bitterness and even hatred. Precede the phrase with the word "armed" and there's no way to describe the range of emotions that came to the surface when black miners arrived at Franklin. Fear was certainly one of them. Cora Jones Flyzik was not quite five on that fateful morning, but she remembered that "there was terrible, terrible confusion and worry . . . there were all of them with guns. All these Blacks with guns."[30]

Jenny Edwards was only about six months old when the black miners arrived, but as a second generation member of a mining family she heard the tale "so many times." She remembered her mother telling her that as she looked at the Green River Gorge Bridge at six in the morning, she was astonished to see "600 colored people, with rifles over their shoulders." Her family decided to leave Franklin immediately and went to Black Diamond.[31]

After seeing the condition of the imported miners upon their arrival, some of the locals, while in no way laying out a welcome mat for them, at least had some understanding of why they came. Cora Flyzik's description of what her mother saw remained in her mind:

> They had terrible clothes just like rags on them. They were awfully poor people. I heard my mother telling about that part of it. . . . I think we educated ourselves and realized what had happened . . . they were starving where they were and wanted to get something better for themselves and that was their only out for them.[32]

It didn't help ease anyone's mind when the *Seattle Press Times*, printed, as one of its front page headlines, "Twelve Armed Companies of Negroes Organized and Drilled." The newspaper declared that "only a few minutes elapsed before the train pulled into the stone quarry, 2 1/2 miles below, where the army of 675 negroes including about 40 women and children poured out of the cars. . . . "[T]he negroes were formed into companies and drilled in the manual of arms, and after the drills they cling to their guns like grim death."[33]

In reaction, one group of white miners led by a former soldier of the German army went so far as to prepare for a "mini war." Carl Steiert, whose parents were first generation miners, recalled the time he asked his mother about a box in their house's cellar:

> One thing that I remember . . . we had a cellar. There was a nice box under there, well made and we used it to keep some tools in it. It said Winchester rifles on it. I said to her one day, "I wonder how come we ever got that Winchester rifle box?" "Oh," she said, "you know, when they brought the Black people to break the strike up in Franklin? Joe Steiert and Pete Boos, they both were in the German Army when they were young men, and they were training the men down here in the field in Morganville where they used to have athletic events. They were marching them around so if they ever got into trouble, they were going to march to Franklin."[34]

Local newspapers were filled with interviews from both whites and blacks. Their statements were contradictory and many times controversial in nature. Some of the related reports were, at best, questionable. One white miner felt

> The company will find it hard work to work the mines with these negroes, most of them I am reliably informed, are offal collected from the slums of the cities, and they will get away from here as soon as they can and flock to the cities.

Almost as a reply to his comment, one newcomer was reported as saying, "There's about 300 miners along and all old hands. I have been mining in Pennsylvania, Illinois and Iowa. They could get 2,000 miners easy if they wanted them. 'Tisn't any trick to get 'em at all."[35]

One black miner, Charles R. Johnson, obviously tiring of the broadside of verbal abuse by the Knights of Labor, wrote a letter to the *Seattle Post Intelligencer*:

> Since their emancipation the doors of the Knights of Labor have been thrown open to the colored man, only to starve him and his family to death. When we were bound to follow our white brothers to Canaan, we got only to the borders, while our white brothers in labor went in and enjoyed the fruits of the land. We could only stand and look on. Then after they had feasted, we took a peep, and were abused for looking on and called "scabs" because we wanted a little morsel to help keep our starving souls as we travel this journey to life.[36]

Many white miners had no doubt in their minds that the newly arrived black men wouldn't survive, that they didn't have the knowledge or experience to mine coal. But superintendent T. B. Corey, the person responsible for importing the black miners, told the press that he expected to lose a few of the men, but he was confident the majority would stay.[37]

Cora Flyzik's father was one of those who were convinced the'"inexperienced" blacks couldn't "do the mining of that coal." It may have been wishful thinking, but as far as he and many other miners were concerned the blacks "didn't know how to do it" and it would only be a short period of time before they all quit. Her father thought that they could wait because the blacks were sure to leave. "But they didn't do that, you see," Cora Flyzik commented.[38]

No, the men didn't leave. They hadn't come to this area just to break a strike; their intention was to settle in an area that was thought to be a 'land of opportunity.' In fact, they had signed agreements to work a certain number of years, and while critics have described the contracts as exploitation, the black miners saw them as an opportunity most never had in the past: good pay (for them) and security. Some men did leave within a short period of time for various reasons, but the overwhelming number remained to work. Furthermore, if the new arrivals had questions about staying, they were encouraged to remain by three of Seattle's black residents. Only two days after their arrival, the Reverend L. S. Blakeley of the A.M.E. Church of Seattle, accompanied by Mr. Blacker and I. W. Evans, traveled from Seattle to address the group, and appealed to them to remain "with the company." Bitterly denouncing labor organizations, the Reverend Blakeley reminded his audience of the difficulty of obtaining the work necessary to support themselves. "The workingmen of the country . . . had never extended a hand of welcome and good fellowship to the Negro, but refused to let him join unions or to work at all because his skin was black," he stated.

Franklin Coal Mine workers, 1902. Courtesy of the Washington State Historical Society.

Following Blakeley's address, I. W. Evans, perhaps to discourage a possible exodus to Seattle if the men quit the mines, told of his difficulty in finding work in Seattle and whites' treatment of other African Americans. "Because we have a black skin they will have nothing to do with us," he said, "and if you boys quit work now you could find nothing to do in Seattle." He also promised that Seattle's small black community would make their stay as pleasant as possible. Mr. Blacker, the last to speak, also condemned the union, but in addition, spoke of the "thousands of acres of unsurveyed land in the state" He said the men and women should not only remain, but they should also consider homesteading.[39]

The three man committee certainly must have been fortifying and probably had a hand in convincing some of those who may have been on the fence to remain at Franklin. The *Seattle Press Times* reported that "the colored delegation which addressed them . . . greatly strengthened their resolution to stick it out."[40]

As if to reinforce the complaints that Reverend Blakeley's party made against white workingmen and more or less provide a smoking gun to justify their statements, union delegates from Black Diamond, Franklin, and Gilman held a meeting at Wilkeson, in which all classes of labor were supposedly represented. Out of that meeting came a unanimously passed resolution that said in part:

That we will no longer submit to the introduction of the negro race amongst us, and that we cannot and will not recognize the negro as worthy of association with us; neither will we submit to association with them in any manner whatsoever.[41]

If there was any hope of convincing the black men that it was in their interest to listen to the pleas of the white miners and leave the mines, that resolution ended it. What better evidence of the truth of the Reverend Blakeley's words could be presented to the black miners than a strongly worded anti-black resolution issued by the very union men he spoke of?

They not only stayed but began work immediately. Among the men there were a host of mining skills they had previously learned. Mine superintendent Williams reported, "that they are not greenhorns by any means." He also indicated that he would put "more miners to work . . . and shall go on adding to the force daily until the mine is fully manned."[42]

During the first month, with the exception of a few scattered incidents, the camp, while tense, remained relatively quiet. It was on June 29, six weeks after the black miners arrived, that the race war many people thought was imminent almost occurred. That morning, a train from Seattle stopped briefly at Franklin, quickly picked up 80 black miners—all armed—and 10 white Sullivan guards, and sped off to the Newcastle mine, where the miners were to be put to work. Though the train was heard and fired upon by striking miners when leaving Franklin, they were caught by surprise, and the black miners arrived safely at Newcastle.[43]

When it was learned that a number of guards had left on the train, some whites thought it was the opportunity they had been waiting for to attack the black miners and attempted to overrun the black encampment, wounding one black before retreating. Infuriated blacks prepared to immediately drive the whites from Franklin, but the intervention of the Sullivan guards averted escalation to the long anticipated conflict. Tempers were still at the boiling point, however, when a train arrived that evening with the returning guards from Newcastle and a dozen new black workers from Seattle. Whites waiting in ambush attacked the train, and the guards returned fire. Franklin's black miners, hearing the gunfire, turned out in force to fight the whites. In the end, after much confusion on both sides, one white was killed and several wounded.[44]

Feelings remained tense in the ensuing years, but life went on—and so did death. Strikes and miners came and went, but families needed to eat, so despite their protestations white miners were employed at the Franklin mine along with blacks. On August 24, 1894, the *Post Intelligencer* reported on a devastating fire in a Franklin coal mine that killed 37 men. Until that time there hadn't been a disaster of that magnitude in a King County mine. The newspaper went into great detail describing the tragedy, and included a list of the miners who died as a result of the fire. The coverage by the *Seattle Press Times* was not as extensive, but it provided what it called a "corrected list" of the dead, shown below:[45]

Newcastle Black Miners Association. Courtesy of the Renton Historical Society, neg. # 1887.

Robert M'Crusky, single, native of Poland
Evan D. Jones, married, native of Wales
Peter Hay, married, native of Scotland
Louis Tarri, single, Italian
Joe Stanish, single, American
Phil Demaro, single, Italian
John E. Johns, leaves widow and four children, Welsh
John Morris, leaves widow and four children, Welsh
John Hale, single, American
Chris Dunker, single, Swede
Charles Stevens, single, English
Jake Oleson, leaves widow and one child, Swede
Frank Larsen, single, Swede
Evan Hughes, leaves widow and three children, Welsh
Rocco Titti, single, Italian
D. D. Jones, leaves widow and four children, Welsh
D. Jackson Jones, single, colored
H. R. Jones, single, colored
Ike Clemmons, leaves widow and three children, colored
Petro Perry, single, Italian
Frank Willis, single, colored
Ed Maxwell, single, colored

R. W. Jones, single, colored
John Grantilli, single, Italian
Joseph Dawson, single, English
H. R. Roberts, single, colored
John Irvin, single, colored
Joseph Casselli, single, Italian
James Gibson, leaves widow, colored
J. M. Johnson, single, Swede
Andrew Engdahl, leaves three children, Swede
John J. Pugh, leaves widow and five children, Welsh
John Q. Anderson, leaves widow and four children, Swede
William Secor, leaves widow and one child, American
Andrew Greer, single, colored
Joseph, Borni, single, Italian

The list indicates that a mixed group of workers including foreign born whites from several countries, American born whites, and American born blacks were working at Franklin in 1894. Whether they actually got along while at work in the mines is a matter of conjecture, but in the end it didn't matter. The fire didn't take the time to distinguish between black and white skin, or different ethnic groups. For the 37 men who perished—more than 10 percent of the miners employed at the time—it was an equal opportunity killer. The miners worked together to save lives, and some of those who died did so in an attempt to save their workmates. The *Post Intelligencer* reported that the call for volunteers to go into the mine was quickly answered:

> The first man to volunteer was George W. Smalley, a negro, and with two others he was lowered down the 1,100 foot slope to the sixth level. There he met men from the sixth level south, who were doing all they could to rescue the men on the north side of the same level. Other rescuers went down from the surface and Smalley, C. C. Todd, John Adams and John Morgan found the body of the first man in the gangway, about 1,000 feet in from the slope.[46]

One miner expressed what many others probably felt at the time when he said, "I thought I had some enemies the other day, but I haven't now. Every man I meet I feel is my friend. I'm so glad no more are dead."

The *Post Intelligencer* started a drive to aid the widows and orphans of the disaster with its own donation of $100, stating: "contributions of those who desire to give, of whatever race or color, will be received at the business office of this paper." It added that "subscriptions to a fund on behalf of the colored people" would be received by J. E. Hawkins, of Seattle, one of the black community's leading citizens."[47]

The miners' ethnic mix brings to the surface an often overlooked point: while labor organizations might have questioned the motives of mine operators, the hard fact is that until World War I, when a dire need for workers arose due to the war, the industrial labor force, in most cases, excluded black workers from meaningful jobs. It was the mine operators, with their policy—regardless of their reasons—of employing—"native whites," European immigrants, and blacks, that gave some African Americans an opportunity to work at an occupation other than the ones to which they were usually relegated.[48]

This is further demonstrated by the *Seattle Republican* 1898 article pertaining to work opportunities in the Newcastle mines.

> In talking to the general manager of the Pacific Coast Company one day this week we learned the following: "Our mines," said he, "would be glad to give employment to 375 or 400 colored miners. As soon as we get the new mine opened at Newcastle we will have one of the finest mines in the Northwest, and will be able to turn out more coal than any other mine in this section . . . As to pay, no mining company in the West pays its men better than the Pacific Coast Company, and I am certain not one as regular. Never since I have been connected with the company has it missed a pay day, and that should cut some figure in the eyes of those who work. *Colored men have always been given work whenever they applied* [emphasis added]."[49]

## OTHER ACTIVITIES AND POLITICAL INTERESTS

Mining wasn't the only interest for the men who came as "strikebreakers." They formed bands, established lodges, churches, and clubs. Some, after a period of years in the mines, homesteaded. In addition, many men were active politically, and while the number of African American voters in King County was very small in comparison to the general population, by working together and with white politicians they sometimes made some measure of difference on the local scene.

Horace Cayton reminisced about one such use of that unified action that included men from Seattle and the mining towns of Franklin and Newcastle. The 1918 article gives some insight of how quickly some miners assimilated into surrounding communities and became active in their political affairs. John Van Horn, a former streetcar conductor, according to Cayton's article, had little use for blacks and engaged in many heated arguments with black passengers while he worked for the Madison Street line. Van Horn eventually entered politics, and in 1896 (five years after the arrival of the Black Train) attempted to win the Republican nomination for county sheriff. However, he had antagonized too many blacks—and they hadn't forgotten. Cayton wrote:

There were not many colored voters in the county at that time, but almost to a man they made a fight to defeat him [Van Horn] for the nomination at the Republican County Convention. There were twelve colored delegates in the convention, six from Franklin, four from Newcastle and two, J. E. Hawkins and H. R. Cayton, from the city . . . The Franklin and Newcastle delegations . . . assisted Hawkins and Cayton in making trades inimical to Van Horn's success. The floor leaders of the colored delegates worked all day . . . and succeeded, so thought Van Horn, in defeating his nomination. So favorable an impression on the convention did the colored delegates make that I. I. Walker was nominated for constable.[50]

## VOICES FROM THE PAST

There are few people alive today who can contribute personal information from the black miners' point of view, few who can look at family records, photo albums, and letters or dig into their memory banks and testify for the miners. In Roslyn the only two African Americans left (as of this writing) who can give firsthand information about the mining families are Harriet Joyce Craven Greenwood and her brother, former Roslyn mayor William Craven.[51] There may be descendants of the Franklin and Newcastle miners still living in the local area, but except for Ernest Moore, the grandson of John Hale, their voices have been silent. Ernest Moore died in Seattle on April 22, 2001, two weeks shy of his 89th birthday, but fortunately he had written a family history before his death, so there is some written family information available. That, along with oral history interviews with a few members of the pioneer families in the mid 1970s, makes it possible to put faces on some of the people involved. Two such people are John Hale, a miner, and Elva Moore Nicholas, the daughter of a miner who worked at Newcastle and Franklin.

**John Hale.** One of the people on the Black Train was John Hale. He was born in a slave cabin but never knew his parents because they were sold to owners of another plantation when he was still a baby. He was four days shy of his 45th birthday when he got off the train, armed, and marched to Franklin on May 17, 1891.

John Hale was an experienced miner. He had gotten his first taste of coal mining after the Civil War when he and his brothers were recruited to work in the mines of the Tennessee Iron and Coal Works. They were promised $1 a ton, payday once a month, and a cabin to stay in. For the Hale brothers, "free and with no place to go," this was a godsend. Though they had no knowledge of coal mining, they learned quickly as they performed a variety of jobs at the coal mine that "were not particularly likeable."[52]

In 1882 John Hale married Fannie Gray, and the couple traveled from mining job to mining job with what few belongings they had. Sometimes their bed was nothing more than some straw on a floor. By the time Hale was recruited to mine at Franklin, he and his wife had three children: one boy, Claude, and two girls, Annie and Melinda.[53]

The train for Franklin departed from Saint Paul, Minnesota, but the miners had to find their own way to get to the point of departure. Whether it meant riding a mule, being on the back of someone's wagon, or some other means, these seekers of a better life, going to a place they knew little or nothing about, managed to find ways of getting to St. Paul. People with little means did what they could to help these pioneers. Neighbors gave Hale's family potatoes, biscuits, and calico material to be used for the girls' dresses. Somewhere during the trek to St. Paul, the Hales met another family of five, and a farmer plowing his field who hadn't "taken some vegetables to the hogs yet" gave them to the two families. John Hale remembered that "Big Jim Shepardson" [sic] was "the man signing up the people" and was "the spokesman for the group."[54]

**Elva Moore Nicholas.** There was probably no disagreement among the black miners that they were in a much better place and situation than they had left—but it wasn't paradise by any means. School life could be an abrasive experience for the younger children, especially girls. Elva Moore Nicholas, who lived in Franklin until she was 8 years old, gave one view of Franklin as she remembered it growing up as a school child. School was somewhat difficult for her, but not because of any problem learning; she was an excellent student academically. Her problems came from some of her teachers' bias against black students, and from older white children harassing her. In a 1976 interview she said:

> We had to fight our way to get to school 'cause they were determined that no Negroes should go to school. And every day if we didn't run like mad, like a demon itself was after us, we'd be beat up. And many times, I've had my hair pulled out, just handfuls, pulled out by the white kids, they'd grab me by my hair 'cause I had long hair.[55]

But all children weren't the same, and Mrs. Nicholas remembered one white boy in particular who always did his best to help her. "Glady Tollman . . . would always stand up for any child that was being molested or beaten up or anything like that . . . Finally his parents moved away. But by that time, we were big enough to defend ourselves to a certain extent."[56]

One teacher who was eventually dismissed told black students she'd "never taught 'niggers' before," and "she just didn't know how to teach black kids." The situation was more serious with a male teacher who physically abused the children on a regular basis and liked to use a hose on them, according to Mrs. Nicholas. "He didn't like blacks. So no matter what grade you got you'd never pass." Once he threatened to beat young Elva because she was "sassy," according to the teacher. Her father, learning of the threat, went to the school with fire in his eyes and gave

Old Newcastle sunday school class. Courtesy of the Renton Historical Society, neg. #1877A.

the teacher a dire warning as to what would happen if he touched his child. What he said remained etched in the family's memory throughout the years.

> You messed up her report card . . . I went along with that 'cause I knew she was intelligent—she got it, you can't take it away from her regardless of the marks you gave her. But you better not put your hands on her, don't you touch her. If you do, I'll kill you! You put one lick on her you're a dead man.[57]

She never had problems with the teacher again, and he didn't return to the school the following year. Not all teachers cared about their students' color. One of Mrs. Nicholas's teachers, Mrs. Tibbert, "treated all the children the same and didn't withhold anything." The memories of Mrs. Tibbert were pleasant. "She taught us music . . . you know, like the other children were having. And we got along pretty good under her."[58]

Like children elsewhere, they had certain restrictions placed on them by their parents. Besides being home by a certain time, not playing in certain areas, and other rules, there were certain houses they weren't supposed to be near. Mrs. Nicholas recalled that years after she arrived at Franklin there was one woman, Mrs. C——, who was referred to as a "lady of the street," and that children weren't allowed to go by her house. "Now, we'd have to go out of our way . . . but we weren't allowed to pass her house. Yeah, we had no business on that street, so we didn't go." It isn't known if Mrs. C——'s clients were of any particular ethnic group or color.[59]

## CONCLUSION

The purpose of my research was to determine if the black miners imported to work at Franklin and Newcastle were actually "inexperienced, ignorant tools of mine operators," as some believed, and, if not, why they came to King County to mine. Each reader will, of course, form her or his own opinion, but my conclusions are: no, they weren't inexperienced; no, they weren't ignorant; and no, they weren't tools.

As has been shown, the men, for the most part, already had mining experience. They came to King County's mines looking for a better life, and that certainly doesn't constitute ignorance. Did they know they were strikebreakers? Some accounts say the men knew they were strikebreakers, and others say they didn't know of any labor problems when they signed up. (Ernest Moore insisted that they didn't know.) It's my belief that even had they known, at the time of their recruitment, that there were labor problems at Franklin, most of the men would have gotten on the train anyway. *Most were fleeing from Southern hostility, poverty, or both.*

But weren't they tools because their actions helped the company in its fight against the union? Before answering, it's important to remember that, at the time, the black miners were not allied with labor organizations. Labor unions, as far as most black workers were concerned, were obstacles to black advancement. Workers, then and now, look for opportunities to advance themselves and try to take advantage of them. That's exactly what King County's black pioneer miners did: take advantage of an opportunity to improve their status. This tells me they were by no means tools. In fact, one could conceivably argue that the company was the tool of the black workers. They used it to flee from unwanted conditions, to obtain decent pay, to find a place where they might be treated as something better than second class citizens.

And once they arrived, what did they do? They worked, got married, had children, told relatives and friends about opportunities to work, homesteaded, formed communities and became parts of larger communities, and were involved with politics. In other words, they lived and acted as did other residents of King County.

## NOTES

[1] Victoria Neufeldt, ed., *Webster's New World Dictionary of American English*, 3rd college ed. Cleveland: Simon & Schuster, Inc., 1988), 1196, 1327.

[2] Robert A. Campbell, "An added objection: the use of blacks in the coal mines of Washing-

ton, 1880-1896" (M.A. Thesis, University of British Columbia, 1978), 67.

[3] Irene Henderson Grayson, "I Always Like to be Free," interview by Esther H. Mumford, tape recording, 20 September, 1976, Washington State Archives, Olympia, accession no. BL-KNG 76-67em.

[4] *Cayton's Weekly*, 19 April 1919; *Cayton's Weekly* was published from 1916 through 1920.

[5] *Roslyn Community Study, Spawn of Coal Dust: History of Roslyn 1886-1955* (Roslyn, Washington: Community Development Program, 1955), 46, 208.

[6] Ibid, 208.

[7] W.E.B. DuBois, "The Propaganda of History," *Writings* (New York: Library Classics of the United States, Inc., 1986), 1037.

[8] Richard K. McDonald and Lucile McDonald, *The Coals of Newcastle: A Hundred Years of Hidden History* (n.p.: The Issaquah Alps Trails Club, 1987), 45.

[9] Ronald L. Lewis, *Black Coal Miner in America: Race, Class, and Community Conflict 1780-1980* , (Lexington: University of Kentucky Press, 1987), 4.

[10] See Ernest Moore, *The Coal Miner Who Came West* (Seattle: n.p., 1982), 1.

[11] Lewis, *Black Coal Miner in America*, 10.

[12] For more insight into the prison leasing system, the relationship between the courts and businesses, "peonage"— considered by many a legal form of slavery — and the conditions under which men and women were forced to continue working for planters and others, see Thomas A. Frazier, ed., "Peonage in the South: The Life of a Negro Peon," *Readings in African-American History*, 3rd ed. (California: Wadsworth Group, 2001), 182-89. The author of the biographical story described his sleeping quarters as stockades that were the "filthiest places in the world" and were "cesspools of nastiness." He ends his tale of peonage in an unequivocal manner when he states that he will "die either in a coal mine or an iron furnace. It don't make much difference which. Either is better than a Georgia peon camp." "Peonage" was originally published in *The Life Stories of Undistinguished Americans as Told by Themselves*, ed. Hamilton Holt (New York, 1906).

[13] Douglas A. Blackmon, "Hard Time: From Alabama's Past, Capitalism and Racism In a Cruel Partnership," *Wall Street Journal*, 16 July 2001, sec. A, p.1.

[14] Blackmon, "Hard Time", sec. A, p. 10.

[15] George C. Wright, *Racial Violence in Kentucky, 1865-1940: Lynchings, Mob Rule, and "Legal Lynchings"* (Baton Rouge: Louisiana State University Press, 1990), 131.

[16] Carter G. Woodson, Ph.D., *A Century of Negro Migration* (Washington, D.C.: The Association for the Study of Negro Life and History, 1918), 156-7.

[17] *Seattle Post-Intelligencer*, 19 May 1891.

[18] "Bulldozing" was a term used to describe the persecution of, and political injustice and violence directed against African Americans. For additional information on its practice and the fear of re-enslavement, see Woodson, 126-7. Horace Roscoe Cayton, the publisher and editor of the *Seattle Republican* (1892-1913) wrote extensively about the conditions in the South. On 10 August 1900 Cayton lambasted Southern states for trying to reduce blacks "to a form of moderate slavery." In the 9 August 1901 issue, Cayton wrote "[South Carolina Senator] Tillman has never gotten over the idea of wanting a black slave at his beck and call, and he still laments that he hasn't one, and for this loss he purposes to murder them by the wholesale and drive them into a form of *slavery*." (Emphasis added.)

[19] Woodson, *A Century of Negro Migration*, V.

[20] Van. B. Shaw, "Nicodemus, Kansas, A Study in Isolation" (Ph.D. dissertation, University

of Missouri, 1951), 8.

[21] Woodson, *A Century of Negro Migration*, 178.

[22] Irene Henderson Grayson, "I Always Like to be Free," interview by Esther H. Mumford, tape recording, 20 September 1976, Washington State Archives, Olympia, accession no. BL-KNG 76-67em.

[23] Gail Davis, interview by author, tape recording, 9 December 1998, Seattle, Washington, in author's possession.

[24] *Seattle Republican*, 30 December 1898.

[25] Harriet Joyce Craven Greenwood, interview by author, tape recording, 13 October 2001, Roslyn, Washington, in author's possession.

[26] Ibid., in author's possession.

[27] Sandy A. Moss, interview by Esther H. Mumford, tape recording, 22, 25 April 1975, Washington State Archives, Olympia, accession no. BL-KNG 75-2em.

[28] Irene Grayson, interview by Esther H. Mumford, tape recording, 17 April 1975, Washington State Archives, Olympia, accession no. BL-KNG 75-1em.

[29] Horace Cayton, *Seattle Republican*, 4 January 1896.

[30] Diane Olson and Cory Olson, eds. "Franklin...Another Company Town," *Black Diamond: Mining the Memories*. Seattle, 1988. 214.

[31] Ibid., 214, 217.

[32] Ibid., 219.

[33] *Seattle Press-Times*, 18 May 1891.

[34] Olson and Olson, eds. "Franklin . . . Another Company Town," 215.

[35] *Seattle Press-Times*, 19 May 1891.

[36] *Seattle Post-Intelligencer,* 5 July 1891.

[37] *Seattle Post-Intelligencer,* 19 May 1891.

[38] Olson and Cory Olson, eds. "Franklin . . . Another Company Town," 217, 218.

[39] *Seattle Press-Times*, 21 May 1891. The Rev. Blakeney was the first pastor of the A. M. E. (Bethel) Church which was organized in 1890 by John T. Gayton and other members of Seattle's black community. Seattle is still the home of some of Gayton's descendants.

[40] *Seattle Press-Times*, 21 May 1891.

[41] *Seattle Press-Times*, 23 May 1891.

[42] *Seattle Post-Intelligencer,* 19 May 1891.

[43] Ernest Moore, *The Coal Miner Who Came West* (Seattle: n.p., 1982), 13.

[44] Ibid., 13-14.

[45] *Seattle Press-Times*, 25 August 1894. The black miners who were killed on August 24, 1894, according to Ernest Moore were Jay Clements, John Dixon, Andy Greer, John Irvin, A. Jackson Jones, R.W. Jones, Edward Maxwell, John Proustille, H.R. Roberts and Frank Williams. See Ernest Moore, *The Coal Miner Who Came West*, 17.

[46] *Seattle Post Intelligencer,* 25 August 1894. In January 1896, the *Seattle Republican*, noted that "G. W. Smalley (deceased)" had been working as a "day top boss" at the Franklin mine.

[47] *Seattle Post-Intelligencer,* 25 August 1894. J.E. Hawkins started as a barber in Seattle who, in his spare time, studied law and became an attorney and political activist. See *Seattle Republican*, 3 January 1902.

[48] Joe William Trotter, Jr., *Coal, Class and Color: Blacks in Southern West Virginia 1915-32* (Urbana: University of Illinois Press), 9.

[49] "Negro Miners Greatly Needed," *Seattle Republican*, 19 August 1898.

[50] *Cayton's Weekly*, 18 May 1918.

[51] William Craven became Washington State's first black mayor when he was unanimously appointed mayor by the Roslyn City Council on 10 June 1975. See Rob Tucker and Rafael Gonzales "Roslyn's mayor has made state history," *Yakima Herald-Republic*, 6 July 1975, 1.

[52] Moore, *The Coal Miner Who Came West*, 2.

[53] Ibid., 3.

[54] Ibid., 6.

[55] Elva Nicholas, "Practically Everyone Carried a Gun!" interview by Esther H. Mumford, tape recording, 22 March 1976, Washington State Archives, Olympia, accession no. BL-KNG 76-42em.

[56] Ibid.

[57] Ibid.

[58] Ibid.

[59] Elva Nicholas, interview by Esther Mumford, tape recording, 24 June1976, Washington State Archives, Olympia, accession no. BL-KNG 76-55em.

# MIRROR OF TASTE

## THE RESTAURANT AS A REFLECTION OF THE CHANGING APPETITES OF SEATTLE

Robert S. Fisher

Over the years the restaurants of Seattle have not only provided sustenance, but also entertainment, camaraderie, new experiences, and new opportunities. As the city has grown, so have its tastes and appetites and its desire to, on the one hand, measure up to other cities and, on the other, become something unique. Born as a dream of a new New York, Seattle has often been compared to cities described as cosmopolitan and world class. Situated in a naturally abundant and lush environment, Seattle's bounty of natural resources were considered a definitive ingredient of its cuisine. Dependent on new immigrants not only to work in its kitchens and dining rooms, but also to found new ones, the restaurants reflected the diversity of the city. This essay will attempt to show some of the diversity of a selection of the city's restaurants over the years, how their offerings have changed, or not, and how they have reflected the history of the city.

Henry Yesler's log cook and mess-house may be considered Seattle's first public eating-house. Built in 1853 to feed the mill workers, the cookhouse was "a low, long rambling affair without architectural pretensions, [and] it possessed a certain homely attractiveness."[1] The report of its demise in the *Puget Sound Dispatch* on July 30, 1866, lists the many functions it served in the early years of Seattle:

It has, at different times, served for town hall, courthouse, jail, military headquarters, storehouse, hotel and church; and in the early years of its history served all of these purposes at once. It was the place of holding elections, and political parties of all sorts held their meetings in it, and quarrelled [sic] and made friends again, and ate, drank, laughed, sung, wept, and slept under the same hospitable roof.[2]

There is no record of what was served at the mess-house but Clarence Bagley, in his early history of Seattle, provides clues as to the diet of the early Caucasian inhabitants. "Late in 1852 Mr. Denny paid $90 for two barrels of pork and $20 for one barrel of flour. One of the barrels of pork was lost on the beach. The settlers lived on potatoes, fish, venison, sugar, syrup, tea, coffee."[3] The interesting fact about this list is that from the very beginning Seattle's new immigrants ate the foodstuffs of their fellow European Americans. For them, as for other immigrants, providing one's native food or a reasonable facsimile was very important. Though the Seattle area was rich in certain foods, these did not, or could not, support the new city, although later they would play an important part in the development of Seattle restaurant cuisine and it's marketing. However, the abundance and quality of the local edible vegetation and aquatic life were recognized and appreciated early on.

> As for fruit, we can very well live without it as the superabundance of berries here will serve as a substitute. We have strawberries, raspberries, dewberries, salal berries, salmon berries, cranberries, whortleberries and wild grapes of a superior kind. There is an abundance of game in the woods, consisting of deer, wild cattle, . . . bears, wolves, panthers, squirrels, skunks, and rats. Pheasants, grouse, gulls, and ducks and crows are as tame as hens at home . . . Salmon are very abundant, cod fish, herring, sardines, oysters, and clams.[4]

It was this natural bounty, combined with their inherited cuisine, that would inspire future cooks and chefs. Yet, it would take years for them and the city to grow into it.

With the advent of trade and the influx of visitors in the settlement, there was a need for boardinghouses that also provided meals. According to the columnist C. T. Conover, David Mauer opened Seattle's first public house in a building owned by Doc Maynard. Captain Felker of the brig *Franklin Adams* secured land located at Jackson and Commercial (now First Avenue) from Doc Maynard and built the first milled lumber building. Painted a brilliant white, the Felker House stood out from the rest of the log buildings. Its controversial proprietor was Mary Ann Conklin, also know as Madame Damnable, possibly due to her rough tongue or because she may also have run a brothel or both. The other early boarding establishment was Our House located on the south side of Mill Street (Yesler) toward the wharf from Commercial Street and operated by Bill Gross. Another African American, Manuel Lopes, opened a barbershop and restaurant on Commercial Street after his arrival in 1852. It was one of the first restaurants in Seattle. His customers were mostly loggers, mill hands, sailors, and miners, and he was known to provide meals whether they had the money to pay or not.[5]

Development of independent public restaurants was slow until Seattle's population grew large enough to support them. The fire of 1889 destroyed practically all of the business district's restaurants, though many were back in operation in tents in a matter of days. The 1890s would see the growth of more permanent structures as well as the beginnings of the early grand restaurants. The fire provided the opportunity to expand to meet the growing needs of the city.

The Maison Riche, later called Maison Tortoni and then Maison Barberis, at

Second Avenue and James Street, was one of the more notorious restaurants of the new era. When it was opened in 1893 the Maison Riche was hailed as "What Seattle Needs." The restaurant was French, with both an *á la carte* menu and a set *table d' hôte* menu with wine for the price of 50 cents. It was described in the *Seattle Press Times*:

> This is the style of restaurant that Seattle is very much in need of, and will be the only first class place in the city where a gentleman can take his wife, sister or sweetheart with that feeling that everything connected with the place is beyond suspicion; is thoroughly respectable and that proper service can be given them.[6]

The report that this was a place that welcomed females in the company of men with no suspicion aroused was important. Prior to Prohibition, and for a time afterwards, the bar and restaurant business catered mainly to men. Working-class saloons as well as high-class bar cafés and restaurants were all-male bastions where whiskey, wine, and brandy flowed too freely for feminine tastes; most hotels had separate entrances and dining rooms for women.[7] In addition, unaccompanied women in restaurants and cafés were often considered to be prostitutes. Seattle needed a place where respectable men and women could go to dine out, though it did not last long. The restaurant, renamed Maison Tortoni was described in an ad in 1899 as "The Only Epicure's Resort." By 1900 the name had been changed once more, to Maison Barberis, after the new owner, Jack Barberis. By 1906 the venue was closed. An article in the *Seattle Post-Intelligencer* on May 6, 1906, offers an explanation in a story of corruption and decline. In 1897 Jack Barberis arrived from San Francisco, where he had run an Italian restaurant. Once in Seattle he became famous for the steaks at his restaurant. His business expanded and he added "private dining rooms." As with the box theaters in the south end of the city, these private rooms allowed patrons to expand on their own "appetites." The quality of the cooking no longer mattered, only the quality of the liquor. The police warned Barberis. "The all-night orgies of the rounders who frequented the Maison became obnoxious to the hotels in the neighborhood. The drunken revels, the inharmonious song and the wild laughter in the closed boxes could be heard on the street." Barberis tried to separate the drinking from the dining by partitioning a separate saloon, but soon the drinks returned to the dining rooms. However, it was the public perception that ended his business as the news spread that only "working" women would be seen entering the Maison. Barberis blamed the newspapers for the decline in business and he closed the restaurant but remained in the private catering business.[8]

## NEW ERA

The crossover of the business of the saloons and cafés was a chronic problem in the early years of the 20th century. As the public turned toward reform, the excesses of the city's nightlife became ammunition for more stringent codes. An exposé in the *Town Crier* in 1913 described the scene in a number of "cafés" where the main order of business was to link patrons and prostitutes. The article admits, "We saw hundreds of persons in good order and good spirits, doing nothing worse than taking a drink now and then. In such a city as Seattle the cafes are 'places to go' where those who know not what else to do may find a measure of entertainment and hospitality . . . ," but concludes, "Decency and innocence may pass through the atmosphere unharmed, . . . but the cafes discover no influence tending to promote the one or to protect the other."[9]

Despite the problems associated with serving liquor, many new Seattle restaurants opened with the object of providing good meals for their patrons. In 1899 a new place opened on Cherry between Second and Third Avenues: Manca's Café. In 1871 Angelo Manca, an immigrant from Sardinia, opened a café in St. Louis. One of his sons, Victor E. Manca, subsequently operated restaurants in Denver, Las Vegas, Salt Lake City, and Pueblo, Colorado, before coming to Seattle in 1899. The original restaurant was razed in 1905 to make way for the Alaska Building, and Manca's moved to 108 Columbia Street. Little changed from that point: the blue-and-white-tiled entrance, oval shaped glass panes, red leather seat cushions, potted plants in the windows, and fluted light fixtures all remained for the life of the business. After Victor's retirement in 1945, his sons Eugene and Vincent operated Manca's. Specialties of the house included Dutch babies—pancakes described by the family as a cross between a popover and an omelet—combination salad and razor clam hash. Manca's also originated the famous poached eggs Vienna and grilled crab legs, making them the talk of the town. The restaurant had a staff of 12, and in one 28-year period no employees were changed. "We have a little place, but we've tried to give our customers the best in foods. We believe that everyone who comes in here is paying us a compliment," said Eugene. Manca's closed August 19, 1955, when the United Exchange Building Corp. decided to demolish the buildings housing Manca's and the National Hotel to make room for the Norton Building. In a story in the *Seattle Times* on the closing, Eugene Manca said that the café business was changing, moving to showmanship, "but there's still room for the old type of restaurant. What we have here is a sort of a club—more of a club than a restaurant—and the membership is open to everyone."[10] For historian Bill Speidel, Manca's was "American cooking in the fine old manner . . . razor clam hash . . . potato pancakes . . . corned beef . . . steamed finnan haddie . . . old time waiters . . . old Seattle surviving because of quality."[11]

Another middle-class eating house opened in 1905 in the Hogue Building. The Rathskeller, named for a restaurant of the German type, offered a sumptuous Ladies Café in the former press rooms of the *Seattle Post-Intelligencer*. Though it

Manca's Café, one of Seattle's longest-lived and popular eating establishments. Courtesy of the Museum of History and Industry.

had separate entrances for men and women, the Rathskeller provided more than nourishment—it provided entertainment. The 400-seat room featured concert music every night of the week under the initial direction of Harry West. According to the *Seattle Mail and Herald*, "Cafés are becoming popular places of amusement both in the east and on the coast. The music alone places it [the Rathskeller] above any other entertainment in the city.[12]

In addition to the Rathskeller another restaurant was vying for the same clientele, the Olympus Café, at 110–112 First Avenue South. Opened in 1897, the Olympus was renovated in 1905. The former one-story building was expanded to three stories, with a seating capacity as great as any on the North Pacific Coast. After the remodel, the Olympus was described in the *Seattle Post-Intelligencer* as "without equal in the Northwest in elegance, cleanliness, general appointments and thorough equipments [sic]."[13] The first floor contained the men's grill and a buffet area with a side hall leading to electric elevators that accessed the second and third floors. The second floor held the main dining area, the Venetian Room, an oblong space with seven dining alcoves on each side. The large window in the front, divided into many small windows of different shapes, was a reproduction of the Students' Café window in Vienna. An orchestra gallery was situated on the same floor; the opening season presented the music of Sharpe & Steiner's Orchestra. Also on the second floor was the Holland Room, with a fireplace and German details, and the private Blue Room. The third floor was leased to the Lumbermen's

Club for their sole use.

Chauncey Wright was one of the best-known Seattle restaurateurs in the early 20th century. Following in the footsteps of his parents, also restaurant owners, he worked the summers in the dining service on boats to Alaska, beginning at the age of twelve. As related in his biography, in *Seattle and Environs*, he opened his first restaurant in Seattle at the age of 19 at Second Avenue and Yesler. According to this biography and other sources, Wright soon left Seattle and spent time in Tacoma and Los Angeles, where his family had lived at some point in his childhood. After Wright returned to Seattle, gold was discovered in Alaska and he took off for Dawson City in 1897. He initially went to work as a cook, but soon opened his own place, the Greasy Spoon, which acquired a reputation for fine food.

> His stories of the high prices obtained in those days (coffee was 50 cents, as was a piece of pie, a sandwich cost a dollar, and a full meal from four to eight dollars) and of his ability to "turn out" any order that was called for, from "ham-and" to *pate de fois gras* or *terrapin*, are among the amusing tales he related of that early invasion of the Klondike.[14]

In 1904 he returned to Seattle and opened his own eponymous place at 164 Washington Street, beginning his restaurant empire. He moved the restaurant to 110 Occidental Street in 1910 and after that established restaurants throughout the city before his death at the age of 47 in 1917.

The early 1900s were fraught with challenges for Seattle restaurateurs. On the one hand the public was becoming more concerned with health, cleanliness, and sobriety, and on the other workers were demanding greater wages and fewer hours. The movement to close saloons by banning the sale of alcohol, supported by many restaurant owners, would eliminate competition but also a sure source of revenue. Restaurants and food purveyors also had to convince the public that they ran clean operations in compliance with the Pure Food and Drug Law of 1906.

In addition, labor was organizing restaurant workers. The Waitresses' Union Local 240 was formed in March 1900. At that time waitresses were working 11 to 12 hours a day, seven days a week, for $5 per week. Once union represented, they got a 10-hour day, with a salary of $8.50 per week, and if they arranged a substitute they could have a day off. Another goal of the union was to provide a place of refuge and rest for its members, and in 1913 Fred Keen gave the union a 14-room house for just such a purpose.[15] By the mid-1930s many Seattle restaurants, as part of a deal worked out by the Seattle Restaurant Association, had become union shops.[16]

In 1906 a French immigrant, Charles Blanc, arrived in Seattle after a peripatetic youth. He worked as a chef at the Rainier Club, the Rainier Grand Hotel, the Rathskeller Café, the New Washington Hotel, and the Savoy, before he eventually decided he was ready to open his own restaurant. On January 6, 1916, in the first year of Prohibition in the state, Charles Blanc opened Blanc's Café at 315 Marion

Street. It was right across the street from the old Martin Van Buren Stacey Mansion, built in 1883 and the former home of the Rainier Club and the Seattle Chamber of Commerce. In 1920 Blanc opened Café Blanc at 509 Third Avenue and renamed the first restaurant Blanc's Le Petite. This new café was also hailed in an article in the *Town Crier* as a place "Seattle has long needed." Blanc later opened the Chantecler Cafeteria at Third Avenue and University Street in 1922 and L'Montmarte Café. The Chantecler, which boasted "An Aristocratic Meal at a Democratic Price," put a new spin on the cafeteria concept with its transformation each night into a ballroom with spring floor and an orchestra under the direction of Tiny Burnett. In 1925 Blanc moved his namesake café to the Stacey Mansion, at 308 Marion Street, which he had recently purchased and renovated. It was his magnum opus, "Where Epicureans Meet" and "Sans Rival." Blanc offered a menu comprising 750 items, from 18 ethnic cuisines. In 1933 he created a replica of a German beer garden in the basement. The Rathskeller, "Where True Bohemianism Prevails," served a truly international menu with a national special each day.[17]

The menus at Maison Blanc, the former Blanc's Café and the Rathskeller were international but heavily favored European and American dishes. However, like most Seattle restaurants, they offered few regional dishes; "Toke Point Oysters" and "Puget Sound Seafood" are listed. As with many of their contemporaries the cuisine of Blanc's restaurants reflected classic European and American fare.

One of the definitive restaurants of early Seattle was Rippe's Café. Frank Rippe opened his first café in 1910 at 314 Pike Street, between Third and Fourth Avenues. By 1924 the restaurant had moved to 1421 Fourth Avenue. Rippe's was the place to go for many locals as well as visitors. "Dining at the restaurant was always a celebration," according to the *Seattle Times*, for business lunches, weddings, or after the theater, opera, fights, or ball games. Scores of famous personalities, from Calvin Coolidge to Jack Dempsey, Texas Guinan, and Jean Harlow, dined there.[18]

Rippe's, "as good as any restaurant in San Francisco," had white tablecloths, heavy silverware, polished mahogany and brass, spacious booths, and skilled waiters, and was open 24 hours a day. The menu included cracked crab and Olympia oysters, ready-to-go meat dishes, melons in season, oysters Rockefeller, German potato pancakes with pot roast, steak, eggs Vienna, oyster stew, and ham-and-eggs Southern.[19] After Frank Rippe's death in 1934, the restaurant remained open under the direction of his widow and son-in-law, until 1940. That's when John G. von Herberg, Seattle theatre magnate, and partner Antone J. Meyers acquired the café property and reopened it as Von's Café, with plans to recapture the restaurant's name for fine food. The restaurant changed hands again in 1949, after von Herberg's death, and was purchased by Seattle restaurateur Gilbert Ridden. It again changed hands in the 1960s and closed for good in 1963. The menu of Von's reads like an inventory of every dish conceivable in the United States at that time, including Crab Meat Cocktail, Quilcene Oyster Cocktail, Pork Chops with Country Gravy, Chicken Livers with Italian Spaghetti, omelets, sandwiches, and Chocolate Ice Box Cake.[20]

Throughout the 1920s Seattle's restaurants adjusted to serving meals without alcohol. Many closed, but most were able to thrive on the growing middle class's need for working lunches and special-event dinners. Many places ignored the prohibition laws, and for a price one could have gin, bourbon, or whiskey brought to the table. It was also possible to drink at some roadhouses and underground speakeasies.

Even after Prohibition ended in 1933, beer and wine were the only alcoholic beverages legally allowed in restaurants in Washington State. Liquor was banned in public eating-houses. At the same time, the Depression was forcing owners to cut prices to entice customers into their restaurants, although the owners also made an effort to band together to hold prices steady. It was in this atmosphere that two of Seattle's best-known restaurateurs entered the fray.

Walter Clark, a veteran of Manning's coffee houses, began business on July 28, 1930, after purchasing Marie's Barbecue, located at 4545 Tenth Avenue Northeast (the street is now known as Roosevelt Way). Clark would own and operate some 53 restaurants over the course of his career, was president of the state restaurant association and the National Restaurant Association, and would be instrumental in establishing some of Seattle's most prominent restaurants in years to come. He opened several major establishments in the 1930s and '40s. In 1931 Clark and his partner, Karl Monson, opened the Salad Bowl, 1325 Fifth Avenue, as a tea room catering to the tastes of women; it was also Clark's first full-service restaurant. Later that year Clark opened the Top Notch at 1121 East 45th Street, formerly the site of a White Spot. The Top Notch kept its predecessor's menu but added some full-course meals. In 1932 Clark and Monson opened Clark's Third Avenue at 1426 Third Avenue and billed it as "New York's latest idea in restaurants," with booths for coziness rather than "conspicuous, old fashioned tables." In late 1932 Clark worked out a deal to take over a space in the Medical-Dental Building at Fifth and Olive, formerly the home of Clare Colgrove's Purple Pup. Clark's Coffee Tavern, at 1628 Fifth Avenue, featured salads, sandwiches, and full dinners similar to those offered by the Salad Bowl.[21]

Dinners served by Clark's restaurants in the 1930s and early '40s included: Shore Dinner of Fresh Crab Meat Cocktail, Fried Native Oysters, Grilled King Salmon, Puget Sound Scallops, Cole Slaw, Tarter Sauce, French Fried Potatoes, and a Hot Roll with Butter for 50 cents; Sizzling Top Sirloin Steak (served on a "sizzling" platter) with French Fried Potatoes, Hearts of Lettuce Salad, French Dressing, and Hot Roll for 65 cents; Fruit Salad with Whipped Cream Dressing; Combination Vegetable Salad or Combination Fruit Salad; Fresh Crab or Shrimp Salad; Cottage Cheese and Pineapple; and Crab or Shrimp Louis.[22]

Clark's menus were simpler than those of Blanc's and Rippe's, but offered many of the same foodstuffs: grilled steaks, veal and pork chops, spaghetti, chili con carne. Clark's offered a local seafood plate and all offered the ubiquitous oysters, but these were standard fare of the times. The menus of Clark's early restaurants also reflect the economic conditions of the 1930s, emphasizing cheaper, lighter meals and better service. Clark's Salad Bowl, described as a tea room, reflected the trend of catering to women in a quiet, clean environment at odds with the old-time male-dominated chop house but also less expensive than the more elegant Rathskeller or Rippe's.

Heavily featured in *Cosmopolitan Seattle*, a *Seattle Post-Intelligencer* restaurant recipe booklet, tea rooms were geared to a specific audience, as this description of The Pine Tree at Third and Pine in the Welles Building shows:

> Home economics trained manager and women cooks! There's the combination that produces all-American cooking typical of American tea rooms. Vegetable plates and cheese soufflés with a la King sauce, generous salads that make most of a meal. Ruth Holland, home economics graduate from the University of Minnesota, guided the culinary destinies of the Pine Tree. Tea room cookery frequently typifies the highest standard of home cookery in the community.[23]

Tea rooms were generally run by women for women, and the owners were often home economics graduates. The Red Candle at 614 Pine Street had as its pastry chef Helen Switzer, who had previously worked at the Washington Hotel and the Washington Athletic Club. Owner Eva Dove earned her degree from the University of Washington in home economics, specializing in tea room and institutional management. She said, "Tea room management is a happy career for a woman to undertake. She earns a living in a pleasant way, works in pleasant surroundings and meets nice people."[24]

Tea rooms did not exclude men and did solicit their business. At the Betsy Jarvis Tea Room, on the second floor of the White-Henry-Stuart Building, at Fourth and Union, the agenda as described by author Elizabeth Herrick was to serve good food: "Just good old-fashioned favorite dishes—no trouble at all to get the man of the family back here, despite his aversion to tea rooms. Once he's tasted their orange chiffon pie and hot biscuits—he's sold. Dinners are 75 cents and usually feature mealy baked potatoes, nice homey dishes like veal birds, chicken pot pie, etc., and always green vegetables and crisp cold salads."[25] Some "women's restaurants," such as Helen Swope's Restaurants in the Edmond Meany Hotel and one upstairs in the Republic Building, at Third Avenue and Pike Street, did include a men's grill.

> "Her [Helen Swope's] family dinners for 50 cents include soup, choice of entrees and her own special desserts, salad, 10 cents extra and every meal features the home made graham bread for which she has become known. The seafood plate for 50 cents is a luncheon feature, and includes oyster cocktail, fresh crab, tuna fish, fresh shrimps, one half a stuffed egg, sliced tomatoes and sardines. The tea room itself is lovely, Early American in feeling and, after all, modern American,

is the best possible tradition in cooking."[26]

Not all tea rooms were run by women. The Dolly Madison, at 1536 Westlake Avenue, offered Southern-style dishes in a room decorated with genuine antiques of the Colonial period. Like many tea rooms it was on the second floor, with cut-glass prism chandeliers, antique clocks, and spool-back chairs. The owner, Arthur Gabler, was known for the artistic designs of his vegetable plates. He admitted, "Each of our plates is planned to make a picture. The eye first devours the food; merely to eat would be a vague function. A wholesome, balanced, vitamized [sic] repast is one of life's keenest enjoyments." One specialty was baked ham with corn pone. Lunch was 35 cents and dinner was 50 cents.[27]

Certainly the most colorful, if not the most influential, restaurateur in Seattle's history was Ivar Haglund. Ivar's Acres of Clams opened in 1946 and soon became a unique Seattle landmark. Haglund, a restless self-promoter, never let an opportunity slip to get his business in the paper. Built on the pier that had been home to his original aquarium, Ivar's never tried to be anything other than a fun place to eat. With its clam chowder, fried and steamed clams, cold or barbecued Dungeness crab, and finnan haddie, Ivar's became an institution. Some of Haglund's later restaurants—the Captain's Table and the Salmon House—were more pretentious, but his original place, filled with years of nautical knickknacks, is a genuine Seattle restaurant.[28]

While Ivar's was all kitsch, Crawford's Sea Grill was all business. Opened in 1940 by C. C. Crawford at 333 Elliott Avenue West (later to become Ivar's Captain's Table), the new structure—built and completely equipped for $31,000—featured a glass-enclosed dining room providing an unobstructed view of Puget Sound and the Olympics. With seating for 118, its slogan was "A Showplace on the Shore of Puget Sound." Crawford said in an article in the *Seattle Times* announcing the opening that "[T]he Sea Grill will specialize in the serving of the widest possible variety of sea foods all prepared on a specially designed broiler with olive oil used exclusively in the preparation."[29] Crawford's aim was to showcase the seafoods of the Pacific Northwest, but the menu includes little local seafood—only Puget Sound clam chowder, salmon and halibut. Louisiana prawns, Alaskan shrimp, rainbow trout, and filet of tuna Mexican style make up the rest of the menu, in addition to other meats and seafood.[30] Even an earlier seafood restaurant, Don's Seafood, 1429 Fifth Avenue, though also offering an extensive menu, featured little local seafood. But appetites were changing. As Don Elhe, the owner, said in 1935, "Thirty years ago we had no fresh raw shrimps or Puget Sound scallops, and most orders were for ham and eggs or steaks[;] today only 5 per cent of our orders are for meat."[31] Still, it would be a few years more for the potential of local ingredients to be realized.

The prevalence of "American" food on Seattle restaurant menus carried over into even the businesses new immigrants opened. At one time immigrants of Greek descent, according to the *Seattle Times* columnist John Reddin, owned and operated more than 75 percent of downtown restaurants and candy stores, even Crawford's, which was run by Nick Zandies after the death of C. C. Crawford. Other Greek-owned restaurants, many of them cafés with refrigerated front windows displaying melons, fruit, meat, and shellfish, included the Sapho at 114 Prefontaine Place, the Golden Gate on Pike Street, the Boston Café, the Busy Bee, the Apollo, and the Acropolis. Asked why so many had closed by 1961, one owner replied, "As for the restaurant business, it's a hard game[;] . . . the old folk are either dying off or have retired and young folk want no part of it, preferring to get an education and a white collar job or profession."[32] As for the food at these Greek-owned cafés, it was standard America fare: oysters, steaks and chops, eggs and omelets, sandwiches, salads, potatoes, and pie for dessert.[33]

The story was the same for many Japanese immigrant café owners. Though some of their restaurants served Japanese food, such as the Maneki at 212 Washington Street, most served Western-style food. In an interview, Genji Mihara remembered,

> I ran the Occidental Café in Seattle for twenty-two years, from 1919 till 1941. There were forty-two Western style restaurants run by Japanese in Seattle . . . ninety per cent of the customers were whites; the Japanese in the city were almost all single men who patronized the eight Japanese-style restaurants.[34]

In the 1920s, '30s, and '40s, many Chinese-owned Seattle restaurants, in addition to the ubiquitous 'American' Chinese food (e.g., chop suey), had an 'American' food column on the menu, with such items as relishes, steaks and chops, potatoes, salads, and sandwiches.[35] It would not be until the 1950s and '60s that non-Chinese patrons could go to a Chinese restaurant in Seattle and not receive a menu with "American" dishes.

## THE 'CLASS' RESTAURANT

Victor Rosellini was one of the most influential restaurateurs of the 1950s and 1960s. According to one account, "the birth of the modern era of Seattle restaurants may be pinpointed . . . to late 1949[36] when the voters finally okayed liquor by the drink and a restaurateur named Victor Rosellini arrived to show his native state how to run a great restaurant."[37]

The gregarious Rosellini returned to Seattle from San Francisco, where he had been working at Bimbo's 365 Club, to open one of the "new" Seattle restaurants in May 1950. Bringing with him a wooden salad bowl that would become his trademark, he decided his new restaurant, Rosellini's 610, would have white tablecloths, chic upholstery, a floorshow, and a boisterous bar. The bar was a center of the business; Victor's first bartender, Paul Pissue, poured giant drinks and allowed patrons to maintain monthly tabs. Rosellini's was one of the first downtown restaurants to open without a lunch counter. For single diners there was a "director's table" that soon became *the* place to sit for regulars. Rosellini's chef, brother-in-law John Pogetti, was an alum of San Francisco's Amelio's restaurant.[38] In the kitchen Pogetti spared no expense or effort. He butchered whole legs of veal, top rounds of beef, and made 50 quarts of pesto at a time. He created new dishes, such as Steak Joanne (the bottom piece of the sirloin marinated for two to three days in garlic, pepper, and rosemary, then broiled and served with a spicy sauce) and Chicken á la John (chicken with artichoke hearts, pimentos, fresh mushrooms, and zucchini in a white wine sauce).[39]

The passage of Initiative 171 in 1948, allowing liquor by the drink to be sold in restaurants, created an impetus for a number of new restaurants and hotel bars to open in Seattle. Profits from selling liquor by the drink would allow restaurateurs to provide higher-priced food, a more upscale atmosphere, and entertainment once they had applied for and received a class 'H' license. In addition to Rosellini, Peter Canlis, Les Teagle, Walter Clark, Jim Ward, and Cliff Waring were among those who opened new restaurants in 1949 and 1950.

In 1949 Peter Canlis joined with Walter Clark, who owned a prime view location on the brow of a hill just south of the Aurora Bridge, to create one of the city's most spectacular restaurants: Canlis, 2576 Aurora Avenue. Canlis, with the aid of the Honolulu architectural firm of Wimberly and Cooke and the Seattle firm of Tucker, Shields and Terry, set about spending more money on the Pacifica-style building, made of cedar and stone, than had been spent on any restaurant in Seattle in 30 years.[40] In *A Gourmet's Notebook*, Canlis is described as "part steak house, part Tiki-Polynesia, part Continental cooking and part Santa Barbara modern home . . . and pitched to that strange hushed dream world inhabited by those who have enormous expense accounts and who prefer a dash of servility from kimona-clad [sic] oriental waitresses."[41] In addition to his Asian wait staff Canlis brought over from Hawaii Joe Ching, who was his executive chef for over 30 years.

The main feature of the Canlis kitchen was the charcoal broiler, with charcoal imported from Hawaii, on which was grilled top sirloin steaks, filet mignon, New York steaks, French peppercorn steaks, lamb chops, and salmon. Canlis also served local clams, oysters, and crab, and was known for its gargantuan baked potatoes and Canlis Caesar salad.

The trend of new restaurants equipped with charcoal broilers, banquettes, bars, and a heavy meat menu continued in the early 1950s: John Franco's Hidden Harbor, 1500 Westlake Avenue, opened in 1950, as did the Cloud Room in the Camlin Hotel. Jim Ward opened El Gaucho at 624 Olive Way in 1953, Walter Clark opened the Red Carpet, formerly the Coffee Tavern, in 1956, and Victor Rosellini opened the 410 in 1956. All offered steaks, oyster and crab cocktails, Caesar salad, and a well-stocked bar. The upscale 'class' restaurant was here. Seattleites felt they finally had places that were comparable to those in New York or San Francisco. In the 410's obituary, the columnist Emmett Watson recalled:

It was always the "safe" place to take somebody from New York or San Francisco. It was no three star on anybody's Michelin, but it was good—often superb—and it measured up to the best in national standards. And to those who could afford it, Rosselini's 410 became a must to local diners-out.[42]

Chinese restaurants began following the same trends. Ruby Chow opened Seattle's first "atmosphere" Mandarin Chinese restaurant in 1949, Ruby Chow's. Later the Hong Kong, at 507 Maynard Avenue South, received a class 'H' license, modernized, and became one of the most popular eating houses in Chinatown. Soon after, Tek Wong opened the Gim Ling at 516 Seventh Avenue South, Art Louie opened his place at 421 Seventh Avenue South, and the Four Seas opened at 714 South King Street.[43]

In 1955 William C. Speidel wrote *You Can't Eat Mount Rainier*, a book about Seattle's restaurants, because he felt the natives did not appreciate what they had. The introduction, entitled "Seattle's Inferiority Complex," berated the natives for not realizing that "national restaurant experts rate Seattle up in the top ten best restaurant cities and at least second-best on the Pacific coast." He goes on to say, "Our restaurant industry—for the most part—is young . . . robust . . . progressive . . . competitive." And the native has no reason to feel restaurant inferiority.[44]

This pep talk was reinforced in 1963 in an article in the *Seattle Post-Intelligencer*: "Fifteen years ago no visitor could spend more than a day in Seattle without being told, 'There is no place to go in Seattle.' Today that same visitor can spend no more than a day in Seattle without being told by at least one proud Seattleite that the city's restaurants are among the best in the United States."[45] Of course, even then there were detractors who thought it absurd to say that Seattle was one of the best restaurant towns in the country as there was no place to compare to New Joe's and Tiny's in San Francisco or Hody's in Los Angeles. There was still the need to measure up to the 'big' cities.[46]

## REVITALIZATION AND REVOLUTION

Putting Seattle on the map as a culinary city, able to keep up with the best the world had to offer, was the legacy of the restaurants of the 1950s and '60s. But there would be little new until the late 1960s and early 1970s. Just as Seattle seemed to be imploding from within when Boeing went bust in 1970, a groundswell of restaurant activity occurred in Seattle that would influence its development for the rest of the century. One instigator was Francois Kissel and his wife, Julia. When they opened the Brasserie Pittsbourg in the former location of the Pittsburgh Lunch at 602 First Avenue in Pioneer Square, a new wave of development began, bringing a renaissance to the area and to Seattle's restaurant scene. In 1969 Francois and Julia Kissel were planning to open a French restaurant called Pomme de l'Amour, but they gave up on it when they saw the Pittsburgh Lunch was for sale. The Brasserie was by all accounts loud, due to the white tile floor, bright, and to some expensive, but at the time it was the new "new thing."[47] Many diners at this time had an increased desire to learn about French food, á la Julia Child, and ethnic and natural foods, and new restaurants provided that education. Instead of looking to the menus of the past, which offered many of the same items, patrons were looking for new experiences. Brasserie Pittsbourg offered many their first lessons in French cuisine. Local writer Roger Downey, apologizing for not being loyal to the Kissels, explained,

> Once you've learned what *bouillabaisse* is, what it tastes like and how to pronounce it, it's more interesting to try out . . . your knowledge on some-one else's product than to keep eating the one you learned from; and when it comes to learning the basics of good dining, of flavors, seasonings, ac-companiments and the like, Dr. Kissel's Culinary College has more grads hereabouts . . . than all the rest put together. His *mousse*, his *paté*, his *vinaigrette*, his *bearnaise* lurk, like Platonic forms, back at the dim begin-nings of our gustatory experience.[48]

Pioneer Square's restaurant renaissance also included Marvin Timberlake's Das Gasthaus at 303 Occidental and Peter Cipra's Prague Restaurant and Gallery at 309 First Avenue South.

If Francois Kissel was a Frenchman bringing French food to a new generation of Seattleites, then Robert Rosellini was an American bringing new American food to the same generation in the guise of French food. In 1974 Victor Rosellini's 410 was still considered by many to be the standard for elegant dining in Seattle. That changed when Victor's son opened The Other Place in the space formerly occu-pied by Walter Clark's Dublin House, at 319 Union Street. The Other Place was immediately pronounced to be "[U]nquestionably the finest restaurant in the Pa-cific Northwest and our one restaurant of major national importance," and "a res-taurant aspiring to and often equaling the highest traditions in European cook-ing."[49] Robert Rosellini and the Other Place blew into Seattle on the winds of change of the *nouvelle cuisine* movement and the local food movement and eventu-ally established the *New American* label in the Pacific Northwest. Rosellini, trained in a crash course in European cookery with restaurateur Jean Schild of Geneva, trained as a butcher as well as worked as a cellar-man and a vineyard manager in France. Upon his return to Seattle he assisted at the 610 and planned his new venture. The plan included importing seeds to have local farmers grow greens and herbs; supporting a game farm for a ready and fresh supply of pheasants, quail, ducks, and geese; and developing a trout farm to supply the restaurant.

The menu of the Other Place offered a choice of prix fixe menus in French with explanations in English. First-course choices offered in 1976 included salmon quenelles, sturgeon, escargot, pheasant liver paté, and Quilcene oysters. Entrées included elk with a sauce reduction with morels and juniper berries; quail stuffed with walnuts, cream cheese, bacon, and cognac; veal with Cognac, cream, and hollandaise; roasted rack of lamb; and trout au bleu. All of these dishes were well prepared and quite good, but well within the confines of French cuisine at that time. However, by 1982, Rosellini was seen not as a classical French chef but as Seattle's champion of the "New American" cuisine. The Other Place was described as "Seattle's most innovative, idiosyncratic restaurant where the motto is, 'the products of the Northwest; the style of France,' and where dedication to Northwest products, even more than to French style, verges on the fanatical."[50]

This change was marked by a profusion of young chefs, usually middle class, who chose to become cooks and were given that opportunity. They did not have to go through a rigorous apprenticeship but learned on the job and then had the freedom to cook as they pleased. A 1981 article in the *Weekly* highlighted some of these young chefs "who are creating a new kind of restaurant in Seattle, one in which the sophisticated developments in French nouvelle cuisine—lighter sauces, less elaborate presentations, exotic combination of ingredients—butt up against a new American style in the kitchen: that of unbridled freedom to do as one pleases."[51] One of the featured young chefs was Bruce Naftaly, then about to open Les Copains, 2202 North 45th Street. Naftaly had worked at the Other Place, beginning as a dishwasher and working his way up to day chef, and went on to high praise at Les Copains, which boasted "Northwest foods cooked in the French manner." Naftaly still presides over his own restaurant in Ballard, Le Gourmand.

Another child of the food revolution of the 1980s, and still one of the most influential restaurateurs in Seattle, is Tom Douglas, whose career brings to a close this study. There are a number of other great restaurateurs at this time, such as Thierry Rautureau of Rover's, Scott Carsberg of Lampreia, Ludgar Szmania of Szmania's, and Kaspar Donier of Kaspar's, but it was Douglas who finally combined the best foods and cuisines of the region and fulfilled the potential of his many talented predecessors in creating what has come to be labeled "Northwest" cuisine.

Douglas began his career in Seattle in 1977 when he arrived from Delaware. He worked at Boondocks, Second Landing, the 1904, and McCormick's. He was hired at Café Sport, 2020 Western Avenue, first as the co-chef and then as the chef and general manager. He was described by Emmett Watson as "an unpretentious, ordinary, hard-working guy, with no formal training, who ranks among the best in the kitchen."[52] Café Sport served a number of innovative dishes, many heavily influenced by Asian cuisine, such as kasu cod, Columbia River sturgeon with a light curry sauce, lamb sausage, pasta with wild mushrooms, the house salad with Oregon blue cheese, black bean soup, and Chilean sea bass.[53] Douglas later installed this type of menu at his own restaurant, The Dahlia Lounge, 1904 Fourth Avenue, which he opened in 1988. A menu from 1994 lists Five Spice Soup, Lobster-Shrimp-Shiitake Potstickers, Local Oysters, Pan Roasted King Salmon, Harry Yoshimura's Fish Selection of the Day, Moroccan Lamb Mixed Grill, and Lap Sang Tea Smoked

Duck Breast.[54] Douglas later opened two more restaurants: Etta's, at 2020 Western Avenue (the old Café Sport location), and the Palace Kitchen, at 2030 Fifth Avenue. His success has been attributed to a "freewheeling style that incorporate[s] Asian ingredients and locally produced food stuffs into easy-to-understand and easy-to-enjoy home-style cooking."[55]

Douglas, an immigrant to the city, immersed himself in the myriad flavors it offered and helped create what has been called "Northwest" cuisine, an original amalgamation of American and Asian foods prepared and served in a European manner utilizing local produce, seafood, and foodstuffs. With unpretentiousness, Douglas continues in the tradition of Charles Blanc, Walter Clark, Ivar Haglund, Victor Rosellini, Robert Rosellini, and Francois Kissel by providing a good and satisfying meal in a city that is not always sure of itself. Fortunately, at the end of the 20th century, there was no longer a need for local restaurants to aspire to be "as good as" those in New York or San Francisco. Seattle's restaurants had come into their own.

## NOTES

[1] Clarence B. Bagley, *History of Seattle From the Earliest Settlement to the Present* (Chicago: S.J. Clarke  Publishing Co., 1916), vol. I, 39.

[2] *Puget Sound Dispatch*, 30 July 1866, quoted in William C. Speidel, *Sons of the Profits* (Seattle: Nettle Creek Publishers, 1967,1990), 64–65.

[3] Bagley, 26.

[4] *Ibid.*, 33. From Mr. Blaine's letter of 6 December 1853.

[5] Esther Hall Mumford, *Seattle's Black Victorians 1852-1901* (Seattle: Ananse Press, 1980), 66, 67; Mary T. Henry, *Tribute: Seattle Public Places Named For Black People* (Seattle: Statice Press, 1997), 70.

[6] "What Seattle Needs," *Seattle Press Times*, 18 August 1893, 4.

[7] Harvey A. Levenstein, *Revolution at the Table: The Transformation of the American Diet* (New York/London, 1988), 185.

[8] "Maison Berberis Closes its Doors," *Seattle Post-Intelligencer*, 6 May 1906, 1.

[9] Forrest Anderson, "One Night in Seattle Cafes," the *Town Crier*, 19 April 1913, 5–6.

[10] "Manca's to Move," the *Seattle Times*, 15 July 1955.

[11] William C. Speidel, *You Can't Eat Mount Rainier* (Portland: Binford & Morts Publishing, 1955), 70–71.

[12] "The Rathskeller," *Seattle Mail and Herald*, 15 April 1905, 10.

[13] "How the Olympus, Seattle's Model Café, Looks," *Seattle Post-Intelligencer*, 19 November 1905.

[14] Chauncey Wright, *Seattle and Environs, Op. Cit.*; "Chauncey Wright Drops Dead in His Home," the *Seattle Times*, 11 December 1917, 3.

[15] Mabel Abbott, "The Waitresses of Seattle," Life & Labor, February 1914, 48–49.

[16] P. E. Tibbetts, *Mr. Restaurant: A Biography of Walter F. Clark* (Seattle: Murray Publishing, 1990), 81.

[17] Robert Fisher, "Charles Joseph Ernest Blanc," *Columbia Magazine*, forthcoming.

**Manca's Café menu**

CATERERS FOR 84 YEARS

*Manca's*

MANCA'S CAFÉ
SEATTLE, U.S.A.

Open from 11:30 a. m. to 8:45 p. m.
Closed Saturdays, Sundays
and Bank Holidays

108 Columbia St.        ELiot 7361

MANCA'S
SPECIALTIES

MANCA'S
SPECIALTIES

**TODAY'S SPECIALS**  August 16, 1955

COCKTAILS  Fresh Shrimp Cocktail 80    Crab Leg Cocktail 90
Tomato Juice 20

SOUPS  Clam Chowder 20  French Onion Soup 30  Minestrone Soup 50

SPECIAL  Mushroom Soup 35
SOUPS  Consomme Clear 35
Chicken Noodles 35

Manca's
Combination
Salad 90c
Half Portion 65c

SALADS  Head Lettuce
Manca's Special
Lettuce and Tomato
Carlyon Special 95
Sliced Tomatoes 40
Celery 40    Jumbo

Dutch Babies
$1.40
with Bacon $1.60
with
Sausage $1.70
Trade Mark
1942

FISH  Fried Halibut
TO ORDER  Halferty's Razor
Grilled King Salmon
Filet of Sole with
Razor Clam Has
Grilled Crab Legs
Fried Ocean Ga

Grilled
Crab Legs,
Tartar Sauce
$1.75

FISH READY  Boiled Fresh K
Grilled Fresh

Grilled
Ripe Tomatoes
Anchovy Butter
85c

ENTREES  Boiled Corned
READY  Braised Beef
Creamed Fre
Salisbury Sto
Fried Fresh
Home-made
Grilled Genu
Frankfurter
Fried Fresh
Cold Corned
Cold Boiled
Hot Prime
Cut of Prim
Potato Pan
Broiled Pr

Fried Louisiana
Shrimps
$1.35

BEERS
(In Bottles Only)
Eastern Beer 35
Western Beer 30

Imported
Tuborg Beer 50c
Heineken Beer
55c

MINERAL
WATERS

Sparkling Water
20c

Gingerale 20c

F
ROCK PO

Broiled, Manca
Half Dozen Fr
Milk Stew
Half and Half
Cream Stew
Plain Pan Ro
Fancy Pan Ro
Fancy Pepper

FRESH A
Salmon Stea
Halibut Stea
Filet of Sole
Salmon Trou
Barbecued
Finnan Hadd
25c Extra S

**dahlia lounge**

**appetizers**

FIVE SPICE SOUP with ginger-duck wonton and roasted
wild rice ~ 5.95

LOBSTER-SHRIMP-SHIITAKE POTSTICKERS with sake sauce
and chili oil ~ 9.95

BARLEY RISOTTO with carmelized turnips, fried artichokes, and
white truffle oil ~ 8.50

DUNGENESS CRAB RICE PAPER SPRING ROLL with cilantro,
holy basil, and bean sprouts with lime-garlic dipping sauce ~ 9.50

radish creme

led housemade

tte ~ 8.95

owa-wasabi

il,

with

ive ~ 17.95

rscapone-
0.95

~ market price

prawns

maftoul

 n ginger

eads,

**MAISON BLANC**
*Seattle*
U.S.A.

MAISON BLANC

SANS RIVAL

(Clockwise from top left) Manca's Café menu, which notes "84 years of service." Dahlia Lounge restaurant menu from the 1980s, Tom Douglas owner, 1904 Fourth Avenue, Seattle. Maison Blanc restaurant menu, January 13, 1937. All collection of the author.

[18] "Famous Rippe's Café is Closed," the *Seattle Times*, 20 October 1940, 11.

[19] John J. Reddin, "Rippe's Café Was THE Place to Go," the *Seattle Times*, 20 October 1965, 20.

[20] Von's menu, 1959, Museum of History and Industry Library, Seattle.

[21] Tibbetts, *Mr. Restaurant*, 50–61.

[22] Top Notch menu for 8 August 1935, and Clark's Salad Bowl menu for 9 May 1941, collection of the author.

[23] Bernice Orpha Redington, *Cosmopolitan Seattle* (Seattle: Seattle Post-Intelligencer, 1935), 26–27.

[24] *Ibid.*, 14–15.

[25] Elizabeth Webb Herrick, *Native Northwest Novelties* (Seattle: Carl W. Art, 1937), 43.

[26] *Ibid.*, 38–39.

[27] *Ibid.*, 37–38; and Redington, *Cosmopolitan Seattle*, 16–17.

[28] David Brewster, "The Other Ivar," the *Weekly*, 9 June–14 June 1976, 11, 14.

[29] "Opening of Crawford's Sea Grill Announced," the *Seattle Times*, 26 July 1940.

[30] Crawford's Sea Grill menu, University of Washington Special Collections, Menu Collection.

[31] "Seafood Café Seat Capacity to be Doubled," the *Seattle Times*, 23 June 1935, 10.

[32] John J. Reddin, "Few Greek Restaurants Left in Seattle Today," the *Seattle Times*, 2 April 1961, Seattle Public Library, clippings file.

[33] Apollo Restaurant menu, 1937, collection of the author.

[34] Kazuo Ito, *Issei: A History of Japanese Immigrants in North America* (Seattle: Japanese Language School, 1973), 548.

[35] Menus from Chinese Garden, 1930s; New Chinatown, 1940s; and Twin Dragon, 1940s, collection of Wing Luke Asian Museum.

[36] Actually, Initiative 171 was on the ballot in November 1948, and the class 'H' licenses were not issued until March 1949. "Restaurants and Hotels Plan Bars," the *Seattle Times*, 7 November 1948, 1.

[37] *A Gourmet's Notebook*, vol. 1, no. 4, March 1973, 25.

[38] Speidel, *You Can't Eat Mount Rainier*, 88–89.

[39] *A Gourmet's Notebook*, March 1973, 25.

[40] *Ibid.*, 22–23.

[41] *A Gourmet's Notebook*, April 1973, 33.

[42] Emmett Watson, "Several Last Suppers," the *Seattle Times*, 19 August 1975, B1.

[43] John J. Reddin, "Chinese Restaurants: Cocoon to Butterfly," the *Seattle Times*, 22 September 1963, 21.

[44] Speidel, *You Can't Eat Mount Rainier*, 1–6.

[45] Geoff Brouillette, "Seattle's Remarkable Restaurant Boom," *Seattle Post-Intelligencer*, 30 June 1963, *Pictorial Review*, p. 5.

[46] Emmett Watson, "How Good Really?," the *Argus*, 23 November 1962, 3.

[47] David Brewster, "A Very Original, Very Traditional Place," the *Argus*, 2 February 1973, 1, 5.

[48] Roger Downey, "For Francois, with love and snobbery," the *Weekly*, 28 December 1977–3 January 1978, 1.

[49] *A Gourmet's Notebook*, October 1973, 25, 29.

[50] Colman Andrews, "The Passionate Chef," *Metropolitan Home*, October 1982, 115."

[51] George Blooston, "Beyond Nouvelle Cuisine," the *Weekly*, 2 December–8 December 1982, 29.

[52] Emmett Watson, "Some of Seattle's Finest Meals Start with a Cream Puff" the *Seattle Times*, 4 August 1988, C1.

[53] Schuyler Ingle, "The Good Life at Café Sport," the *Weekly*, 14 March–20 March 1984, 61–62.

[54] Dahlia Lounge menu, 1994, collection of the author.

[55] Greg Atkinson, "The Tom Douglas Touch," the *Seattle Times*, 26 November 2000, *Pacific Magazine*, 43–44.

# THE THEATRICAL HISTORY OF SEATTLE TO 1930

Eric L. Flom

Today, at the beginning of the 21st century, Seattle's theatrical scene is thriving. National touring companies regularly play venues such as the 5th Avenue, the Moore, and the Paramount. Several local organizations (ACT or the Taproot Theatre Company, for instance) enjoy national, not simply regional reputations. In addition, innumerable smaller groups stage works ranging from the traditional to the avant-garde to the just plain strange—all of which might describe the city's annual Fringe Theatre Festival, now in its 12th year.

With such a lively theatrical scene, it's hard to imagine a time when the stage formed an even more central part of the city's cultural milieu. And yet, almost a century ago, theater in Seattle was even more vibrant and colorful, not to mention the city's most popular form of public entertainment. In an age before the mass appeal of television, radio, motion pictures, and major sporting events, the theater stood as a focal point in Seattle's recreational, social, and artistic life. Regardless of whether local audiences were drawn to opera, Shakespeare, "blood-and-thunder" melodrama, or minstrelsy, through World War I the stage held a significant position in the lives of Seattle's citizens, both young and old, upper class and working class.

An overview of Seattle's theatrical history to 1930 demonstrates theater's importance not only to the city's cultural heritage but also to the development of the American stage. Although Seattle was a young city located far from the New York theatrical establishment, it nonetheless made its mark on stage entertainment during the 19th and early 20th centuries, when drama in all its forms (traditional plays, stock, and vaudeville) reigned supreme as the public's chosen form of entertainment.

## PIONEER BEGINNINGS

While Seattle would eventually see its share of name performers, in the 1850s, when the city wasn't much more than a few wood-frame buildings, popular entertainment was largely provided by the settlers themselves. Whether log-rolling contests, prayer meetings, or dances, community gatherings of any sort were a welcome respite from the rigors facing Seattle's early residents. Adding a touch of Eastern sophistication to their rugged surroundings, pioneers in the Northwest were quick to embrace amateur theatrics, as Alice Henson Ernst noted in her 1961 book *Trouping in the Oregon Country.*

> Going West, [in] those restless days, was far more than a slogan: it was a state of mind. Tucking a hasty script or two into capacious carpetbags, the troupers arrived soon after the exhausted settlers. They found it native land. But even before the stage folk climbed up on makeshift platforms, curtains had been raising in the new frontier, often without the benefit of footlights. Folk entertainment—eager, spontaneous—does not always await the proscenium arch. [1]

For the first decade or so after Seattle was founded, professional engagements were the exception, not the rule. By the late 1860s, however, a handful of professionals were regularly traveling the region. These early engagements were infrequent, with perhaps no more than one or two visits per year, often with little advance notice. For instance, Edith Mitchell gave what is believed to have been the city's first known professional engagement, a Shakespearean reading at Plummer's Hall in April of 1864, but performed only because she was stuck in Seattle waiting for a ship to take her elsewhere.[2]

Not all early engagements were as highbrow as the Mitchell performance. Once traveling acts began arriving with some frequency, it was not unheard of for an evening's entertainment to include such diverse offerings as a scientific or political address, some rudimentary magic, a farce, and a blackface routine all in one night.[3] The itinerant nature of these early performers, who returned season after season to the same general locales, made them popular both onstage and off. Not only did they provide much-needed entertainment, but they also gave Seattleites a connection with other localities in the Washington and Oregon Territories. With no established rail line until 1883, few overland wagon routes, and the prohibitive time and expense of water travel, few pioneers strayed beyond the local countryside once they had settled. The arrival of performers from elsewhere often provided a tie to the outside world that they only rarely experienced themselves.

Limited modes of transportation not only kept people in, but also kept people out. Coupled with a sparse population base along Puget Sound, this fact made it impossible for larger, more established theatrical troupes to tour profitably in the Pacific Northwest for many years. During the pioneer era most performers tended to work as single or double acts (with the occasional small troupe), their box-office take in any given locality providing a modest sum that, ideally, left enough for water travel to the next settlement and the next series of performances. The dual problems of thin population and lack of cheap, convenient transportation were obstacles both to Seattle's growth as a city and its growth as a theatrical center.

## Building a City and Its Cultural Institutions

The first makeshift performance hall in Seattle was the Yesler mill cookhouse, a tiny log structure built in the winter of 1852–1853 as a mess hall for mill owner and city founder Henry Yesler. For many years, the cookhouse was the city's only site for meetings, court proceedings, and other types of gatherings, including theatrical engagements. In 1859, merchant Charles Plummer built a larger hall above his store at the corner of Commercial (now 1st Avenue South) and Main streets, while Henry Yesler eventually built comparable venues such as Yesler's Hall (1861) and Yesler's Pavilion (1866).[4] (Although each was an improvement over the old cookhouse, the term "larger" was a relative one. A crowded house at Yesler's Hall was said to have been a mere 40 people.[5]) The conditions in these early "theaters" veered sharply toward the minimal: performances could employ very little in the way of scenery, and the stage (if there was one) had to be lit with candles and oil lamps.

Even so, larger and more elaborate productions began arriving in Seattle as the city continued to grow. The 1870s saw the rise of theatrical combinations, forerunners of the road shows and traveling repertory companies of a generation later. Combinations featured established performers in their signature plays, many of which originated in San Francisco, fast becoming the theatrical center of the West Coast. One such combination was the Sawtelle Dramatic Company, which played a weeklong engagement at Yesler's Hall beginning November 29, 1876. Led by Mr. J. A. Sawtelle, this troupe of 13 players offered several dramas typical of the period, including *East Lynne, David Garrick, Rip Van Winkle, Rosedale,* and *Under the Gaslight.*[6]

The increasing appearance of combinations such as the Sawtelle Dramatic Company eventually led to the erection of Seattle's first legitimate theater in November 1879. This was Squire's Opera House, built by Watson C. Squire, later governor of the Washington Territory and a U.S. senator. Located on Commercial Street between Main and Washington, Squire's Opera House had 1,200 square feet of stage area and seated almost 600, including 12 box seats on either side of the stage.

Unfortunately, construction of the Opera House was somewhat shoddy, and it lasted a mere four years as a theater. Arguably, it was too big for Seattle at the time—there simply weren't enough touring companies arriving in the Northwest for Squire's to remain financially viable—and the building was remodeled into the Brunswick Hotel. Later, after rail service came to Tacoma in 1883 and Puget Sound became more accessible for theatrical companies, developer George Frye erected Frye's Opera House on 1st Avenue at Marion. Frye's Opera House seated approximately 1,300 and was said to have been the largest theater north of San Francisco when it opened in 1884.

## THE POPULARITY OF BOX-HOUSES

Although a traditional or "legitimate" theater on the scale of Frye's Opera House was a source of pride for the community, the growth in Seattle's stage-centered businesses during the mid to late 1880s was not in legitimate theaters like Frye's, but in so-called "box-houses." Essentially, box-houses were saloons with stages attached. Although legitimate theater continued to exist in Seattle, box-houses (forerunners of variety and vaudeville) saw tremendous growth in the late 19th century, despite becoming the subject of constant scorn from religious and civic groups.

To Seattle's more genteel citizenry, the very premise of a box-house was fraught with sin. They were called box-houses because the balcony section and/or sides of each establishment consisted of isolated box seats that could be curtained on all sides, so patrons could watch the show or otherwise enjoy themselves in total privacy. This wasn't objectionable in and of itself; however, such establishments made money not by charging admission, as a traditional theater would, but through the sale of alcohol. Worse, the drinks were hustled by young women, many of whom doubled as chorus girls in the various stage offerings. The combination of alcohol, pretty girls, and privacy shocked most decent citizens—particularly since these very features attracted scores of single men, not only from Seattle but from outlying communities as well.

Box-houses were rowdy, with frequent reports of fighting, some were ill kept, and reformers alleged that many of the women serving drinks were actually prostitutes. Subsequent historians have debated the actual conditions in Seattle's box-houses, in particular the charges of prostitution. Author Murray Morgan, for instance, in his landmark Seattle history *Skid Road*, noted that the city's early box-house establishments willingly turned a blind eye toward girls who enhanced their income with a few "extracurricular" activities. Even though such venues do not appear to have had a stake in the practice, in Morgan's words, at least, it was good business for a box-house manager to employ "entertainers whose talents were not the type to appear to the best advantage on a stage."[7] Besides, as Morgan also pointed out in *Skid Road*, throughout its colorful past Seattle was home to a number of brothels, some of which enjoyed long and prosperous existences.[8]

The conditions in local box-houses were probably comparable to those in similar establishments, such as saloons. However, because advertising their shows gave them a higher profile in the community, box-houses became a lightning rod for criticism.

The key factor distinguishing box-houses from the variety/vaudeville theaters of a later period was their reliance on alcohol for revenue, as opposed to the sale of tickets. Packed houses and quick audience turnover, so critical to financial success in vaudeville, were not always a concern in Seattle's early box-houses. On the contrary, the typical box-house manager did just about anything to keep customers in the house, and would even push drinks into the wee hours if there were patrons still willing (or able) to part with their hard-earned money.

One of the longest running box houses, the Standard Theatre (here circa 1885) located at 2nd Avenue and Washington. MSCUA, University of Washington Libraries, neg. # UW14559.

Under these conditions, the entertainment portion of the typical box-house was a secondary consideration. But, in an effort to distinguish their houses, managers gradually began to separate the stage show from the "floor" show. Although the performers themselves may not have been the main attraction, box-houses typically offered singing and dancing acts, comedy skits, minstrel shows, and the occasional play, although such productions were hardly on the scale of a traditional stock company or traveling show. Newspapers rarely covered the entertainments offered in local box-houses, however, no matter how talented the performers. With alcohol and the various other "amenities" as the obvious draw, these businesses typically catered to a boisterous, lower class clientele—unbecoming to an ambitious young city just starting to make its mark on the world. "Variety was to struggle long to free itself of the stigma of its association with the saloon and honky-tonk," wrote historian Eugene Clinton Elliott. "The fact that it did succeed in becoming respectable [under the guise of vaudeville] speaks highly of its vitality and should earn it the right to be seriously considered as an art form and a true expression of the temperament and mind of a nation."[9]

Box-houses (together with brothels) may have been an unavoidable by-product in the development of early Seattle, but they could, at the very least, be controlled through geography. At the time, the downtown area was divided at approximately Yesler Way, otherwise known as "Skid Road." (Lumbermen for the Yesler mill had earlier used the thoroughfare to drag logs from their cutting areas to the waterfront.) South of Yesler Way stood most of the brothels, bars, and box-houses; proper citizens generally stayed north of Yesler. Particularly during its early years, when Seattle was dominated by lumbermen and miners, the Skid Road area, which today encompasses much of the historic Pioneer Square district, was not only one of the least respectable places in the city, but also one of the most dangerous, particularly after dark.

## ROAD SHOWS COME TO SEATTLE

The arrival of the railroad in the Pacific Northwest in the 1880s had a tremendous impact on the region, not only in terms of economic and population growth, but in terms of theatrical growth as well. As the transcontinental railroad began linking Seattle and other western cities to the East Coast, for instance, the old theatrical combination gave way to its larger, more elaborate cousin, the road show.

Most often organized in the East, road shows gave other sections of the country the opportunity to see the stars and the productions drawing raves in the theatrical world. Unlike a repertory actor touring with a collection of plays, each performed on successive nights, the road show put all its eggs in one basket: one play, with all the trimmings. The expanding rail networks allowed Broadway producers to mount national tours, taking shows to the larger theaters in the larger cities, and sometimes with the personnel and equipment used to stage the original New York or London productions. With generous pre-engagement publicity, producers found that audiences outside the East responded enthusiastically to plays that were already proven hits.

This was certainly the case in Seattle. Writing in the April 1937 edition of *Pacific Northwest Quarterly*, Bernard Berelson and Howard F. Grant counted a total of 15 road productions that played the city during 1870, a figure that did not include variety shows that may have appeared in Seattle's smaller venues. Ten years later, in 1880 (and three years before the rail connection in Tacoma was established), this figure had grown to only 21. Yet by 1890, one year after the Seattle fire had destroyed much of the city's business core and with four (albeit small) theaters in operation, the number of touring shows leapt to 178. By 1900, this figure had again skyrocketed, much like the city's population during the same period. Berelson and Grant identified 606 separate touring productions playing Seattle that year, despite the fact that the number of legitimate theaters in operation had dropped from four to three.[10]

Certainly, factors other than the railroad aided this explosive growth. Continued westward migration and the Klondike Gold Rush (which began in July 1897) contributed to these swelling numbers. Nonetheless, the expanding American rail system was the catalyst allowing this to occur.

Even with these increasing numbers, early on the theatrical industry lacked the organization to fully coordinate these tours. Prior to 1895, Seattle managers had a difficult task securing a season's worth of stage productions, due in part to the city's distance from the New York theatrical establishment. Even though book-ing arrangements for individual shows were made several months in advance, fi-nancial, travel, and logistical problems frequently developed as troupes moved from city to city along the way. As a result, many shows were unable to keep their sched-uled Seattle dates, and some never made it to the Pacific Northwest at all.[11]

This situation began to change in the late 1890s. In Seattle, it was John Cort, long one of the city's most prosperous box-house managers, who was largely re-sponsible for bringing a new era of road show attractions to Seattle. By the time the Klondike Gold Rush was on, Cort recognized that box-houses had no long-term future and began plotting an ambitious move into the world of legitimate theater. He selected the perfect moment to change his business focus.

While the Gold Rush was changing the complexion of Seattle, prominent men in the East were moving to establish large circuit systems in an effort to coordinate road show tours nationwide. These organizations, commonly referred to as "syn-dicates," looked to organize and consolidate theatrical bookings in return for a box-office cut at each house. By formalizing national booking arrangements, syn-dicates provided a steady, predictable stream of touring shows to localities all across North America. Although the move can be easily (and truthfully) depicted as an effort by certain business moguls to seize control of the industry, it was also a legitimate effort to bring order out of chaos. "It was a necessary development that was taking place," maintained Eugene Clinton Elliott. "The confusion in booking, with hundreds of small theaters independently operated scattered all over the coun-try and with every producing unit existing by itself, increased the hazards of man-agement many times and could not be allowed to continue indefinitely."[12]

Even while a box-house manager, John Cort recognized that organization was the key to expanding and thriving in the theatrical business. By the late 1880s, he had spearheaded efforts to coordinate the booking of talent with other Northwest box-houses, a significant factor in his ability to draw acts from the opposite coast. Even prior to the Seattle fire of 1889, through connections forged with other West Coast theaters, Cort could book acts for a guaranteed run of 16 weeks, traveling a route that took them to major cities such as San Francisco, Portland, and Seattle, followed by an eastern swing through Spokane to Butte, Montana, hitting smaller towns all along the way.[13] Cort's regional "circuit" positioned him nicely with syn-dicate forces a decade later. By purchasing or forging business ties with theaters all along the coast (he controlled 37 outright by 1903), Cort made himself a key figure to reckon with when the Eastern interests looked to expand their road show tours into the Pacific Northwest.[14]

Shortly after 1900, John Cort signed an agreement with Marc Klaw and Abraham Erlanger, then the preeminent booking agents of dramatic talent in America, to bring their circuit shows to Cort's houses. The move firmly estab-lished him as the top theatrical manager in Seattle, if not the entire Pacific North-west. That same year, he also completed the local venue that would house these road show attractions: the Grand Opera House, built at a cost of nearly $40,000.

Cort's new house stood as the jewel of the city's entertainment venues, usurping that title from the Seattle Theatre, built in 1892, which stood less than half a block away. Until competing houses such as the Moore (1907) and the Metropolitan (1911) were constructed, the Grand hosted the largest and most elaborate road productions playing the city. Located on Cherry Street between 2nd and 3rd Avenues, it seated 2,278 people and was hailed upon completion as one of the best theaters on the entire West Coast.

But while John Cort's new house and his agreement with syndicate forces initially were a coup for his business interests, the quality of the road shows that arrived in Seattle polarized the local theatrical scene. Although many were stellar productions, after only a few seasons theater patrons (and a handful of vocal journalists) began to complain that Klaw and Erlanger tended to deliver quantity over quality, while actively preventing independent touring companies from playing the Pacific Northwest. Many syndicate offerings, critics complained, were substandard productions whose sole purpose was to keep the circuit houses from going dark. Worse, the play selection hinged more on box-office potential than artistic merit. "Ever since Klaw & Erlanger first began to throttle independent theatrical attractions there is no question but that the tone of the stage [in this city] has been lowering," the *Argus* complained in a 1909 editorial. "Scenery, costumes and stage settings have taken the place of ability. A playwright with a good thing has been obliged to accept the dictated terms. The same old chestnuts have been served up year after year."[15] James William Ladd, in his 1935 survey of legitimate theater in Seattle, made a similar observation.

> In their desire to fill [the syndicate's] costly theatres over the country, acting companies were thrown together in haphazard fashion and hustled out for road consumption. Whenever a hit appeared on Broadway duplicate companies, from one to ten in number, were hurriedly assembled to play the circuits, often with far inferior actors. As a result of this policy audiences in cities such as Seattle, and throughout the country, were increasingly dissatisfied with the legitimate theatre.[16]

Syndicates like Klaw and Erlanger's brought order to the national booking system, but they also brought a business ethic to the dramatic arts that didn't always play well with theatergoers, whether in Seattle or elsewhere. "The theatre became controlled by businessmen, as the policies of the syndicates evidenced," Ladd continued. "Their sole object was the making of a profit . . . art became a business."[17]

Typical of the road shows put forth by the syndicate (albeit a good one, in this case) was the March 1905 production of Owen Wister's *The Virginian*, which starred matinee idol Dustin Farnum. *The Virginian*, successful as a novel, stage play, and eventually as a motion picture (in multiple versions), focused on a Wyoming rancher pitted against the local bad man. It also included the requisite love story (essential to holding the interest of female audience members) between the title character

A scene from Act I of "The Virginian," which opened at Seattle's Grand Opera House on March 9, 1905. This still (taken from the 1907 road show production) features, from left to right: Frank Campeau (seated), Joe Callahan, Thomas Medock, Dustin Farnum, Bennett Musson, and Frank Nelson. MSCUA, University of Washington Libraries, neg. #UW21565z.

and Mollie, a New England schoolteacher who meets her true love after being rescued from a runaway stagecoach.

The show made its Seattle debut at the Grand Opera House, and the syndicate's advance publicity was so impressive that the *Daily Times* actually recommended *The Virginian* sight unseen, given its reputation among the circuit houses where it had already played.[18] The *Star*, at least, waited until its theater critic had actually seen the show before praising it; their reviewer certainly couldn't knock the production, save for a few minor technicalities.

> Its well-earned reputation had preceded it and with the first flourish of the orchestra there was a bulging house with an overflow of "standing room onlies" in the rear. If one were to pick out the elements that make for such a splendid production one would have to include author, playwright, cast and stage director, though the latter comes in rightly for censure for the interminable waits between acts, for which there appears to be no reasonable excuse. The audience, however, was indulgent . . .[19]

The play, produced by the Kirk LaShelle Company for the Klaw and Erlanger

circuit houses, brought Seattle a first-class road show, but the producers and circuit forces also knew they had a good product. As a result, they exploited the play
in typical syndicate fashion: following its 1905 debut at the Grand, *The Virginian*
visited Seattle seven times over the next nine theatrical seasons, the quality the
stage company diminishing with each successive engagement.[20]

Audiences quickly tired of substandard road productions and repeat engagements. John Cort was not unaware of the situation, and in 1910 he led a rebellion
by forming the National Theatre Owners' Association, a group representing 1,200
theaters in the West, Midwest, and South that bolted from Klaw and Erlanger's
control by booking independent shows.[21] After several months of pocketbook pressure, Klaw and Erlanger eventually cut a deal with association members, allowing
them to book both independent and syndicate attractions at their houses.

By that time, however, the sheer cost of mounting road show productions and
taking them city to city was becoming too great for all but a handful of shows, and
the frequency of touring presentations across the United States went into sharp
decline. During the early teens, large theaters such as the Moore and the Metropolitan, both designed to showcase road productions, sat idle for weeks at a time or
were forced to fill scheduling voids by booking local companies or feature-length
motion pictures. "As the public refused to accept the mediocre standards offered
them, [they] turned to other forms of entertainment," commented
James William Ladd. "[T]he syndicates, after destroying the legitimate field in
Seattle, were themselves eventually destroyed by the very system they had set up."[22]

## The Rise of Stock Theater

Often a worthy alternative to local road show attractions, stock theater also thrived
for a period during Seattle's early theatrical history. Stock differed from theatrical
combinations or road shows in that companies were resident troupes of their re-
spective houses, a stable of performers presenting different plays on a regular basis. Although the actual troupe may have been hired from outside the Pacific Northwest, stock companies were routinely booked for runs of a few weeks to an entire
season, sometimes longer.

Stock was an ideal training ground for young actors, but it was also a consum-
ing lifestyle, even with the grind of frequent travel largely removed. Days without
matinee performances were spent rehearsing upcoming productions, while evenings were taken up with the play at hand. Sundays and holidays—any day of rest
for the masses—were typically busy days for stock actors, as was also the case for
vaudevillians. Within the troupes, typically made up of eight to 10 regular players
(additional actors were hired as needed from the community), typecasting was the
norm. Each of the company's principal players was generally suited for a specific
type of role (a hero or a heavy, for instance), and often played similar parts in each
succeeding show. Each production generally ran for no more than a week at a time,

A rainy Seattle afternoon following a matinee performance at Third Avenue Theatre, corner of Third and Madison. MSCUA, University of Washington Libraries, neg. # UW871.

although some ambitious troupes changed plays more frequently.

An extreme example of this ability to juggle multiple productions was the engagement of the Chase Stock Company at the Third Avenue Theatre in March 1896. At the time, poor economic conditions in the Pacific Northwest had left the Third Avenue with dwindling audiences. Coupled with an ongoing program of audience giveaways (gold watches, among other items), the interest of local theatergoers was piqued by the prospect of the Chase Company attempting to change shows nightly, rather than on a weekly basis. "The Chase Company can play a new play before the public every night for an entire month, their repertoire running from burlesque to classic tragedy," wrote the *Post-Intelligencer* on the house's change in policy. "The amount of study required to properly memorize thirty plays would frighten any lawyer or professional speaker, yet in the old days of drama, it was a common thing."[23]

Thus, over the next 42 days the Chase Stock Company undertook the daunting task of producing a new play each evening at the Third Avenue, although the troupe actually gave only 27 different selections during that time. Several productions were changed or repeated, for instance, after the company's leading lady, Hettie Bernard Chase, mistakenly drank ammonia shortly before a performance. (She reportedly mistook the bottle for a cough remedy.) Chase sat out an entire week while the other female cast members stepped up into new, sometimes unfamiliar roles.[24]

Newspaper accounts of the Chase Company's offerings during the endeavor were fairly lenient, considering the difficulty of their undertaking. Generally, the actors seem to have acquitted themselves very well, despite the occasional muffed line or other mishap, as the *Post-Intelligencer* observed during a performance of *A Kentucky Thoroughbred* on March 11, 1896.

> The dramatic force of the finale in the racing scene, where the villain shoots the jockey who has won the race, was somewhat marred by the failure of the pistol to go off. The villain, after snapping his weapon four times, with rare presence of mind, rushed on his waiting victim, and 'dashed out his brains.'[25]

For the more typical stock engagement, however, weekly production schedules (coupled with limited resources) were the norm. Yet while stock productions, often popular melodramas, sometimes lacked the polish of a notable road show presentation, these troupes could nonetheless present amazingly good shows. In addition, with theatergoers returning week after week to the same houses, many stock actors managed to establish a bond over time with the audience, something that only a handful of traveling performers enjoyed. "Plainly, better results for both actors and the public could be achieved by professional groups resident at the larger playhouses," Alice Henson Ernst observed. "With proper time for rehearsals, adequate backstage facilities and a skilled director, greater finish was possible. The public could enjoy a planned series of standard plays, staged with rewarding care . . . Spurred by the shoddy output of many road shows, resident professionals became worthy and formidable rivals."[26]

In many ways, stock theater in Seattle didn't follow the traditions of Eastern stock, an attribute that at least one local historian, Mary Katherine Rohrer, attributed to the city's provincialism.[27] For example, local stock companies rarely performed new plays, as was often the case in the East. Instead, local audiences preferred established favorites and proven successes, some of them decades out of favor. These productions also rarely toured, even locally. Finally, the employment of guest stars, a popular technique to raise interest in particular shows, wasn't typical for Seattle until after 1910, when the city's theatrical scene was beginning to feel pressure from other forms of recreational entertainment.[28] A credible argument can be made, in fact, that stock scene in Seattle was simply an offshoot of the flourishing (and much more "traditional") stock theaters of neighboring Portland. Not only was Seattle's first stock company from there, but two of the city's longest-running and most successful stock companies, the George Baker and Henry Duffy troupes, were also organizations based out of Portland.

It wasn't until 1890 that stock theater debuted in Seattle. This pioneering troupe was organized by John Cordray, a businessman from Portland looking to expand his theatrical interests northward. Late that year, Cordray took over the Madison Street Theatre at 3rd and Madison, gave it a reported $20,000 facelift, and promptly named the venue after himself. Cordray was adamant about providing family-style entertainment—no liquor, no rowdiness, and no profanity. Even peanut eating was not allowed. "[A]nyone who can't comply with the rules . . . must not be surprised if they are invited by [the] Police Officer of the house to vacate immediately," he warned in his early programs.[29] Thus, when the 1,172-seat Cordray Theatre opened for business it was exactly the type of entertainment that many civic reformers and box-house opponents had longed to see. Debuting on December 1, 1890, with *The Lady of Lyons*, the Cordray troupe began a nearly three-year run of stock productions.[30]

With the difficult economic conditions of the mid-1890s, however, John Cordray abandoned his Seattle theater to William M. Russell and Edward Drew, who continued Cordray's vein of family-style entertainment well into the 20th century, hosting mostly stock companies and independent touring shows. Renamed the Third Avenue Theatre in 1896, the venue was a haven for the type of "blood-and-thunder" melodrama preferred by the working classes, and by 1904 it was easily the most popular theater in the city, despite competition from larger and more elaborate houses. Tickets for the Third Avenue were sometimes in such demand that young boys made extra money by spending the day lined up outside the box office, holding a place in line for someone else.

The Third Avenue, Seattle's primary venue for stock theater, continued its success until early 1907, when the house was demolished—a victim of the regrading projects that were transforming Seattle's downtown. Stock theater continued to enjoy broad appeal for another three years or so, particularly at the Lois, located at 2nd and Seneca, but eventually gave way to other forms of popular entertainment such as vaudeville and motion pictures. As Mary Katherine Rohrer observed of Seattle's early stock theaters:

> The stock theatre was a family theatre; its plays were tried and true, not old enough or good enough to be termed classic, yet successes because they appealed to the average taste. The companies attracted few stars and soon lost those to greener fields, but they developed such a following that three or four companies could exist in Seattle at one time, as was the case in 1908, 1909, and 1910. They served as buffers to the trusts and syndicates; they furnished entertainment when every other source failed; and they filled a very real place in the hearts and lives of people of that period.[31]

## VARIETY GRADUATES TO VAUDEVILLE

An outgrowth of Eastern variety shows, vaudeville was to have the most significant impact on Seattle and its theatrical reputation during the early 20th century. This style of entertainment, formerly seen only in the city's box-houses, remained popular despite the fact that fewer and fewer box-house establishments were in operation after 1900. Variety entertainment was fast outgrowing the saloon, proving attractive not only to the usual crop of men but also to women and children. "Up to five years ago there were only three theaters in Seattle north of Yesler way," the *Post-Intelligencer* observed in 1907. "About that time the craze for 10-cent vaudeville swept over the country and did not skip Seattle. Half a dozen stores were vacated for the 10-cent houses, which were followed by the Orpheum, the Star, later [Alexander] Pantages' theater, and more lately a number of others. The Coliseum[32] was reconstructed from a skating rink into a 'ten-twenty-thirty' house last summer by Sullivan & Considine."[33]

Vaudeville, of course, centered on a series of live acts, or a "bill," each act independent of the others and each varied in terms of style and content. A dramatic playlet, for instance, may have headlined a show that also featured a knockabout comedian, a juggler, a contortionist, trained bears, a knife-throwing exhibition, and a high-wire act. Diversity was a key attribute of vaudeville; as historian Anthony Slide has noted, crowds returned to their favorite theaters week after week because "[a]n audience could sit through fifteen minutes of a second-rate comedy routine, secure in the knowledge that the next act would probably be a good one."[34]

A testament to vaudeville's diversity is the Orpheum circuit show that began on June 23, 1918, at the Moore Theatre. Headlining the bill was 73-year-old stage legend Sarah Bernhardt, making the fourth and final Seattle appearance of her illustrious stage career.[35] She performed two playlets during her engagement, both entirely in French. (For theatergoers who weren't fluent in Bernhardt's native tongue, the Moore program kindly provided an English translation of each plot so audiences could follow along.[36]) From Sunday to Tuesday the Divine Sarah performed *Du Theatre Au Champ D'Honneur* (*From the Theatre to the Field of Honor*), while the Wednesday through Saturday performances were given over to an excerpt from Alexander Dumas' *Camille*.

Recognizing it was perhaps the last time Seattle audiences would have the opportunity to see Bernhardt in the flesh, local papers were generous in their praise. "Though speaking in a foreign language and handicapped by the hand of time and infirmity, Sarah Bernhardt, at the Moore theatre Sunday, moved a great audience to patriotic exaltation by her art," wrote Charles Eugene Banks in the *Post-Intelligencer*. "Sunday's initial audience was deeply impressed with both the play and the actress. There is an acceptable company of seven people, and the bar of language is forgotten."[37] Other acts supporting the great Bernhardt included a pair of comic sketches, a musical comedy, and soprano Marion Weeks. All were fairly representative of the types of performers who frequented the vaudeville stage. Of particular note, however, was the show's opening act, or at least the first live act to follow an overture by the house orchestra: Albert Donnelly, a man who billed himself as "The Silent Humorist—The Fellow Who Talks with His Fingers." While Sarah Bernhardt was impressing audiences with some of the finer details of the dramatic arts, Donnelly's specialty was to cast shadow animals on the backdrop of the Moore stage.

As was the case with legitimate drama, the establishment of circuits was a key factor to gaining a foothold in the emerging vaudeville business, from the standpoint of both performers and managers. Vaudeville performers existed as individual units, for instance. They coordinated their own travel, made shipping arrangements for their gear, and were responsible for their lodging and meals, all of which was paid from their own pocket. Guaranteed playing time on a circuit of vaudeville houses was an essential element to a performer's survival, particularly in the West, where the jump between cities was sometimes considerable. The situation was equally important to managers, however, who found bargaining power in the ability to sign acts on a long-term basis. "Vaudeville [was] one of the most expensive forms of theatrical entertainment ever offered to the general public," noted Eugene Clinton Elliott. "The players of seven separate acts, each, so to speak, a star, and the musicians, stage hands, electricians, and management personnel necessary for the presentation of such acts, are an aggregate commanding an astounding weekly expense. In order to support such a crew one essential is an assured audience, best obtained by moving from city to city throughout the country along a regularly assigned route."[38]

As the business developed, in fact, circuits became such a vital element of Western vaudeville that they multiplied much faster than their Eastern counterparts—the exact opposite of legitimate theater, where circuits were largely organized and controlled by the eastern syndicates. This is exactly where Seattle showmen such as Alexander Pantages and John Considine made their mark. "All in all, the most important contribution of the Northwest to the national theatrical business was the origin and development of popular priced vaudeville circuits," Bernard Berelson and Howard Grant have argued. "The stock companies and road shows spread East to West; vaudeville, from West to East."[39]

Notable among the Northwest vaudeville magnates was Alexander Pantages. An immigrant from Greece, Pantages was a latecomer to the city's theatrical scene, not even arriving in Seattle until 1902 after having worked as a waiter, barkeeper, and theater manager in Dawson, Alaska. His first theatrical enterprise locally was the Crystal Theater on 2nd Avenue, an immediate hit with the public. Pantages had a particular gift for measuring the taste of his audiences, and the popularity of his house was such that in 1904 he built a much larger venue, which he named after himself. Located at the northeast corner of 2nd and Seneca, Seattle's Pantages Theatre was the first of many venues throughout America that would eventually bear his name. (Later, in 1914, Pantages built an even more modernized Pantages

Vaudeville magnate Alexander Pantages during his Seattle tenure. MSCUA, University of Washington Libraries, neg. # UW2242.

Theatre at the northeast corner of 3rd Avenue and University Street.)

The growth of Pantages' vaudeville holdings was remarkable. In 1906, two years after opening the original Pantages Theatre, the showman erected the Lois Theatre a short distance away, named in honor of his wife. There he housed various stock theater companies, in addition to the occasional vaudeville bill. He even had the foresight to swoop into San Francisco after the 1906 earthquake and fire, buying six small houses on the cheap (the flagship theater of the small chain had been destroyed). By 1909, seven years after opening the Crystal, he could offer acts a run of 26 consecutive weeks in his circuit houses. Two years later, thanks to agreements forged with other regional circuits throughout the United States and Canada, this had increased to almost 60 weeks.[40]

Alexander Pantages' success came in a rather cutthroat field. Managers like Pantages were known to blacklist troublesome performers, break acts apart so they could rehire the portion they liked, or terminate the contracts of certain performers while they were on the road, in the middle of nowhere, knowing they would have little choice but to sign a new contract at a fraction of their original salary.

Sometimes the tables were turned on the managers, however. Seattleite John Considine, a significant competitor in the field of popularly priced vaudeville, briefly made a habit of stealing acts from the Pantages circuit by offering salaries that he knew Pantages could not or would not match. This worked in the short term, until Alexander Pantages countered by sending men to the train station to locate each performer's gear when he or she arrived in town. If someone then announced the intention to jump to a rival circuit, Pantages threatened to retaliate by destroying their costumes and props, for many vaudeville acts the key to their livelihood.[41]

Pantages' astonishing success came not because he knew how to play hardball, but because he was simply a better businessman and a better showman than most of his competitors. If someone else was planning to offer a notable high-wire or animal act, for instance, Pantages often located a similar one and played it a city or two ahead of his rival, thus taking the wind out of his competitor's prize discovery. Furthermore, Pantages tended to book talented but lesser-known acts, saving on costs while his business counterparts sometimes emptied their pocketbooks on high-profile performers.

In the early 1920s Alexander Pantages moved his business offices to Los Angeles, but Seattle was nonetheless the birthplace of the famous Pantages vaudeville circuit, which grew to cover most of the United States and parts of Canada. Toward the end of the decade Pantages began selling his venues to RKO and Warner Bros., but remained a prominent show-business figure right up to his death in 1936.

## THE END OF AN ERA

Seattle was never much of a creative center for the American stage, but through the business endeavors of men such as John Cort, John Considine, and Alexander Pantages, it held a prominent place in national theatrical affairs during the early 20th century. Seattle had also gained the reputation of being an excellent show town, a fact that the *Post-Intelligencer* trumpeted in 1907.

> Fifteen years ago Seattle had but one real theater, Cordray's. Fourteen years ago it had but two, Cordray's and the Seattle. Seven years ago it had three, with the addition of the Grand. Now it has more than fifteen, including ten-cent [vaudeville] houses, all playing to a profitable business. Fourteen years ago the theaters of the city combined to seat but 2,200 people. In 1907, on Sundays or holidays, Seattle's playhouses frequently played to 30,000 to 40,000 people, including the matinee and evening performances . . . [A]s [William M.] Russell [manager of the Third Avenue Theatre] observes, "Seattle is the manager's Mecca of the West.

A week stand in Seattle assures any company's railroad fare back to the Missouri river."[42]

But regardless of the theater's popularity with local audiences, Seattle was not immune to industry trends, and as the booming conditions that fed the American stage through the early 20th century began to wane the city began to see less and less in the way of professional stage talent.

Through the teens, road show tours (whether syndicate or independent productions) became fewer each season, a decline attributable to both the sheer cost of mounting such lavish shows and the growing popularity of feature-length motion pictures. In Seattle, the trend was sharp and measurable. During the first decade of the 20th century, road show companies had appeared on a regular basis, yet in 1912 the Metropolitan Theatre was dark a full 20 weeks, while the Seattle and the Moore Theatres were empty 15 and 12 weeks respectively.[43] According to research compiled by James William Ladd, between 50 and 75 touring productions played Seattle during 1910, while only six arrived during all of 1935.[44]

Stock theater, too, was hard hit during the 1910s and 1920s, even with fewer road show attractions against which to compete. After the demise of the popular Third Avenue Theatre in 1907, Alexander Pantages' Lois Theatre seemed to fill the void, and it ran continuously until 1910 when it was destroyed by fire. But the demise of the Lois marked a clear end to the popularity of stock in Seattle—never again would stock theater hold the same sway over the theatergoing public. Despite a handful of troupes operating after 1915 (including the venerable Wilkes Company out of Portland, which eventually left town in 1922), most efforts to revive stock theater failed after just a few seasons. As America moved into the Jazz Age, the audience for stock was no longer there, siphoned away by changing times and competing forms of entertainment.

Like road show and stock productions, vaudeville faced its own challenges during the 1910s and 1920s. Recognizing the public's fascination with film, many local vaudeville houses began to alter their formats after World War I, offering a feature film in addition to a bill of live entertainment. The move was not just good showmanship, considering the growing popularity of movies, but it also made sound economic sense. Vaudeville houses could still provide an entire "show," but cut some of their enormous overhead by employing fewer live acts and, consequently, fewer theater personnel.

Throughout the 1920s, however, the emphasis in Seattle's vaudeville houses gradually shifted. Early on motion pictures were a supplement to the live bill, but by the end of the 1920s, at the Pantages, the Palace Hip, and other venues, the films typically held the spotlight. The stage portion became less of an audience draw, and was gradually shortened to the point where some houses could accommodate a pair of first- or second-run films in addition to an abbreviated stage program. At the same time, many of Seattle's downtown motion picture houses were engaging live acts to diversify their own shows, a move that blurred the line between Seattle's early film and vaudeville establishments.

The death of vaudeville in Seattle wasn't officially recorded until the doors shut on the Palomar (formerly the Pantages Theatre at 3rd and University), which continued to offer live stage acts in support of feature films into the early 1950s. Even so, by the time the Palomar closed vaudeville hadn't been a popular draw in about 15 years; the house was clearly a vestige of past times, drawing on a small and mostly nostalgic crowd of older Seattleites.

## CONCLUSION

Although by the Depression organized theatrics in Seattle paled in comparison to its former greatness, the dramatic arts did not disappear after 1930. Rather, the stage underwent a metamorphosis, one that left some traditions behind while adapting others to suit a new era and new artistic forms. The Federal Theatre in the 1930s, the rise of the University of Washington Drama Department in the 1930s and 1940s, and the growth of community theaters (such as Black Arts/West) in the 1960s and 1970s demonstrated that drama in Seattle could adapt and thrive, one period giving way to the next, each breathing new life into the local theatrical scene.

Today Seattle maintains its reputation as an important theater town. Yet in some way, its current success is an extension of the city's historical connection to the stage. Gone are the days of a century ago, when theater was such a popular attraction that some of Seattle's religious leaders sought to ban Sunday performances, given that an increasing number of locals were choosing aisle seats over pews.[45] For at least 50 years in Seattle's early history, a trip to the theater was a regular weekly outing for much of the population. Those days may be over, but the city's unusually rich theatrical history has left a long-standing legacy, one that continues to color Seattle's cultural scene.

# NOTES

[1] Alice Henson Ernst, *Trouping in the Oregon Country: A History of Frontier Theatre* (Portland: Oregon Historical Society, 1961), 1.

[2] See program, Plummer's Hall (23 April 1864), J. Willis Sayre Collection, University of Washington Special Collections. In the absence of an existing program, J. Willis Sayre typed a record of the engagement from an unknown source. See also Howard F. Grant, *The Story of Seattle's Early Theatres* (Seattle: University Bookstore, 1934), 7–8.

[3] Eugene Clinton Elliott, *A History of Variety-Vaudeville in Seattle: From the Beginning to 1914* (Seattle: University of Washington Press, 1944), 5.

[4] See Grant, 7–13. See also James William Ladd, "A Survey of the Legitimate Theatre in Seattle Since 1856" (master's thesis, State College of Washington, 1935), 17–19.

[5] Information on Yesler's Hall taken from photo caption in Elliott, between pages 8 and 9. Much of the information in Elliott's study came directly from newspaper clippings and theatrical summaries compiled as part of the Federal Theatre Project, a Works Progress Administration program that researched Seattle's early stage history in the mid- to late 1930s.'

[6] See programs, Yesler's Hall (29 November–5 December 1876), J. Willis Sayre Collection, University of Washington Special Collections. In the absence of existing programs, J. Willis Sayre typed a record of the engagement from an unknown source.

[7] Murray Morgan, *Skid Road* (New York: The Viking Press, 1951), 125.

[8] Ibid., 59–61, 80, 169–76.

[9] Elliott, 10.

[10] See detailed chart of performances in Bernard Berelson and Howard F. Grant, "The Pioneer Theater in Washington," *The Pacific Northwest Quarterly* XXVIII (April 1937), 124. Berelson and Grant are careful to note that their figures do not include shows that played local box-houses or amateur performances.

[11] Edward Leonard Nelson, "The History of Road Shows in Seattle from Their Beginnings to 1914" (master's thesis, University of Washington Drama School, 1947), 81.

[12] Elliott, 45.

[13] Ibid., 22.

[14] Ibid., 46.

[15] "Opening of the Alhambra," the *Argus*, 17 July 1909, 1.

[16] Ladd, 48.

[17] Ibid., 45.

[18] See "Attractions of Merit," *Seattle Daily Times*, 5 March 1905, Magazine Section, 8.

[19] "The Virginian," *Seattle Star*, 10 March 1905, 7.

[20] See play index, J. Willis Sayre Collection, University of Washington Special Collections.

[21] Elliott, 47. See also Mary Katherine Rohrer, The History of Seattle Stock Companies: From Their Beginnings to 1934 (Seattle: University of Washington Press, 1945), 21–22. Like Eugene Clinton Elliott, Rohrer pulled much of her research material directly from the newspaper clippings and summaries compiled as part of the Federal Theatre Project.

[22] Ladd, 57.

[23] "Third Avenue Theatre," *Seattle Post-Intelligencer*, 8 March 1896, 11.

[24] "Miss Chase Drinks Ammonia," *Seattle Post-Intelligencer*, 11 March 1896, 8.

[25] "A Kentucky Thoroughbred," *Seattle Post-Intelligencer*, 12 March 1896, 5.

[26] Ernst, 118.

27 Rohrer, 1–3, 27.

28 Ibid., 27–28.

29 See "Auditorium and Theatre Notes," program, Cordray Theatre (1 December 1890), 2, J. Willis Sayre Collection, University of Washington Special Collections.

30 Rohrer, 6.

31 Ibid., 30.

32 The Coliseum, the first permanent home for Orpheum vaudeville in Seattle (and formerly known as the Dreamland Skating Rink), should not be confused with the Coliseum Theatre, built at the corner of 5th and Pike in 1916, which was devoted exclusively to motion pictures. As a vaudeville theater, the Coliseum was said to have been the largest venue west of Chicago, taking up an entire city block at the corner of 3rd and James, and seating upwards of 1,800 people.

33 "Theaters Mark Seattle History," *Seattle Post-Intelligencer*, 29 December, 1907, 5. "Ten-twenty-thirty" is vaudeville slang for the ticket prices charged by the house—ten cents for general admission, up to 30 cents for a box seat. Ten-twenty-thirty theaters were also known as "popularly-priced" vaudeville houses.

34 Anthony Slide, *The Encyclopedia of Vaudeville* (Westport, Conn.: Greenwood Press, 1994), xv.

35 See play index, J. Willis Sayre Collection, University of Washington Special Collections.

36 See program, Moore Theatre (23 June 1918), J. Willis Sayre Collection, University of Washington Special Collections.

37 Charles Eugene Banks, "Bernhardt Thrills Big Audience at the Moore," *Seattle Post-Intelligencer*, 24 June 1918, 7.

38 Elliott, 45.

39 Berelson and Grant, 118–19.

40 Elliott, 60.

41 Ibid., 59.

42 "Seattle is the Best Show Town in the Country," *Seattle Post-Intelligencer*, 29 December 1907, 5.

43 Rohrer, 25. See also Nelson, 149.

44 Ladd, 50.

45 See "Sunday Theatres," *Seattle Daily Times*, 23 August 1908, Section III, 40, and "Sunday Closing of Theatres," the *Argus*, 10 October 1908, 1.

# THE SCANDINAVIANS IN KING COUNTY[1]

Marianne Forssblad

Few Nordic immigrants came to the Northwest before the Civil War or even before the 1870s, but following the completion of the Northern Pacific Railroad's western terminus in Tacoma in 1883 the flow of Nordics increased rapidly. King County saw clusters of Nordic immigrants settling in Preston, High Point, Coal Creek, Newcastle, Black Diamond, Bothell, Enumclaw, Issaquah, Hobart, Kent, Ballard and, of course, in the city of Seattle. The region offered opportunities in occupations familiar to the immigrants such as logging, fishing, mining, farming, as well as in the trades such as construction, wood and millwork. The early urban settlers were often common laborers, but by the turn of the century trade and commerce increased as sources of employment. Soon the Nordics, in particular the Norwegians, began to play dominant roles in the fishing and maritime industries. They have owned and managed packing companies, canneries, boat building enterprises, large fishing vessels and steamers, and have held responsible positions in cooperatives and trade unions in the fishing industry. Nordic immigrant women were to a large extent housewives and domestic servants. A relatively small number worked as seamstresses, boarding house managers, and teachers. In Seattle, Swedish Hospital offered unique opportunities for nurses.

Present day immigration from the Nordic countries is only a trickle, yet the heritage has strong roots. In order to document this heritage the Nordic Heritage Museum, in collaboration with the Ballard Historical Society and the Swedish Finn Historical Society, set out to collect oral histories from what we call the Vanishing Generation. The resulting book, *Voices of Ballard: Immigrant Stories from the Vanishing Generation*, edited by Lynn Moen, is the product of a two-year effort to capture the spirit and feel of Ballard, a community known for its Scandinavian legacy. The excerpts found in these pages are devoted to the Nordic stories, although a large number of non-Scandinavian narrators contributed to the larger project. These stories provide a wonderful window into a past that is no longer but actually was not that long ago. They throw light on a lifestyle that was not devoid of hardships but was also very rich in its sense of community and family values.

*Voices of Ballard* came about through the cooperation of many people who wished to preserve the memories of the older generation who had seen the community grow and who had helped make it what it was and what it is today. The individual voices come through loud and clear but often with the same message— a love for the community in which they lived.

Marianne Forssblad
Director, Nordic Heritage Museum


## Excerpts from the Vanishing Generation Project[2]

### Olufina Duesund Andvik (1891–2001), Norway

I came to this country in 1924. This fellow that I married was a widower with two children. He had worked on the streetcars here in Seattle for many years, and he liked to take a trip home and thought he was going to take over his folks' farm. So he lived there for a few years on the farm, and he found out that was too hard to make a living. And so he liked to go back to this country. When he told me how he wanted to go back to America, I said, "OK. I suppose I can make it like others have done." I wasn't too excited about it.

The ship came to Bergen. And we went from there over to this country. It took us eight days. And then I had three children to take care of, the two stepchildren and Bjarne, my oldest, who was born in Norway. He was a year old when we came, and the two stepchildren were also small. We were on the ship for eight days with three kids, and another week from New York to Seattle on the train.

Everything in Seattle was new, and it was a little hard to get used to it, but I made it. By and by, I got acquainted with the church people. I attended Norwegian Lutheran Church and I got acquainted with some of those people. After a little while my husband got his job back at the streetcar company. The First World War had been on and those fellows who had been in the war were in front of him. We bought a house on North 65th [Street] and Greenwood [Avenue] after he got settled in his job.

We lived very simple, and we never had much money. The Norwegian people got along with very meager things in those days.

I didn't have much problem with the language. Bjarne, my son, was home, and the two stepchildren went to school. Bjarne learned the language much sooner than I did. I never went to school in this country to learn the language. I took it all by and by. I always liked to read. So I read quite a bit and learned something by that. I'm surprised at myself sometimes when I think how I was able to read the English. Now I read the New Testament and the church paper. I can't read too long because I just see with one eye and I get tired.

One of my grandsons, his mother went in a hospital for something. And he came—he was just a little guy, maybe four years old, came and he asked me, "Where

Mr. And Mrs. Andvik in front of their Greenwood home, 1935. From left to right, John Quam, Laura Quam, Olufina Andvik and Martin Andvik, with Bjarne Andvik in front. Courtesy of the Nordic Heritage Museum.

is Mommy?" "Oh, she's in the HOOS-pital," I said to him. "*Bestemor*," he said—in Norway *bestemor* is "grandma"—"don't say HOOS-pital. Say HOS-pital." And he has been in language work ever since.

### Bjarne Andvik (Olufina's son) (1923– ), Norway

When the family moved from Norway to Seattle, they began to attend the First Norwegian Lutheran Church on Boren and Virginia. After a few months Dad bought a house out on Phinney Ridge, at 6513 Greenwood Avenue. Dad bought the house in 1924 for $3,000. We grew up there. Dad sold the house in 1954 when he retired.

Dad was a streetcar driver and conductor. Some of the streetcars had secondary conductors, but later one man handled both jobs. Before I started school, Dad would sometimes say, "If you'll take a nap today, I'll let you go along with me on my tripper this afternoon." A tripper was a single round trip during the rush hour. Dad worked a split shift. He'd go for a couple trips during the morning rush, come home, have a nap, then go back for a tripper in the evening rush hour.

He would take me to the car barns, and I got to see all the streetcars in or out of the barn. Then I'd stand with my fingers on the edge of the windowsill at the front while he drove the streetcar. On the Fauntleroy route we'd go down a road called End-O-Line. The barns were in the Denny Regrade area, somewhere near

[the] Broad Street substation. There were streetcar lines on 15th Avenue and 24th Avenue Northwest, and I think as far west as 28th Avenue. They cut Eighth Avenue Northwest through the backyards of homes in 1927 or '28, maybe a few years later. The city limits at that time was 85th Street. One streetcar ran across 85th Street from Golden Gardens east to Greenwood, and perhaps further east.

In those hard times we ate lots of salt herring. We'd come home from school hungry as could be, and Mother would have herring for dinner. I often got a herring bone stuck in my throat. I never looked forward to a herring meal. We'd have a keg of salt herring almost every year. A full keg of salt herring lasted a long time.

Dad had a lot of fisherman friends who provided us with salmon, halibut, and other fish, and we enjoyed that. Dad was not so great on *lutefisk*. Years later I found *lutefisk* to be very delicious. We also had a lot of meat-and-potato meals, pot roast, meatballs. Leg of lamb was very popular with our family. Mother and Dad had a vegetable garden, with peas, carrots, onions, radishes, and lettuce.

One favorite Norwegian meal was *raspeboller*, also called *kumle* or *raspekake*. It was made of ground-up potatoes and flour wadded into a ball with a piece of ham in the center, then cooked in ham water. When it was all done you also had a nice soup that it had been cooked in. We'd dip the *boller* in hot bacon grease for a real flavor.


## Dagney Petersson Stevenson (1907– ), Sweden

I was 14 and a half when some people left home in Bonäs. They had come home from America two years earlier, but they were going back. I guess my mother thought that would be an ideal time to send me. My mother had eight children, and my grandmother had eight children, and they all came to the United States. My mother was here two years and she just loved America, but she was engaged to my dad and I guess she felt bound to marry him, so she went back. I think she had a baby every other year. My dad liked it much better in Sweden, where he could work on the farm, and he did a lot of business too, which he couldn't do here.

All my mom's and my dad's siblings were here, too. So when she asked me if I wanted to go to America with these people, I thought it would be interesting. So we took a boat from Norway. It was terribly windy and I was sick the whole time. It was terrible.

We landed at Ellis Island, and the officials there wouldn't let me go with those people. I was stuck at Ellis Island for a whole week. Didn't have anybody to talk to. I didn't know a word of English, and nobody there was Swedish. They had to get word from my aunt that she would send me to school until I was 16. It took a week. They didn't telephone then. It's terrible not to be able to talk or understand. I didn't understand a word of English. They had high bunk beds for us to sleep in. We got three blankets: one for the bed, one for the pillow, and one to put on. I always got the highest bunk. They showed movies there, too. You know, my parents were very religious, and seeing a movie was wrong. But I saw two movies in that week.

And then they told me I could stay in America. It didn't matter too much to me whether I got in or not—I'd get my trip home, you know. But my aunt said I'd be welcome there, and so they took me to the train. I was going to Minneapolis, and when we got to St. Paul they had all those train cars that said Minneapolis, so I thought this must be it. So I got off. Luckily, it wasn't far from Minneapolis, so they could take the streetcar and meet me in St. Paul.

My relatives in Seattle sent me money for a train ticket and asked me to come here. So on my 16th birthday I took the train to Seattle. I went to Ravenna School and I graduated from there. I think it took two years. It was kind of fun and I enjoyed it. I also did housework; I was a maid. It was hard work, but I didn't mind. I had to get up early, work and do my homework, and come home after school and work. I stayed in the home where I was working. I got room and board and about $10 a month. I was so broke.

When I got to be 18, 19, I got tired of going to school, and I quit. I didn't have time for any fun at all. I just stayed home and worked. I did go to church on Sundays most of the time. This was almost 80 years ago. And then I started going to dances, and to my parents that was a sin, too. But I did go. I met my husband, David Stevenson, at a dance at Norway Hall. He was from Sweden, too. He came over around 1924 or '25. He spoke English when I met him.

We bought a house in Ballard, on 13th Avenue Northwest. We paid $1,300 for that house in the midst of the Depression. It was a good house. We fixed it a lot.

Dave made a little money, but he didn't work that much at the time. We tried to save, too. I saved a notebook. I made a schedule of what we paid for groceries. I looked over that once and I just couldn't believe it. You know, eggs, I think, a loaf of bread—a dime. I think he [Dave] made $25 a week or something like that. But we skimped. Every penny counted.

David was a glass blower at a place where they made asthma medicine, Stansbury Chemical. And I worked at a caterer's that served meals in the Highlands and all over. We were in charge of the tables—they had to serve swanky. And we washed the dishes afterwards, and cleaned up and everything. I think we started with 50 cents an hour; then I got up to 75 cents or a dollar an hour by the time I quit. But I didn't make much. This must have been in the '50s. But I kind of enjoyed that kind of work. I like to move around. I don't like a sitting job. When I did that catering, it was late at night. Sometimes we worked eight to 10 hours.

We usually brought out a little of the Swedish traditions at Christmastime. We even had a few Swedish Christmas songs. I fixed *lutfisk*[3] when my husband was living. I enjoyed having it once, at Christmastime. What most people have against it is it smells so awful. I didn't mind it. We sort of looked forward to it at Christmas when we were little. It wasn't Christmas without it.

We used to go across the Sound on Sundays to Virginia; you know where that is? [Its] very pretty. It's across the bay from Poulsbo. We had friends there that had a cabin, and we went there quite a bit. The boats stopped at all those little places on the Sound. It was the most beautiful ride on a sunshiny day. It really was a nice ride. One ferry left from Ballard at that time. That's why we could take it. It certainly wasn't very expensive, and you could get to all those places. It was wonderful.

My oldest sister came over, too. She was a little older than I, but I was the first one to come. None of my brothers came to the United States. It was better in Sweden by that time. They got jobs and then cars came into existence, so they could get places.

I know it was hard on my mother to send me here, because I was a pretty good worker, a good help. And I wanted to tell her, "Thank you, for sending me to America." I never regretted coming to [the] United States. I was grateful. I wanted to tell my mother.

### Herbjorg Sortun Pedersen (1915– ), Norway

My father came to America alone in 1925. He made up his mind before he went back home that he wanted to take his family to America. He came home and prepared us all for leaving. It took about a year. My mother was very reluctant. She didn't really want to leave her family. He said, "You know, with seven girls, what do you think is going to happen to them in this little valley? They would have many more opportunities in the United States." And she said, "OK, Martin, whatever you say." That was my mother. She said that quite often.

Bergen was our first stop along the way. We stopped with my aunt, who had a rather large house. We were leaving late in the afternoon the next day, but the next morning, at nine o'clock, we were on our way to town. My aunt insisted we couldn't go all the way to America without a hat. She bought caps for the boys. We girls got hats that were all alike. They were light blue and we thought they were very pretty.

We left Bergen on the *Stavangerfjord*, landed in Halifax, Canada, and from there we took the train to Seattle. We were very hungry on the train trip because we had not had much of an appetite on the boat because most of us were seasick. When the train stopped my father would run and get apples and a loaf of bread and a jar of jam or something. We thought it was the most delicious food we had tasted in a long time. We loved the apples.

From Seattle we went to Kent where my father had already arranged for a place for us to live. Before he went back to Norway, he had gotten a promise from a farmer who was about to sell his farm to let my father buy it. My father and mother lived there until they died many years later.

We came in 1929. The Depression was already very much a fact at the time. My father's relatives were concerned about us coming because they felt this was such a difficult time.

I learned English unbelievably fast. My father's cousin brought me about 20 comic books and told me, "Just read them and look at the picture, and figure it out. And every time you have a chance to talk to someone who knows, ask them." I could read those comic books very early, before I could speak English. "Li'l Abner" was one, and the man that flew around from tree to tree? Tarzan. I used to laugh at Tarzan. I had never seen comic books before I came to America.

We had probably been here about a half a year when I went to work for some people we knew from Norway. They had a boardinghouse on Fairview Avenue [in Seattle] and had 12 boarders. The woman had a baby, so she had to have help, so I became the nanny. The boarders were all Norwegian; they worked in the woods mostly. They would often be gone during the week and come back on weekends. Quite a few of them had breakfast—they had to shift for themselves for lunch—then they came home to dinner. I was there for about a year or a little more. Then I went home to Kent for awhile. Then I got another job in Seattle for Herbert Carroll, of Carroll Jewelers, in his home. His wife was bedridden and very ill.

I met Einar Pedersen on Snoqualmie Pass, skiing. The very next Saturday night, we met at a dance at the Swedish Club. That was the beginning of our romantic life. We got married in 1937 and rented a house on lower Sunset Hill. Our first two children were born there. We have four children: Susan, then Einar Jr., Mark, and Ingrid. When they were small, my life was dedicated to caring for them. Einar was a fisherman, often gone for months at a time, then home maybe three days and gone again for three weeks. When our son was born, Einar was out fishing. Ballard Oil sent a ship-to-shore radio message to all the boats out there to tell Einar he had a son.

Einar was very aggressive and hardworking. He had an intuitive sense about fishing, and he worked hard. We never had money because we saved enough to buy another boat from time to time. We had several boats when he died that my family are still using. He went from halibut fishing to trawling on the Sound, and tuna fishing and shark fishing in California and the Oregon coast. He was involved with several fishery organizations. He served for six years on the U.S. government's American Fishery Advisory Committee, and I went with him to meetings at San Diego, to Boston, to Galveston, Texas, Washington, D.C., and Key West, Florida.

I had two sisters who lived in Ballard. All three of us married fishermen, so we lived the same kind of life. And they had children at the same time. My sisters and I had a wonderful relationship with our children and with each other. While our husbands were gone we relied on each other to watch the children, if we had to be away.

After Einar passed away in 1989, we continued on. We still have his boats. My grandson is running the *Mark I*. And Einar Jr. is managing the rest of our boats, especially on our mother ship. The mother ship is a boat where the fish are processed. Then we have catcher boats that catch the fish for the mother ship. There are several owners in the mother ship. And they also have catcher boats. The boats actually bought the mother ship.

I've had a very interesting life. Looking back on it, I think I've had a very rich life. My husband taught me one thing: "If you want to do something, just try and do it and not worry about if it will work out." If you want to do something, you are ready to do it was his philosophy.

## Anna Jensen Kvam (1897–1999), Denmark

When my grandma came out here, she had to come across in a boat from Denmark to Ellis Island. And then they put her on a train and they had a tag on her—her destination, name, and nationality. And at the stoppings, a lot of times they'd have somebody who could speak Danish to reassure them, let them know they were going the right direction, and ask them if they needed things, and just cheer them up a little bit. She came by herself.

When my father built this house, there were no streets, just a wagon trail winding in and out, and then trees all over. He came to Ballard because somebody he knew had told [him] it's nicer here. He found a job at the Ballard Stimson Mill. We were just two children, my brother, 91 last June, and me, I was 90 in September. I was born at home. You had just a midwife. She'd just come for that time. You couldn't go to the store and get a loaf of bread. You baked all your own. You baked everything. And you canned vegetables. They had kind of a root cellar to keep all their vegetables and things. They raised everything, from potatoes and fruit. We had apples and pears and peaches and prunes.

In the summer we went barefooted. We never wore shoes in the summer months, unless we had to go someplace. We had to help with the work, too. There was berries to pick—loganberries, blackberries, currants, gooseberries. And the garden to help with.

My father had chickens and ducks, and there were streams going through. And they had pigs and they had cows. My mother sold quite a lot of chickens, young fryers. And they'd come and get them and she'd kill them right while they were there. There were some Jewish people living in Ballard. And they'd want big, fat chickens. Then they'd take it to the rabbi and have it blessed. This would be the only place they would buy their chickens. Later on my father sold milk. He had regular customers. He just had a little wagon he pulled, and sold the milk by the quart. They had a regular little milk house where they had water and everything to sterilize the stuff with.

We carried in every bit of water we used from the pump. We had no washing machine. Clothes had to be washed on the board, and we always boiled the clothes. We used wood in the stove. If you bought it in the summertime, you bought it wet. And you had to haul it in and stack it up outside to get dry, then put it in the woodshed to have it for winter. Here on the hills there were bears around, even. They weren't that plentiful, but there were bears.

## Marie Anderson Malone (1915– ), Sweden

My parents came here to Ballard in 1908. They both came from the Skee parish in the Bohuslan province of Sweden. My father came to North Dakota and my mother came to Chicago. They did not really know each other in the old country although their families were known to one another.

He was 35 and she was 28, and she didn't know if she should get married because she didn't know him that well, but she said, "Oh, everybody says, If you've got a chance to get married, get married," because that was about the only way women had.

They were married December of 1904 in Minneapolis. They were four years in New Rockford, North Dakota. She had the one child and was pregnant with the second one when she made the trip here. She remembered the lights of the city at that time and she thought it was wonderful, because she didn't care for a small town.

They rented a place for four years; then they moved to the home where I was born, and five years later they moved next door. It was all woods up there when they came here. There were not even gravel roads, just dirt roads and no sidewalks at that time.

My parents didn't go to church, but I went to Sunday school. I started when I was 5. It was a Swedish church. At Christmas they had a Swedish service, Julotta. My mother thought she'd like to go to Julotta when I was 9 years old. At five o'clock in the morning we walked to church in the snow. Of course, I didn't understand it.

My brother Bus started working for Mr. Jackson at the grocery store on 68th and 32nd when he was 11 years old [in 1919]. People would call in their order and he delivered with his wagon. Later he had the whole store and he ran it. Bus's store had fresh vegetables, and for ice cream they had a two-hole freezer. Ice cream would be in two flavors. When people bought a quart of ice cream he had to scoop down, and he had these paper cartons that he put the ice cream in. He probably gave more to people he liked by tapping it down a little bit more. A little later the ice cream came in blocks, like a quart of ice cream. Bus would go down to Pacific Fruit, down on Western Avenue, to pick up the fresh vegetables for the day. For meat, they dealt with Kastner's. The [customers] would call Kastner's to have them deliver it up here so when the people got their groceries they could get their meat there, too. Kastner's meat market was on 20th and 56th in Ballard for years and years. It was a Kastner family store, run first by the father, and then his three sons continued on. They did a lot of orders for fishing boats and they had many steady customers. They had as many as four or five butchers working there. Bus sold his store to Victor Anderson in 1939.

In 1931 Ballard High School had a class in retail selling for the first time. They took in 33 students. The teacher, Marion Candee, worked with the downtown department stores: Frederick & Nelson's, Rhodes, and J.C. Penney. We had to give a reason why we wanted to work for a store; I wrote something like "My father was a painter and there wasn't any work and I could use some money."

I worked for the J.C. Penney on Saturdays from the middle of October till Christmas. I was in the women's glove and hosiery department, and the pay was two and a quarter a day. No Social Security. We got our lunch hour, but no coffee breaks at all. At Christmas they gave us white tissue paper and red ribbon. If [a customer] would like [something] wrapped, we would wrap. There was no such thing as Scotch tape then, and we had to tie with this red ribbon and make a bow right at the counter. Of course, there was no pantyhose then, there was silk hosiery and they did carry some cotton. The silk stockings were what we call full-fashioned, cut with a seam in the back of the stocking. In the cheap hose, the stitch was tightened at the ankle, then larger at the calf. They really didn't fit. Full-fashion hose was 59, 79, and 98 cents a pair. A little later they had a very sheer hose. It was only two threads of silk. And they were $1.19 a pair. They were surprisingly strong for being so sheer.

I started in 1931. I worked there until I graduated from the university in '36, and I continued working there until January 1937, when I got a job with a lumber broker.

I took French in high school from Miss Beulah Russell in my senior year. She took me aside one time and she said, "You know, Marie, I really think you should go to college. Even if you get married the day you graduate, I think you should go to college."

I never thought of going to college. My brothers didn't go. One day I told them what the teacher said. And Bus says, "Well, would you like to go?" and I said, "Well, I guess I would." And he thought I should go. I graduated from the university in '36.

I love it here in Ballard. I really like it here, and I like being close down at the water. And I thought, whenever my husband and I went shopping, we always went down along the water to come home. And I bet if I could have a nickel for every time we went down along the water I'd be rich.


## Holger Berg (1916–2001), Finland

Canada was a barren place as far as people were concerned, and they were anxious to get anybody who could work over there. Many who wanted to immigrate to the United States, if they weren't allowed because of quotas, would come to Canada, and after five years they could immigrate from there. It was probably in 1920 my family left Canada and came to Seattle. Aunt Sigrid and Arthur Carlson came first and met us and brought us to their house on Capitol Hill. Later my folks and the Carlsons found a house on Phinney Ridge between 60th and 65th. It was a huge house, and all the Carlsons lived upstairs and the Bergs lived downstairs. And newcomers that came into Seattle came here, to find out which was a good logging company to work for or who was hiring fishermen and so on. We stayed at that house, and I went to John B. Allen School. Then we moved to Ballard, to just off 11th NW and NW 62nd. I was in about the third grade. It was quite a hike to West Woodland School, but it didn't seem to hurt us any.

When I was in the seventh grade, I met James Sully. We were talking at lunchtime, and he said, "Holger, did you ever go trout fishing?" And I said, "No. I don't know even how to go about it." "Well," he said, "I have some common pins I bent into hooks. You want to go fishing?" I said "When?" He said, "Now." I thought, gosh, tomorrow morning we'll really catch it when we come back to school. "Ah," he says, "come on."

So we legged it out to Piper's Creek Canyon, running all the way, and we dug up some worms. I never had so much fun catching fish in all my life. I had a little paper bag full of fish, probably seven, eight inches long. So we finally said, "Hey, it's about time to go home; school has got to be out."

I came home with these fish, and my mother wanted to know where I got them. No use lying about it. I said, "This kid talked me into running away from school today to catch fish." I guess my dad didn't think too much of that, but he looked them over and said, "Well, there must be a lot of fish up there." I said, "There sure is."

Years ago the *P.I.* paper had free swimming classes. My mother decided my brother and I should learn to swim. I remember some bitter cold days in that water with the wind blowing. But after you got dunked a few times, it really wasn't that bad, but it was cold. We'd stay and have our dinner there. My father met us after work and took us home. I talk to my contemporaries, and I say, "You know, Ballard was the greatest place in the world to grow up. There were a million things to do and nobody was shooting one another."

My brother Hakan and I were always fascinated by logging locomotives. They just exuded power to us kids. On 15th Avenue NW, there was a single streetcar track that went from the Ballard Bridge to 85th. I wondered why they never ran streetcars on that track. It had the wire up in the air. Then a fellow told us, "They bring the freight train from Everett down this track every night about one a.m." I thought, a freight train coming down 15th? This, I gotta see. My brother and I talked to our folks and we walked the two blocks from our house to 15th and sat there and waited. Pretty soon here comes this electric train, with boxcars and log cars and cattle cars, everything you can imagine.

I could not figure out how they got to 15th Avenue. Later it was explained to me: they came on the interurban tracks from Everett. Then they had special turns behind buildings because you cannot take a freight train around a 90-degree curve. When the train got to the Ballard Bridge, a locomotive was waiting. The electric locomotive would unhook and get out of the way, and the steam train would take over. I don't know where it went from there, but to us that was most fascinating.

At that time my father was longshoring. He would come home from work and say, "Well, boys, that silk train is going to leave about four o'clock tomorrow afternoon, and if you want to go see it—." So, boy, we would jump on our bikes and go all the way over to Shilshole, park our bikes, and sit there and wait. These trains, the *Mikado*, would really roll through there. They had baggage cars plus a combination car on the end that had some U.S. marshals, 'cause the train was hauling raw silk skeins and they didn't want anybody hijacking it. This train beat the records going to the silk mills in Paterson, New Jersey. It took precedence over any train— mail, passenger, freight; they had to get out of the way. Several railroad companies had these silk trains. The silk came from Japan. The Nippon Yushon Keisha (NYK) Line had ships going into California, Oregon, and Washington, and the silk needed to get to the mill fast.

After my Uncle Arthur passed away, my aunt married another Norwegian fisherman, who had his own boat. One time he saw a skiff floating, so he brought it home and gave it and a set of oars to my brother and me. Oh, we were top dogs; we had our own rowboat. So then, we were watching people out on the log booms peeling bark off the logs. You know, the bark used to be five, four, six inches thick? And you had to have a rope tied to your crowbar, because if you let go of it, you lost it. We would bring bark to the foot of 22nd Avenue NW and stack it up, and I'd run home and tell Dad, "We got a load of bark for us." We'd save it to burn in the heating stove,

There were all these mills. Seattle Cedar was the biggest, and there was Bolcom. I think Bolcom had these old chain-drive trucks, with a greyhound on the side of the cab, like the Greyhound Bus. And underneath it said, "Speed gets 'em." That was their motto for delivering wood. That was pretty neat.

The folks bought what were called edgings, the trimmings off the logs. They were three to six inches thick and 20 to 30 feet long. We'd get a load of those in summer, and my brother and I would stare at it and say, oh, boy, because we had a bucksaw and a crosscut saw. My dad wanted us to split the wood and fill the woodshed right up to the ceiling. I was glad to see when the last piece was cut. Oh, mercy! That took a lot of time, yes.

A man who had a grocery store at 61st and Eighth Avenue NW came to our house and asked me to work for him. And I said sure. He told me after I got to the store he'd pay me $18 a week for six days a week.

My dad was still out of work so that's where my money went. I got to drive a brand-new Ford V-8 panel delivery truck, pretty jazzy for a young guy. I picked up supplies from the wholesalers. I arranged the groceries in the truck in the order I would deliver them. I had my receipt book and cash to make change. Some people bought on a tab they paid weekly or monthly and then some paid cash. So I had to be writing receipts, too. That was a good job. I was there for some months, probably through the winter. Then here comes Dave Beck. You drive a truck; you have to belong to the Teamsters Union. It cost $50 to join the union and $12 a month in dues. No way could Mr. Nelson pay me that kind of money. And he had two ladies working there. At the end of the week, if the bananas didn't look too good, Mr. Nelson would say, "Why don't you and the ladies divide the bananas? They're getting a little overripe." So we each got a big bag of bananas. We got our groceries at cost, so this helped a lot. But when Dave Beck came, that was the end of that.

### Elsie (1924– ) and George (1920– ) Norman, Denmark and Norway

**Elsie:** I came to Seattle in 1942 to work at Boeing as a machinist. I was the only woman working on milling machines, both here and in Wichita. After I finished high school, a friend had told me about the National Youth Administration. I applied, and got in. They asked me if I'd like to learn something to help the war effort. I said, "Sure, why not." They gave me a math test. So I became a machinist. It involved a lot of trigonometry and so on. After I finished my course I was offered several jobs. I had relatives here, so I came to Seattle. I think we were 18 young girls who came here.

I worked at Boeing till 1945, the end of the war, earning money for college. I met George at college and we came to Seattle in 1951, during the Korean War. He got a job at Boeing. George and I had been married three years. He had graduated and started his master's degree. I had been in nurse's training. I'd had three and half years of college. By 1957 we had two children. So we bought a house in Ballard and moved in there.

We were involved with the Danes all the time. We were active in St. John's Lutheran Church. It was then composed of Danes, primarily. A lot of our friends were Danes. There was a Danish old people's home out on Des Moines Way. When it was sold, the proceeds went to buy a building and it was decided to establish a Danish Foundation. My husband and I were both on the committee to get the foundation started. Their primary purpose when they bought this three-story office building—part of it is a culture center—was to keep elderly in their homes as long as possible so they don't have to go into retirement homes.

Our children were both involved in Scouts, and we were also involved. And for several years our daughter represented the Danes in the Swedish Lucia pageant. There were representatives from each ethnic group—Norwegian, Finnish, and so on. I'm sure the queen was always Swedish, but she'd have her attendants. So we went to all these events, to listen to them sing the Santa Lucia song.

We were also involved in many Ballard activities, like the festivals. When the Nordic Heritage Museum was started in Ballard, we were in on getting the Danish Room organized. The museum organizers wanted representatives of the Danish community. So we had big parties and fund-raisers and that type of thing; I'm the archivist for the Danish Room. We collect all these artifacts and have them catalogued, and so on. Nora Olsen worked with me on that, too.

In 1964, I went back to school to Seattle Pacific University and earned a B.A. and master's degrees and started my doctorate. I became a reading specialist in junior high for a while and then moved to elementary in the Highline District. I taught remedial reading. I quit because they wanted me to go into administration.

They offered me a job taking charge of 19 schools. I'd rather work with children.

We lived on Sunset Hill, 75th and 31st NW. We bought the home from Gene Mittelstadt, who was a mortician. When we moved in, we found he had left behind a lot of ribbons and things such as baskets for floral arrangements. Our kids thought that was wonderful. They told their friends that's where he kept the dead.

We really enjoyed our home in Ballard. Our children say that was their favorite home. One of the best things was we had such wonderful neighbors. The neighborhood was full of Norwegians.

When the pastor of St. John's Lutheran Church, Richard Sorensen, came to Seattle in 1957 or so, the parsonage wasn't ready, so they moved in with us. It was cozy. They had three children; we had two. And one bathroom. A morning schedule outside the bathroom door listed who got in first. George was first, because he had to go to work at Boeing, and so on down the line. They stayed three weeks. That was rough, having one bathroom for nine people.

I don't really cook Danish foods. One Danish custom is at Christmas you put an almond in the rice pudding. And whoever gets the almond gets an extra gift. Well, we didn't like rice, especially me. So we put it in the mashed potatoes. We still do that to this day.

Although my grandparents and my father were born in Denmark, my mother was born in this country, so we ate American foods. One time my daughter's Girl Scout troop had an ethnic progressive dinner. And she announced the night before, "Mom, the Girl Scouts are coming to our house for dessert, and it has to be Danish." Oh, wow, you know, here I'm working. So I thought, I'll make *rød grøt*—that means "red pudding." It's made with berry juice and a thickener, and you serve it with cookies. So I quick made that up the night before to serve the 12 Girl Scouts. And they liked it. They really didn't care for the Norwegian fish balls they got at another home.

**George:** We've been busy in retirement, much more than I thought we'd be. We travel a lot and have many activities. We're not a bit bored with being on our own.

**Elsie:** We both belong to a Danish singing group that meets once a month. It's anywhere from 25 to as many as 60 people, with more singers at Christmas. We get together and sing Danish.

**George:** People may question talent of the singers, but we have a good time. And nobody gives us a hard time.

**Elsie:** I was thinking about the masquerades [*fastelavn*]. People would dress in costume, like they do in New Orleans. And that was always a lot of fun. It was a Mardi Gras thing. One year George went as a German admiral. He wore a wig and shoes that must have been size 15. And no one knew who he was all evening. Another time George went as a lady. He and another man came dressed as women wearing high heels and wobbling all over the place. It was hilarious.

**George:** This other man and his wife lived in West Seattle and we were from Ballard. He and I agreed we were going in costume—people wouldn't know us at all, dressed as we were. But he was worried about what would happen if he had a flat tire on our way to the party and he had to change a tire dressed as a woman. I was smart. I didn't dress up until we got there.

### Helen Pekonen Hill (1926– ), Finland

I was born in 1926 in Ballard in a house near Market Street. My father went out to get the doctor, and by the time they got back, I was there. My father, Victor Pekonen, was a carpenter, and we didn't have a whole lot of money. We moved to a little house in a great big lot near 32nd NW and NW 85th, three houses from our only relatives in the area. I think a lot of babies were born at home. Medical care wasn't that available then. And they couldn't speak English anyway. Not very well, just a little bit, you know, a little "Finn-glish," as we called it.

When I was 4, we went to Finland, because my mother, Lily, was lonesome for her parents and her family. We came back to Ballard when I was 7. I had to go to school, but I couldn't speak English, only Finnish. It took me about six months to learn English. As a young child, you just kind of absorb things as they go.

My parents spoke very poor English, so, when I got a little older, I was their interpreter. All through their life I interpreted for them when they were stuck. They got better because they had to get their naturalization papers. They had to study all this stuff. They knew more about our government and how it works than I did by the time they finished going to school and taking all those classes.

Three times a week my parents would go to a dance, right on 15th NW, the Veliaseurra Hall. It was a Finnish hall. In those days you'd take your kid with you. They would almost always have live music. Somebody knew how to play a violin or a piano or something. My mother and dad would be dancing, having a good time, and I'd be sleeping right next to the band. If the band stopped, I would wake up. As long as it was playing, I slept like a baby. They loved to dance. That's where they met all their friends.

By the time I was old enough to walk, I was out there dancing with my dad. That was fun. They had a stage in that old hall where they put on plays. I used to crawl around backstage, going through all these powder puffs and lights and pretending I was a star.

In Ballard they have a Finnish Lutheran church, on NW 85th and 13th NW, which is very active with Finnish gatherings. I go every November to the Nordic Heritage Museum and get all my coffee bread for the Christmas season because there's some woman there that can bake that coffee bread so good. I buy every one I can find, and I put it in the freezer. Cardamom makes the difference.

Golden Gardens was my really fun place to go with my mother and father and all their Finnish friends. Finnish people, like a lot of people, are clannish, mainly because of their language. They would all contribute something to this big pot of stew. Go down there in the morning, bring their kids, bring their cards, and cook this stew there at the stoves, which are still there, and play pinochle. This was during the Depression days, so you just didn't have a whole lot. That was a great activity for those people. They all got there, and laughed and joked and told stories. And that's where I learned to swim because I didn't want to sit there watching them play cards all day. I'd go down to the beach and paddle around. Pretty soon I was able to swim all the way out to the raft, which they had at that time.

### Naomie Fredeen Bulloch (1926– ), Sweden

I'm pretty sure my parents met at the Mission Covenant Church in Bellingham, one of the Swedish emigrants' churches, which still exists. In Sweden my adoptive grandmother was a devoted member of the Salvation Army, which she referred to as *Frälsnings-Armén*. I spent summers with her in Ballard in the 1930s. She played guitar and accordion, also played the drum in the Salvation Army band. Some times she took me with her when the Ballard Corps conducted a Sunday-afternoon street meeting in Pioneer Square. I followed my grandmother as she played in the band. She looked quite charming in her navy blue Salvation Army uniform, with a wonderful bonnet with satin ruffles under the brim framing her face.

We had moved to Seattle because my father hoped to find job opportunities here. Through the Swedish Covenant Church he met Mr. Strom and became his partner in his floor-covering business, Strom Fredeen. Later my father owned the business.

At Ballard High I was taking a botany class when World War II came upon us. The garden behind the school immediately became a victory garden. I worked in the garden and have a picture which was reprinted in one of Paul Dorpat's *Seattle Then and Now* series. The picture, dated February 1943, shows the victory garden with me and others working. The caption says we're harvesting. I think we were probably preparing for a new planting. The garden helped supply the school's cafeteria with fresh vegetables. Dorpat wrote, "The garden in 1942 produced 800 pounds of pumpkins, 300 pounds of tomatoes, cabbages, carrots, onions, beans, lettuce, beets, radishes, Brussels sprouts." At Ballard I was on the staff of the yearbook, the *Shingle*, and the newspaper, the *Talisman*. Both were terrific experiences. We went to the *Ballard Tribune* Tuesday nights to put the paper together. It would be typeset there, and we'd paste up the pages, then send them to the presses. It had news about new students, new teachers, what the Honor Society was doing, and lots of sports. Ballard had some very good teams, including the city-championship football team when I was there. Henry Bendele was the coach.

When I was 14, I started getting part-time jobs. The summer of '42 I worked at Mr. McWorter's toothbrush factory a couple of months, then moved to Ballard Plastics, which was making parts for the Navy. I left that job after several months because the acetone they used gave me headaches. So when I had the chance to become a movie theater cashier, I took it.

The Ballard chapter of Salvation Army officers, circa 1937. The banner in the background reads "Salvation Army" in Swedish. Courtesy of the Nordic Heritage Museum.

I worked at the Grand Theater on 85th near Greenwood. People were flocking to the movies for relaxation, since everyone was working so hard. Because their parents were both working, we saw huge bunches of kids at the theater. I'd get telephone calls at the box office from parents looking for their kids. "Is Betty in the theater right now?" Sometimes the sheriff came to round up someone reported missing. If the kids recognized someone coming in who might haul them home, they'd get up and run. We'd have kids darting out the door, behind the screen, trying to get out to the back. It got pretty chaotic sometimes, but it was kind of amusing—no violence involved, just silly kids trying to get away with something. It became a real problem on the street around there, and the sheriff decided something had to be done about kids out on the streets at night. As a result, the Boys Clubs were organized. They started in Seattle and then spread around the country. Later they added the Girls Clubs.

Wherever we went—to the ice arena, to the Trianon Ballroom, a movie theater—we saw soldiers and sailors, so it was easy to meet fellows from all over the country. When I went to the University of Washington, the Navy was using a lot of University facilities for the V-12 program. The young men in that Navy program had the rank of ensign and wore their uniforms to class.

At the university I joined a group of what were called "town girls," who lived off-campus and who created their own sorority, Phrateres. It was sponsored by the dean of women, May Dunn Ward. We sometimes volunteered at the USO downtown. And that's where I met my husband. I ran the soda fountain, served hamburgers, coffee, milk shakes, that kind of thing. A girlfriend of mine came up and said, "These two young Army Air Corpsmen would like to meet us." We went to a booth and she introduced me. They invited us to sit down and talk. Douglas Bulloch, from New York, was based at Boeing Field in the B-29 program. He eventually flew 35 missions over the Pacific and Japan. He was a gunner. That was very dangerous work.

During World War II, gasoline and food were rationed. We saved aluminum foil and rubber bands. We saved cooking fats and took them to the butcher shop to be recycled. Even pots and pans could be recycled. We couldn't buy silk stockings, and dress styles reflected the shortage of fabric: everything was cut along skimpy lines.

And we worried about being invaded—I'd hear an airplane and think about Mussolini's planes. We'd heard they bombed Ethiopia, and they must be very powerful. Probably because of Boeing, we were terribly aware of the idea of air power. And after the Japanese bombed Pearl Harbor, I think everyone felt they might attack the West Coast. My mother volunteered to spot and identify airplanes flying overhead. Security was tight. After D-Day in 1944 everybody just prayed that it would succeed. We felt vulnerable. We didn't have any sense of being the "superpower" that we've been painted ever since.

I think my parents' generation all wanted to be American. They had a drive to become fluent in English and to be seen as modern Americans. My mother particularly wanted to be identified not as a Swedish immigrant but as a young woman in 1920s America. That's how she saw herself. My mother-in-law, of the same generation, emigrated from Scotland. They both had a need to be contemporary, to appear fashionable and to have a modern home and household. My mother was always researching things like vacuum cleaners and refrigerators. She would have loved to have an automatic dishwasher.

My dad was typical of a lot of men in that he tended to be away, very involved in his business and church activities. So his wasn't really a strong presence. And when the war came along he traveled a lot on business. At church he was on the board of deacons and was sort of a lay minister, too. He was invited to other churches to speak. It was a very important thing in his life. And he was one of the founders of CRISTA Ministries in north Seattle. When I came back to Seattle with my family, after I'd married, he was involved in starting King's Garden Schools, the living facilities and all the rest. He and Mike Martin were the movers and shakers who got it established. It's quite a monument to my dad.

My mother liked needlework a lot. She embroidered tablecloths and napkins, and she made quilt squares, lots of them. She had had a very sad life at times, and needlework is kind of soothing. She felt deprived as a young person, and in the '20s fashion became a very big thing and she was just the right age to be a flapper. She disgraced the family when she bobbed her hair. It was always clear that she loved beautiful jewelry, things like that—gold and rhinestones. One Christmas I bought her a sequined beret with a matching belt, both very bright and glittery—and my sister bought her the same thing. We both knew what would appeal to her.

## Jon Marvin Jonsson (1928– ), Iceland

After grade school I spoke both Icelandic and English, but prior to that time just Icelandic. We weren't allowed to speak English in the home, only Icelandic. If we accidentally forgot we'd get slapped with a wet dishrag, and that continued until I was maybe 14 or 15. Then I started speaking English, but my mother still only spoke Icelandic. At that age I knew everything and could get away with it. My dad spoke Icelandic because he was more comfortable with Icelandic. But I think my mother sort of ran the show.

About my nickname, Bobo, my sisters called me *bróðir* [*ð* is pronounced 'th']. The kids couldn't pronounce that and they ended up calling me Bobo, and the name Bobo stayed with me, all the way through law school.

There was an Icelandic church on NW 70th and 23rd NW, and the sermons were in Icelandic. And they had an Icelandic organization called Vestri, which means "westerners." Sometimes I had to go with my parents to the Vestri meeting. Vestri had a book society. You could borrow books in Icelandic. Vestri was strictly social, and it continued until around 1960. At that time, I incorporated the Icelandic Club of Seattle, which took over what Vestri had been doing.

I built a kayak at home when I was in junior high school. And I would say that I built it properly and correctly. I took the plans from *Boys' Life* and spent the winter building the kayak. It had ribs 12 inches apart, and they varied in size because they started as a point, came out to the cockpit area and again diminished down. I did all the steps you're supposed to do: shrink and coat the canvas and make it watertight and then paint it. And Andy, or Bud, Hjellen, who lived across the street, he too built a kayak. But, as it turned out, his kayak was a foot shorter than mine because the ruler he used was only 11 inches—he thought it was 12. But you know, you don't throw away a ruler if you break it, you just cut off the end.

When I was in junior high school, I had a *P-I* [*Seattle Post-Intelligencer*] carrier route. And I would get up at 3:30 [in the morning], would get my papers, and I'd always be there. I didn't sleep in. And then, when the war started in 1941, most of the people who were *P-I* carriers were seniors in high school. It was a desired job because you'd get money. There were no other jobs. The war started on Sunday. On Monday, three [carriers] went down and joined the military. All of a sudden their slots were empty, including the shack manager. And I was then made the shack manager, which meant I got paid $10 a month, maybe. It would be my job to make sure that everybody was there. And if they weren't, I'd go wake them up. And if I woke them up, I would get to charge them 50 cents.

If they were noisy or caused a disturbance, I would then tell them to be quiet. And if they weren't quiet, I could assess them 50 cents. Now, here I am, a kid in junior high, dealing with people in high school. Do you see? Do you see the prob-

On the stage at Ballard's Icelandic Church, circa 1936. From left to right, Anna Magnusson, Jon Marvin Jonsson, and Dyrlief Arnason. Courtesy of the Nordic Heritage Museum.

lem? OK. So the next thing that happened is I would get pantsed. Do you remember that procedure, take your pants off? OK. I would get pantsed. And I would put up resistance, but you can't put up much of a fight with—and it wasn't a serious fight, no one's getting black eyes. You know, it was more a tussle, yeah, and I would get pantsed. And I would then charge them each 50 cents. And then I concluded, I can make money from this. So what I would do is, I would wear a pair of pants I didn't care about and hide a good pair. Then, in case they took my pair and threw them up in the telephone wires, at least I had another pair to put on.

And then, when I'd be through with the route, I would go by Kannitzer's Bakery on NW 24th and 63rd NW. And I would go in there and I would give them a newspaper, a *P-I*, and I'd get four maple bars. I'd bring the maple bars home, and I'd wake up my parents and I'd give them each a maple bar and I had two for myself.

I graduated from Ballard High in January of '46. The war was over August 14, 1945, but they were still showing up at school with their programs to encourage people to enlist in the Army and the Navy. And then, in October, the Navy came with a program called V-5 and V-12. A program that, if you enlisted, you would go to a regular university, like Stanford, for a two-year program there. Then, if you were in the flying bit, V-5, you would then go to flight school and finish your four-year enlistment as a pilot.

That was very attractive to me. There was a three-day test, and just a few were accepted. Then you were sworn in the Navy, though you're still in high school. And when you graduate, the Navy would send orders where to show up. So I graduated in January and was waiting for the Navy to send me my orders. Well, I received a letter from the Navy, saying in so many words, "We don't need you. Here's your discharge." But that made me a World War II veteran before I turned 18.

After high school, I was in the Marine Corps 14 months. The G.I. Bill paid my way through the first quarter of law school. That was a wonderful program. And because I was married, it paid $110 a month. I then had a job managing the Neptune Theater building—not the theater, but the building, on NE 45th Street and University Avenue. Then I went to law school.

I was elected to the state Legislature in 1958, '59. I don't know that there were any big issues. The breakwater was coming in, and Dwight Hawley was primarily responsible for it. He lost the election, which didn't make sense, but there was an issue on the ballot when I ran that bothered the Unions—right to work—so they got the union vote out, a Democrat vote. I came in on that Democrat sweep. The next time around, that issue wasn't there, the Democrats stayed home, the Republicans voted, I lost, and Dwight Hawley came back in.

Around 1967, '68, I became consul for Iceland, and in 1984 I became consul general. We've been to Iceland maybe 20 times, if not more. My dad was the only one of seven siblings to come to America. The rest are in Iceland. I was raised in Ballard, and I didn't have any cousins. Never had any family, except my mother, dad, and sisters. And then to go back there, and I had just a vast number. Maybe 200.

These stories are selected pieces from the book *Voices of Ballard: Immigrant Stories from the Vanishing Generation*, edited by Lynn Moen. That publication is a result of the Nordic Heritage Museum's collaborative and extensive oral history project with the Ballard Historical Society and the Swedish Finn Historical Society and completed with the help of numerous volunteers. The pieces chosen for this present publication illustrate only a small section of the ethnic make-up of a close-knit community. The book is for sale at the Museum and select bookstores in the Seattle area. The Museum is presently planning to extend its oral history project beyond Ballard, into the further reaches of King County.

# NOTES

[1] For further readings on Scandinavian peoples in the Pacific Northwest see, Jorgen Dahlie, "Old World Paths in the New: Scandinavians Find Familiar Home in Washington" *Pacific Northwest Quarterly* 61:2 (1970), 65-71. Bob H. Hansen, *Norse to the New Northwest: A Sesquicentennial Saga* (Seattle: Norwegian American Anniversary Commission, 1975). Janice L. Reiff, "Scandinavian Women in Seattle, 1888-1900: Domestication and Americanization" in *Women in Pacific Northwest History: An Anthology*, Karen Blair, ed. (Seattle, Wash.: University of Washington Press, 1988 Edition), 170-184. Also of interest is Richard D. Scheuerman, "Washington's European American Communities" in *Peoples of Washington: Perspectives on Cultural Diversity*, ed. Sid White and S. E. Solberg (Pullman, Wash.: Washington State University Press, 1989), 25-74.

[2] These excerpts are taken from Lynn Moen, ed., *Voices of Ballard: Immigrant Stories from the Vanishing Generation* (Nordic Heritage Museum, 2001), based on the Oral History Project of the Nordic Heritage Museum, the Ballard Historical Society and the Swedish Finn Historical Society.

[3] This is the Swedish spelling. The Norwegian spelling is lutefisk.

# "IF I AM ONLY FOR MYSELF, WHAT AM I?"

## TWO SUCCESSFUL JEWISH WOMEN'S ORGANIZATIONS IN KING COUNTY

### Jacqueline B. Williams

The proverb "If I am not for myself, who will be for me? But if I am only for myself, what am I?" comes from Hillel, the great Hebrew sage and teacher who lived circa 60 BC and 9 AD. Customarily referred to as *tzedakah* (righteousness and justice), this fundamental idea is an important aspect of the Jewish religion. Whether giving alms or organizing systematic and careful programs, which today might win the approval of a funding organization, Washington's secular and traditionalist Jewish pioneers retained this age-old tradition of helping people in need.[1]

An exemplary philosophy, however, was not the only factor that created the Seattle Ladies' Hebrew Benevolent Society and the Ladies' Montefiore Aid Society, in the 1890s, and the National Council of Jewish Women (NCJW), Seattle Section, in 1900.[2] Political situations, such as the changing roles of women; the growing King County Jewish community; an influx of immigrants fleeing Europe, Turkey, and the island of Rhodes between 1880 and 1924; and the failure of the city and the county to provide relief for those in need, spurred Jewish women to create these early self-help institutions in Seattle.

During this time frame it was common practice for ethnic and religious groups to provide general assistance, and many American cities set up Charity Organization Societies. In 1891 Seattle joined that roster. Under the leadership of D. C. Garrett, pastor of Trinity Church, Seattle created the Bureau of Associated Charities (changed to Charity Organization Society of Seattle in 1896) so that complete records could be kept on all who requested assistance. By monitoring the amount of help people received, the Charity Organization Society felt it would discourage some people's practice of going from one charitable organization to another seeking help. "A case should be left in the hands of one church or agency, and the fact be so recorded at the central bureau," said Virginia McMechen, secretary of the Charity Organization Society.[3] The agencies called the people, usually men, who engaged in such activity "agency tramps".[4] Leo Kohn, a charter member of the Seattle Hebrew Benevolent Association, a group that would merge with the

Seattle Hebrew Ladies' Benevolent Society in 1917, and Lizzie Cooper, one of the founders of the women's society, served on the Board of the Charity Society Organization between 1902 and 1910. They were also vice presidents of the Charity Society, attesting to an early involvement in charitable works by the Jewish benevolent societies.[5]

Adapting to the changing structure and interests of a growing community, Seattle Jewish women in 1892 began organizing independent and self-governing voluntary associations with multiple purposes. The beneficiaries of economic affluence and increased free time, the women were no longer content with limiting themselves to such traditional activities as preparation of the dead for burials or placing flowers in the temple. Joining a women's society concerned with urban social problems gave them a way to fulfill ambitions for outside-the-home achievement.[6] The tribulations of new immigrants swelling the urban neighborhoods provided a ready target for middle-class women reformers.

Though their activities in the beginning were limited to fund-raising events and distributing gifts to the poor, women very quickly became proficient at managing organizations and directing volunteers. More than 100 years after their founding, the Seattle Ladies' Hebrew Benevolent Society (today's Jewish Family Service) and the National Council of Jewish Women, Seattle Section, have become multifaceted agencies providing social services to both Jewish and non-Jewish people living in Seattle. The Ladies' Montefiore Aid Society adhered to more traditional ways by remaining a small organization of Orthodox Jewish women who raised money to distribute to the poor with no questions asked. It was led by Goldie Shucklin and disbanded a few years after her death in 1935.

Jews first settled in Seattle in 1868.[7] Less than 10 years later, in 1876, Seattleites elected Jewish entrepreneur Bailey Gatzert as their mayor. Between 1885 and 1910, a period that saw Seattle's population increase from slightly less than 4,000 to 237,194, the Jewish population grew from a little more than 200 to approximately 4,500, or 1.9 percent of the city's population.[8] This 25-year period overlapped with the period of "mass migration" (1880 to 1914) when approximately 2 million Southeastern European Jews migrated to the United States. It also overlapped the Progressive Era, roughly from the turn of the century to America's entrance into World War I, a time when reformers across the country confidently grappled with a broad range of issues associated with urbanization and industrialization.

The Seattle Ladies' Hebrew Benevolent Society and the National Council of Jewish Women, Seattle Section, the two philanthropic clubs that are the subjects of this essay, were founded as independent volunteer organizations. They were managed solely by the members, and followed written bylaws and established parliamentary procedures. The women controlled their own finances and raised money by adopting an American novelty, fund-raising events such as card parties and teas. This was a significant break from past traditions, which, according to historian Charlotte Baum "had existed within the traditional Jewish community . . . [and]

had always been communal activity, controlled and executed by men."[9] Neither group was affiliated with religious institutions, although both used Temple De Hirsch, Seattle's Reform temple, for meetings and other events, and many of the club women were also active members of that temple. While both the Hebrew Ladies' Benevolent Society and the National Council of Jewish Women emphasized social service over religious activities, they did so within a Jewish framework. NCJW's motto, "Faith and Humanity," signifies that social work and political action are a part of religious expression.

Moreover, it was this close affiliation with the temple that caused Rabbi Samuel Koch in 1916 to declare that "in spirit, therefore, the Temple De Hirsch and the [Ladies' Benevolent Society] must ever have been one," so they should call themselves the Ladies' Hebrew Benevolent Society of the Temple De Hirsch. The name change "cannot but increase the prestige of the society in many ways and harm it in none," he wrote in "The Temple Tidings," the temple's newsletter. Despite the fact that Koch promised the temple would not interfere with the society, the ladies turned him down.[10]

The Hebrew Ladies' Benevolent Society was local whereas the National Council of Jewish Women, Seattle Section, was part of a national organization. The groups had similar goals, leaders, and memberships. Lizzie Levy Cooper, a founder of the Hebrew Ladies' Benevolent Society, served as president of the NCJW, Seattle Section, in 1903. Early on, both organizations focused on helping new immigrants adjust to American society, and during their formative years they were made up almost exclusively of women who adhered to Reform Judaism, the liberal branch of Judaism.[11]

In contrast to the more traditional Orthodox Judaism, Reform Judaism encouraged women's broader participation in their religious institutions and the community. Many of the Jews who adhered to this philosophy had emigrated from Germany during the first half of the 19th century and were now well acquainted with American ways. Among them were the first Jewish people to settle in Seattle.

## Seattle Ladies' Hebrew Benevolent Society

Esther Levy and her daughter Elizabeth (Lizzie) Cooper, along with 37 other women, founded the Seattle Ladies' Hebrew Benevolent Society in March of 1892. Esther and her husband, Aaron, had moved to Seattle from Idaho in 1889. Lizzie's husband, Isaac Cooper, joined the Levy family to open a retail and mail-order grocery and hardware business. Cooper-Levy became the leading outfitter for prospectors going north to the Yukon gold rush in 1897. Both Esther and Aaron, who had been in the United States since 1850 (Esther came in 1846), were part of the large German immigration that came to America between 1820 and 1880. Esther Levy's and Lizzie Cooper's roles in organizing Seattle's first Hebrew Benevolent Society followed the example begun by Jewish women on

Esther Levy, with her daughter Lizzie Cooper founded the Ladies Hebrew Benevolent Society in 1892. MSCUA, University of Washington Libraries, Jewish History Project, UW neg. 1110.

the East Coast in 1819.

Rebecca Gratz and others who saw the need to provide home relief and, eventually, medical care for the local Jewish poor organized the first Hebrew Ladies' Benevolent Society, in Philadelphia. The women, observed Paula Hyman, "saw their efforts as a safeguard against Christian missionaries who knocked on the doors of poor Jews to offer assistance accompanied by proselytizing."[12] Upwardly mobile German Jewish immigrant women in the second half of the 19th century considered Gratz, who is alleged to have served as the model for Rebecca in Sir Walter Scott's *Ivanhoe*, a paragon of virtue. By the end of the 19th century most cities with a large Jewish population had a Hebrew Ladies' Benevolent Society. In smaller towns it was common for the synagogue and the benevolent society to be the only two Jewish communal institutions.

Early on, Seattle Hebrew Ladies' Benevolent Society members sought to accomplish their constitutional goal of bringing "relief of the Jewish poor and to ameliorate distress in general" by visiting families.[13] Called "friendly visitors," the women trudged up and down hills with baskets of food on their arms and clothing from their own homes to bring aid to Jews in need. In addition, they sought to

Lizzie Cooper, MSCUA, University of Washington Libraries, Jewish History Project, UW neg. 21A.

impress on immigrant mothers the values of cleanliness and a well-run household. Teaching middle-class values was seen as the best way to aid immigrants as they adjusted to American life. When money instead of services seemed more appropriate, events such as dances and card games raised funds for a variety of charitable causes both inside and outside the Jewish community. One event enabled the society to send $167.25 to survivors of a mine explosion in the central Washington town of Roslyn.[14]

Some construed the "friendly visitors" as merely playing at lady bountiful, saying that the women "would complain if the homes weren't kept as their homes were," but most really wanted to help, said Bernice Degginger Greengard, the society's first long-term paid staff person, who came on board in 1921.[15] "It was a question of money mostly. It was helping the foreigners find an American way of living, a Western way of living . . . They got what they needed most. After all, you can't teach a person traditions or anything else when their tummies are empty. They had to have jobs and they had to have money first."[16] Greengard stayed with the agency until 1927 and was replaced by May Goldsmith, who served as executive secretary until her retirement in 1945.[17]

In 1917, the Ladies' Hebrew Benevolent Society joined with the Seattle He-brew Benevolent Association, a men's organization that provided relief to Jewish men, and became known as the Seattle Hebrew Benevolent Society. The women, however, remained as officers, board members, managers, and volunteer workers. The men formed an advisory committee to help as needed. They were not admit-ted as board members until 1947.[18]

By the time the Progressive Era ended, problems for the poor had become more complex, and social services at both the national and state level began to decline. According to Arlien Johnson, who during the mid-1920s served as secre-tary of the Washington State Conference of Social Work, "county relief was over the counter and it was really punitive."[19] In order to help the many Jewish immi-grants coming to Seattle, the women understood they would have to change the focus of the benevolent organization. Giving money and handing out new clothes was not enough. "Providing material needs is only a dose to be administered as a treatment . . . we must restore families to society, making them self-supporting and self-respecting citizens. This change in policy is not confined to our organization alone, but is taking place throughout the country, and we would not be abreast of the times if we did not reflect this tendency," said Gertrude Shopera in her annual report for 1928–1929.[20] Shopera also suggested changing the name of the organi-zation to the Jewish Social Service Agency as "the aim of our work is 'family ser-vice,' which deals with problems of delinquency, medical social work, and ramifi-cations of case work."[21]

Shopera's suggested name did not win approval, but the women understood that "benevolent" was an obsolete term and changed the organization's name to the Jewish Welfare Society (JWS) in 1929. They also added the words "engage generally in social service work upon the broadest principles of humanity" to their mandate.[22] The change of name to Jewish Family and Child Service (JFCS) in 1947 and finally to Jewish Family Service (JFS) in 1978 reflected the role the orga-nization played in working with families.

In 1929 the society had a budget of $19,000, of which $14,000 came from the Community Chest (the predecessor to United Way). As members of one of the first groups to become part of the Community Chest, the active women of the society played a key role in raising money for that organization. Soliciting money to support the JWS's many programs consumed much of the volunteers' time. Deficit spending became a way of life. "From month to month our disbursements are from $200 to $300 more than our income," reported the society's Ways and Means Committee in 1925. [23]

During the Great Depression, unemployed people overwhelmed the system. Washington State, like the rest of the nation, faced unprecedented relief problems. Moreover, Washington Governor Roland Hartley saw relief as a moral issue and rejected any notion of obligating the state in providing assistance. The Jewish Welfare Society, with the help of all the other Jewish organizations, cared for many who needed food and shelter. In 1931, the JWS noted "all our transients are sent to the Central Registry for men . . . and single men and unemployed family men are registered for what public works are available, but so many men are out of work and so few jobs listed that the agencies are taxed to their limit."[24] Granting emergency relief under guidelines set forth by the National Conference of Social Service, the JWS stated, "We wish the community to realize that every applicant is received with sympathy . . . if mistakes are made it is preferable to err on the side of mercy."[25]

The JWS became part of the federal, state, and county welfare system during the Depression and used most of its funds and volunteer help to supplement government money. "Today we have very little time for Social Service. I can say that families applying now are asking for relief. There is no such thing as rehabilitation of a family," May Goldsmith reported in 1932. A year later she added:

Federal Aid gives food ($1.20 per person per week), fuel (wood), some clothing, and lodging. Are these all that our Jewish families need? Can you visualize a family of five, mother, father, and three children, living on five dollars and sixty cents a week? This includes bread, milk, meat, and all grocery supplies. Often a family needs some extras, [and] the JWS provides this when necessary. [26]

Determined to provide relief, the women worked hard at raising money, collecting food, securing housing, and joining sewing groups to make clothes for needy children. During the first three months of 1932, the organization looked after 1,659 individuals, an average of 553 per month. "We have had to secure for ourselves a new viewpoint, a new education, a new attitude . . . So many of the things that we had learned in the past have had to be discarded, and adjustments made to meet the demands of the times," reported president Jessie Danz in 1934.[27]

Throughout those turbulent times, one of the JWS's main strengths was its ability to collaborate with other Jewish organizations. For example, it administered the funds allocated to the Ladies' Montefiore Aid Society by Seattle's Community Chest; worked with the NCJW, Seattle Section's Americanization program to assist refugees trying to establish citizenship; collaborated with the NCJW, Seattle Section, to establish a scholarship to pay the cost of a second-year student studying social work at the University of Washington; and in 1941, in partnership with the Jewish Welfare Board, began assisting servicemen.[28] In 1937 the Community Fund of the Community Chest increased the JWS's budget by $2,000, proportionately the largest increase made to any agency, in "recognition of our fair dealing with them in the past."[29] The increase allowed the organization to hire another worker, but most committees and organized activities were still staffed by volunteers.

The turmoil in Europe that followed the Great Depression brought in more immigrants. Once more, the JWS called on volunteers to integrate people into the community. Volunteers helped immigrants fill out their citizenship papers, assisted

Jewish servicemen stationed at Fort Lewis, and helped Jewish veterans reenter the workplace.

When World War II ended, the JWS found itself the main Jewish welfare agency focusing on family problems, such as conflicts within the family, physical and emotional illness, unemployment, and foster home care for children. "The clients come to the office for consultation just as they would go to a doctor's office. The trained social worker is able to work out their problems with them . . . It is rehabilitation of the person," Goldsmith wrote when she left the agency in 1945.[30]

It was more than that. By the 1940s and '50s voluntary agencies began emphasizing a multidisciplinary approach that would improve standards of living, such as better diets and quality of housing. Social workers had to consider the applicants' social needs as well as their medical needs. Again the Jewish Welfare Society needed new rules, as it now was a member of the Family Service Association of America, an organization of social welfare agencies. This agency maintained membership requirements, such as broad community representation.

To keep up with the times, the agency changed its name to Jewish Family and Child Service, hired a professional executive director, and for the first time elected men to its board. It also attracted controversy. One of its key financial supporters, Eugene Levy, son of Esther Levy and brother of Lizzie Cooper, the trustee administering Isaac Cooper's will, disagreed with the board on the way to administer funds. Isaac Cooper, Levy's brother-in-law and husband of Lizzie Levy Cooper, one of the founders of the Seattle Hebrew Ladies' Benevolent Society, had bequeathed half of his funds to JFCS (about $40,000 per year in 1948). According to Levy, the new executive director, Ann Kaufman, had increased expenses "to build up a big organization to promote herself." Angry about the agency's new direction of providing social services along with direct aid, Levy sued. After a three-day battle in King County Superior Court, Judge Malcolm Douglas ruled in Levy's favor, deciding that the "funds of the Isaac Cooper Estate must be used exclusively for providing direct material assistance to the poor and needy, in the form of money, food, clothing and housing and that a semi-annual statement must be rendered to the Trustees."[31]

Much of the controversy centered on the definition of "poor and needy." The board took a broad view. They did not believe families had to be destitute to be eligible for financial aid. On the other hand, Levy maintained the money should only be used "to help people in real need and not to provide a better living standard for people who have a modest income barely sufficient to provide the living essentials."[32] Considerable correspondence passed between Levy and JFCS concerning the allocation of funds, but Levy never changed his thinking.

However, a basket of food was no longer sufficient. New institutional and ideological ideas made changes necessary. By the 1950s, Jewish Family and Child Service, with a staff of 12, supported a range of humanitarian issues and lobbied for increased welfare support. With continued growth JFCS expanded its services to serve a changing community. It pushed for home care and assisted living for the elderly and offered a multitude of counseling services.

Since that time, women have shared responsibilities for governance with men, an enlarged professional staff manages the day-to-day activities, and funding comes from both government and private sources. But volunteers, now representing all branches of Judaism, still serve on the board, raise money, and assist professionals in providing care. Implementing new and better ways to manage the agency has been as important as utilizing new technologies and business practices. That ability to change and integrate the concerns of the organization with those of the greater Seattle Jewish community and a common belief in voluntarism and the power of people working together have enabled Jewish Family Service, the name adopted in 1978, to remain productive into the 21st century.

## NATIONAL COUNCIL OF JEWISH WOMEN, SEATTLE SECTION

The National Council of Jewish Women was started in Chicago in 1893 to prove that Jewish women working together could achieve results.[33] The NCJW was committed to "social justice, the preservation of Judaism and the Jewish community in the United States, and a vision of religion that combined the two," said Charlotte Baum.[34] The founding leadership overwhelmingly identified with Reform Judaism. Furthermore, the NCJW, unlike some Christian women's organizations, did not see poor immigrant girls as "fallen" and in need of saving. Rather, they felt their clients just needed help to overcome unfortunate circumstances.

In Seattle, Babette Schwabacher Gatzert suggested to some of her friends that they form a local section of the National Council of Jewish Women. At the first organizational meeting, on November 19, 1900, at Morris Hall, 34 women elected Merle (Dolly) Degginger president.[35] The Seattle Section was organized around religious, educational, and philanthropic interests. Early programs included setting up study circles and establishing committees to support progressive social legislation, such as the 1906 Heyburn Pure Food and Drugs Act, and joining the Women's Legislation Council of Washington in 1926. In an era when women had limited formal political influence (they could not vote in Washington until 1910), the NCJW gave them a place to influence social policy. It is a tradition that continues with the very active Public Affairs Committee, which, for example, in 1983 supported the Washington Religious Coalition for Abortion Rights and urged compensation for Japanese-Americans interned during World War II.

From the beginning, the Seattle Section's Philanthropic Committee played a major role in extending aid to the needy. At first members visited hospitals, sent flowers to funerals, and tended neglected graves. Within a few years, after being chastised by Blanche Blumauer, a prominent member of Portland's NCJW, the committee decided they had the expertise to open a settlement house.[36]

The settlement house movement, which flourished between 1900 and 1915, originated in England in 1884 and emerged in the United States in 1886. It was enthusiastically seen as the main vehicle to bring about social reform before the rise of professional social workers and well-organized charitable agencies. In America, settlement workers advocated for social reforms and concerned themselves with the material welfare of newly arriving immigrants and their social and cultural assimilation into American life. Chicago's Hull House, founded in 1889 by Jane Addams, is credited with being the prototypical American settlement house.

With money raised through rummage sales, luncheons, vaudeville performances, card parties, and dances, Seattle's NCJW in 1906 opened Settlement House in the lower part of a rented house at 924 Washington Street. "It aims to be a civic center," Mrs. Emar Goldberg, chairman of the Philanthropic Committee, wrote in her first report in 1909. "Whatever the Settlement attempts to do, it must do in answer to a real need of the neighborhood . . . [E]arnest study of the family groups and an endeavor to improve these is the real settlement work."[37]

The first projects, a sewing school for immigrant girls and a free Sabbath school for Jewish children, had a slow start but soon attracted so many new immigrants that in a year Settlement House moved to larger quarters.[38] At the sewing school, Sara Efron recalled, "we were taught every single seam and every single stitch and we had a sampler book . . . everything was done by hand, no sewing machine—we had to make a pair of bloomers which incorporated every stitch. You had to make button holes . . . it [the sewing course] took two years."[39]

Within two years of the founding of Settlement House, the council hired Hannah Schwartz, who had experience in working with immigrant families in San Francisco, and moved to a bigger building at 17th Avenue and Main Street. Schwartz remained for 14 years. Large numbers of Jewish immigrants took advantage of Settlement House's free religious school, sewing school, night school for English instruction, branch library, citizenship classes, free baths (the first in Seattle), funding of a district nurse to visit homes, medical care, and social clubs for young people.

Many of the people who joined in the activities at Settlement House considered it the place to learn how things were being done in America in comparison to the way they lived at home. Indeed, instilling middle-class aspirations was a key element of settlement houses. For example, in addition to celebrating Jewish holidays, such as Hanukkah and Purim, the immigrants were introduced to Halloween and Mother's Day. Schwartz taught the girls how to sit and speak properly and cook American-style. And in order for Settlement House participants to benefit from the current thinking in areas of hygiene and sex, NCJW volunteers attended lectures given by professionals. In 1913 a speaker from the Society of Social and Moral Hygiene lectured the women on "Sex Hygiene"; another spoke on "Protection of Girls."[40]

Some immigrants suspected that the volunteers looked upon their work in Settlement House as a duty to "uplift" the newcomers so their behavior would be less embarrassing to the Jewish community. Most probably felt that statements such as "it is for us who are fortunate in the possession of education—of leisure— of wealth—and of talent—to make ourselves **permanently** useful to our **less** fortunate brethren [bold print in the original]" seemed patronizing.[41] The reaction frequently depended on the individual immigrant's expectations, the personality of the settlement workers, and the quality of the programs.[42] But regardless of what people believed or the fact that some women were indeed patronizing, what is remarkable in retrospect is not the tensions that developed but rather the speed with which the dedicated NCJW members made Settlement House an active, beneficial locale for young and old.

Realizing the need for a larger site to serve immigrants fleeing anti-Semitism in Europe and the devastating destruction of World War I, the Seattle Section raised funds to finance a new and larger facility. Called the Educational Center, the new building opened in 1916 at 304 18th Avenue South with six classrooms, a library, a clubroom with kitchenette, two emergency bedrooms, a medical clinic, and a ballroom with a stage and motion picture gallery.[43] Two big bathtubs, each in its own compartment, a shower, and a steam room made it possible for the center to continue providing free baths. A medical and dental clinic opened in 1925, and just a few years later the center reported that 1,440 treatments had been given to 1,116 children and 325 adults. To manage and supervise programs when Schwartz retired, the NCJW, Seattle Section, in 1920 hired social worker Anna Bragman from Syracuse, New York. She was the center's first professionally trained supervisor.[44] In 1922 the Educational Center became a member of the Community Fund, which subsequently supplied a major source of its income. Rentals to outside groups, memberships, and gifts made up the balance.

Seattle Section's largest program, the funding and management of the Educational Center (Settlement House), moved forward through the Roaring '20s, the Great Depression, and World War II. With so many refugees coming in after World War I, the mainly volunteer staff had much to do. "There is surely no body of women in any organization that has striven with more unity of purpose, thinking only of efficiency and service," said Anna L. Holmes, president of the Educational Center's board.[45]

As people attended the clinics; learned English; signed up for drama, music, art, literature, and dancing classes; attended plays and recitals; and waltzed and fox-trotted in the spacious ballrooms, instructors had to be found and classes scheduled. Funds from the Federal Works Progress Administration paid the salary of out-of-work actors, artists, and musicians who taught at the Center, as did money from the Community Chest (now United Way). In the early years local doctors donated their services, but as the clinics grew, the city paid the doctors' fees and all the supplies. The center's board also contracted with the city to have their adult clients attend English classes at the Washington School while they provided child care. In addition, the entire Jewish community supported the Educational Center, and often committees representing several organizations, such as the Jewish Welfare Society and B'nai B'rith, joined together to raise money.[46]

When the Jewish population in the neighborhood represented a minority of persons using the center, the Educational Center board on January 1, 1948, changed

In 1916, the National Council of Jewish Women, Seattle Section replaced the old Settlement House with a new facility, The Educational Center (pictured here), at 304 18th Avenue South. It had six classrooms, a library, clubroom with kitchenette, two emergency bedrooms, a clinic, and a ballroom with a stage and motion picture gallery. MSCUA, University of Washington Libraries, Jewish History Project, Council of Jewish Women, #3, UW neg. 1556.

the name to Neighborhood House. They also recommended that the center "aim to involve more of the neighborhood people in the administration and responsibility for the Educational Center program."[47] By 1953 the National Council of Jewish Women no longer dominated the Educational Center board.

In addition to helping immigrants at the Educational Center, the Seattle Section worked on the national organization's Port and Dock project. This required women to station themselves at the docks to greet unprotected girls and women, give friendly aid, and if need be find them shelter. It also helped the national organization keep a record of Jewish immigration. Even when the restrictive immigration laws of 1921 and 1924, passed by the U.S. Congress, drastically curtailed Jewish immigration, the council's work with immigrants continued. They advised people on filling out official papers, discovered misplaced relatives, and found housing and work for those who managed to slip in under the quotas.

The Port and Dock Committee again became active in the years before World War II, helping to relocate people escaping from Hitler. "We would have a boat coming in almost every day . . . We had this marvelous committee with Hilda Guthman and Minnie Bernhard . . . I speak German, so I could communicate with them, and I speak a little Yiddish, and some of them spoke a little Yiddish,

Sewing classes at the Settlement House were very popular and seen as a way to learn to be self sufficient and American. MSCUA, University of Washington Libraries, Jewish History Project, Gold, Rita #1, UW neg. 1127.

so that was quite an exciting time and a very busy time [from 1939 to 1941]," said Florence Flaks.[48] Once the people arrived, Seattle Section found them lodging, provided clothes for the children, and generally helped them become acquainted with American life.

Another successful NCJW program, the Vocational Scholarship Program, began in 1922 to provide financial aid to students who would otherwise be forced to drop out of high school and go to work. Though the money was a gift from the Educational Center board, not a loan, many recipients voluntarily repaid and kept the fund solvent. Later the program expanded to include college scholarships.

In 1952, working with the University of Washington Department of Nursing and Jewish Family and Child Service, Seattle's NCJW spearheaded the drive to open a nursery school for immigrant children. The money came from the Bonham Galland Fund, established in 1915 and never before used, as the will stipulated that the money should "remain intact until it amounts to $50,000."[49] At the school, housed at Temple De Hirsch, preschool-age children of Jewish immigrants played and learned with American-born children of all races and religions. Leone (Mrs. Harvard) Kaufman chaired the project, and council members, after receiving 12 hours of training, volunteered to work in the nursery school.[50]

NCJW, Seattle Section, also established the "Council Workshop and Salesroom to provide incoming 'displaced persons' with a shop in which they could be retrained and re-educated," reported the *Jewish Transcript*.[51] The workshop eventually became a thrift shop with a store in the Pike Place Market. And in 1972, in a joint project with the Federal Department of Housing and Urban Development, the organization opened Council House at 1501-17th Avenue, a residential apartment facility for seniors of modest means and younger people who are physically handicapped.

Another program, Shalom Bayit (House of Peace), opened up a warehouse and office to serve domestic violence survivors in the fall of 2000. Here clients have their pick of furniture, kitchenware, linens, and other household items with which to furnish their homes. It is a variation of the "friendly visitor," with a modern twist. Instead of dashing to people's homes with discarded items from their own homes, the Jewish women volunteers have staffed and filled a place with usable items, some used, some new. The clients, all sent by approved agencies, have the freedom to shop for what they need.

## CONCLUSION

Certainly both Jewish Family Service and the National Council of Jewish Women, Seattle Section, can take pride in continually instituting new and better ways to manage their agencies and serve their target clientele. Both provide a case study of how volunteerism works within an ethnic community and clearly show that in order to survive it is important to adjust to innovations within the social network. Reporting that the JFCS board had granted men the privilege of board membership in 1947, president Mary Louise Reiter called it a "worthwhile change." Working with the American Association of Social Work, JFCS formulated new acceptable staff guidelines as well as "providing ways and means for staff members constantly to improve their own professional competency."[52]

Over the years these strong-willed women established varied and extensive programs to relieve human suffering. Until Franklin Roosevelt set up relief programs during the Depression, neither the federal nor state government had the resources or the will to deal with impoverished people, so the dedicated volunteers made a difference. Whether providing a bed to immigrants fleeing their homes simply because they were Jewish or finding funds to pay the rent for unemployed people during the Great Depression, the ability of these philanthropic organizations to shift their focus and accept new challenges made them effective for more than 100 years.

As the women who managed the organizations and implemented the policies learned to deal with budgets, politicians, governments, changing times, and public apathy, they transformed their own lives and the community they served. Taking their place in community organizations such as the National Council of Jewish Women and Jewish Family Service, based on their own talents, not their husbands, and gaining administrative expertise, they had the satisfaction of knowing they could change social policies. Though the volunteers of 1900 could not have imagined the vast number of programs their organizations would manage in the first years of the 21st century, they would have recognized that *tzedakah* is still an agent of change.

## NOTES

Portions of this chapter will appear in *Family of Strangers: Building a Jewish Community in Washington State* (Seattle, Wash.: Washington State Jewish Historical Society in association with University of Washington Press, forthcoming).

[1] C. G. Montefiore and H. Loewe, *A Rabbinic Anthology* (New York: Schocken Books, 1974), 412. See also Ewa Morawska, "Assimilation of Nineteenth-Century Jewish Women," in *Jewish Women in America: An Historical Encyclopedia*, edited by Paula E. Hyman and Deborah Dash Moore, (New York: Routledge, 1998). For explanations about how *tzedakah* has been and is part of Jewish belief, see Charlotte Baum, Paula Hyman, Sonya Michel, *The Jewish Woman in America* (New York: The Dial Press, 1976).

[2] The Ladies' Montefiore Aid Society, organized by Goldie Shucklin and Mrs. J. Friedman around 1895, was made up of Orthodox Jewish women. It is not included in this essay because the organization dissolved a few years after Shucklin's death in 1935. At one time, however, it was one of the largest Jewish organizations in Seattle. In 1911, 250 women belonged.

[3] The *Seattle Daily Times*, 8 November 1910.

[4] Russell Hollander, "Our Brothers' Keepers," *Columbia*, vol. 3 (Spring, 1989), 12–20.

[5] A letter dated July 13, 1908, lists both Leo Kohn and Lizzie Cooper as vice presidents. File 35110, Seattle Municipal Archives.

[6] See Baum et al., *The Jewish Woman in America*, for a discussion of the Jewish organization woman.

[7] The *Seattle Post-Intelligencer*, 12 November 1905, lists a Mr. H. Uhifelder, J. Brunn, and A. J. Brunn as coming in 1868 and David Magnus, Sam Frauenthal, D. Kaufman, Bailey Gatzert, Jacob and Joseph Frauenthal, Simon Davis, and Jac Davis coming in 1869.

[8] Evyatar Friesel, *The Atlas of Modern Jewish History* (New York: Oxford University Press, 1990) reports that in 1880 there were 200 Jews living in Washington Territory, but it is difficult to assess the accuracy as the United States census did not ask for religion. In 1902 the number stood at 2,800, and most lived in Seattle. For more information on the census numbers, see Julie Eulenberg, *Jewish Enterprise in the American West: Washington, 1853–1909*, (Ph.D. dissertation, University of Washington, 1996).

[9] Baum et al., *The Jewish Woman in America*, 30.

[10] "The Temple Tidings," May 1916, Box 13, Temple De Hirsch, Acc. 2370-18, MSCUA, University of Washington Libraries.

[11] Shucklin, the founder of the Ladies' Montefiore Aid Society and a very Orthodox woman, belonged to both the Hebrew Ladies' Benevolent Society and the National Council of Jewish Women. In 1914 the Montefiore Society was a member of Seattle's Central Council of Social Agencies.

[12] Paula E. Hyman, *Gender and Assimilation in Modern Jewish History* (Seattle: University of

Washington Press, 1995), 31.

[13] The goal is stated in the society's first constitution.

[14] Dramatic programs and dances were popular ways of raising money in the 19th and early 20th centuries.

[15] Greengard, who was not a professional social worker, replaced a professional caseworker from New York. The New York woman did not like Seattle and left after a few months.

[16] Transcript of interview, Bernice Degginger Greengard, Acc. 2403-2, MSCUA, University of Washington Libraries.

[17] Prior to becoming executive secretary for the Ladies' Hebrew Benevolent Society, May Goldsmith had worked for 11 years as a "friendly visitor," but she was not a professionally trained social worker.

[18] Historical materials, Jewish Family and Child Service, Box 1/1, Acc. 2003, MSCUA, University of Washington Libraries. The merger became official January 19, 1926. Minutes from 1917 that discussed combining with the men's group have been lost.

[19] Hollander, "Our Brothers' Keepers," 20."

[20] Annual Report of the President, 1928–1929, Jewish Family and Child Service, Box 6/18, Acc. 2003, MSCUA, University of Washington Libraries.

[21] Jewish Family and Child Service.

[22] Jewish Family and Child Service, Minutes, November 20, 1929, Box 6/19.

[23] Jewish Family and Child Service, Ways and Means Committee Report, October 5, 1925, Box 6/18.

[24] Jewish Family and Child Service, Annual Report 1930–1931, Box 6/40.

[25] Jewish Family and Child Service, Annual Report, 1926–1927, Box 6/18.

[26] Jewish Family and Child Service, Report of Executive Secretary, October 18, 1933, Box 6/42.

[27] Jewish Family and Child Service, Annual Report, 1934, Box 6/43.

[28] Jewish Family and Child Service, President's Annual Report, October 20, 1937, Box 7/2.

[29] Jewish Family and Child Service, President's Annual Report, October 20, 1937, Box 7/2.

[30] Jewish Family and Child Service, "History of Jewish Family and Child Service," Box 6/20.

[31] Eugene Levy to William K. Blethen, March 27, 1950, Box 12/4, Cooper-Levy Family, Acc. 2366, MSCUA, University of Washington Libraries.

[32] Cooper-Levy, Eugene Levy to Mrs. Bernard L. Reiter, January 25, 1949.

[33] Baum et al., *The Jewish Woman in America*, 48–49.

[34] Baum, 48–49.

[35] Copy of original minutes, "Temple Tidings" (May 1925), Box 6, Temple De Hirsch-Sinai, Acc. 2370, MSCUA, University of Washington Libraries.

[36] William Toll, *The Making of an Ethnic Middle Class: Portland Jewry Over Four Generations* (Albany: State University of New York Press, 1982), 76.

[37] Report of Committee of Philanthropy, 1909, Box 1/1, National Council of Jewish Women, Seattle Section, Acc. 2089-29, MSCUA, University of Washington Libraries.

[38] "From Settlement House to Neighborhood House, 1906-1976" 5–6, Jean Devine, Acc. 2632-2, MSCUA, University of Washington Libraries.

[39] Transcript of interview, Sara Efron, Acc. 2535, MSCUA, University of Washington Libraries.

[40] 1913–1914 Yearbook, Box 5/7, National Council of Jewish Women, Seattle Section, Acc. 2089-29, MSCUA, University of Washington Libraries.

[41] Efron, Acc. 2535, Abe Hoffman, Acc. 2744, and Sol Esfeld, Acc. 2018-3, are just a few who give their views about Settlement House days, MSCUA, University of Washington Libraries.

[42] See "Settlement Houses," cited in *Jewish Women in America*, 1231–36.

[43] Devine, "From Settlement House to Neighborhood House, 1906-1976" 5–6.

[44] Report of Committee of Philanthropy, 1919–1920, Box 1/1, National Council of Jewish Women, Seattle Section, Acc. 2089-29, MSCUA, University of Washington Libraries.

[45] National Council of Jewish Women, President's Report, Box1/1.

[46] See monthly reports, National Council of Jewish Women, Seattle Section, for detailed reports of activities, located in National Council of Jewish Women, Seattle Section, MSCUA, University of Washington Libraries.

[47] Devine, "From Settlement House to Neighborhood House, 1906–1976," 23–30.

[48] Transcript of interview, Florence Flaks, Acc. 2519; 2519-2, MSCUA, University of Washington Libraries.

[49] Bonham Galland Will, Box 38, Cooper-Levy Family, Acc. 23662, MSCUA, University of Washington Libraries.

[50] Board minutes, August 15, 1951, Box 17/2, National Council of Jewish Women, Seattle Section. The *Seattle Times*, 5 October 1952.

[51] *Jewish Transcript*, Seattle, 18 December 1950.

[52] President's Report, March 29, 1948, Jewish Family and Child Service, Box 4/18.

# BUDDHISM COMES TO SEATTLE

Ronald E. Magden

## INTRODUCTION:
## THE TEMPLE RESOUNDS BOLDLY, STRIIKING NEW HORIZONS

Though the year 2001 marked a full century since the founding of the Seattle Buddhist Mission, the Buddhist presence in the Pacific Northwest has been but a brief interlude in the 2,500-year history of the religion founded by Siddhartha Gautama. Spreading eastward through China and Korea from its birthplace in India, Buddhism reached Japan 1,000 years after the Buddha's time. By the time another 1,400 years had passed, 56 primary Buddhist groups had become integral parts of Japanese culture. Ten of the groups belonged to Jodo Shinshu, the Pure Land branch founded by Shinran Shonin. Nishi and Higashi Hongwanji emerged as the largest of the Jodo Shinshu groups.

One hundred years ago Jodo Shinshu leaders in their headquarters at Nishi Hongwanji, Kyoto, pondered whether to make the next great leap eastward across the vast Pacific Ocean. To investigate the possibilities of extending their teachings to North America, Jodo Shinshu sent the reverends Eryu Honda and Ejun Miyamoto to San Francisco. They arrived July 6, 1898, and in just eight days the two missionaries and 30 *Issei*, first-generation Japanese in America, organized a Young Men's Buddhist Association. The YMBA rented a house to provide a wholesome environment for young immigrants and to serve as a hall where Jodo Shinshu could be presented to the public.[1]

But when Honda and Miyamoto journeyed to Seattle, their reception was much less enthusiastic. Japanese Consul Miki Saito believed the American government would not tolerate the entrance of a foreign religion. Moreover, he feared that the introduction of Buddhism to America would complicate Japanese-American commercial relations. So Honda and Miyamoto made no attempt to start a YMBA in Washington State.[2] But at least one Japanese immigrant would not have been dissuaded by any diplomat's reticence. Jiro Iwamura, already two years in the country, felt a strong obligation to do whatever he could in this new land to honor and observe the teachings of the Buddha.

## THE FOUNDERS

Iwamura was just 23 years old, determined and ambitious, when he stepped off the ship *Annedale* in Seattle on August 22, 1896. He was an adventurous, physically strong, and inwardly spiritual man. He had come to America to earn enough money to go back to Japan and buy farmland. He found work selling rice cakes to fellow countrymen working in Puget Sound logging camps.[3]

Because Seattle had no Buddhist minister, Iwamura took it upon himself to conduct memorial services for Japanese who died from sicknesses or accidents. After performing the tribute he would send a consoling letter and a burial photograph to the bereaved family in Japan. But after two years the task of tending to the spiritual needs of Japanese immigrants threatened to overwhelm him. Iwamura wrote a plaintive letter to the Jodo Shinshu headquarters at Nishi Hongwanji, asking that a missionary be sent to Seattle. The events he set in motion with that letter constitute the beginning of the Buddhist missionary era in the Pacific Northwest. Nishi Hongwanji did not respond as Iwamura had hoped. Instead, it sent ministers to San Francisco to help the YMBA there expand its services to new arrivals from Japan.[4]

During the summer of 1900 Nishi Hongwanji dispatched an unofficial minister to assess the situation in western Washington. The Reverend Shodo Hatano toiled alongside cannery workers in Blaine, Washington, awaiting the end of the salmon-processing season before moving to Seattle. One of Hatano's coworkers, Tatsujiro Akiyoshi, gave a firsthand account of Hatano's intent in his memoirs:

> There were about fifty Japanese with me. One of them was a Mr. Hatano from Yokohama, and he was in reality an ordained priest of Buddhism. He was my roommate in the camp at the cannery. One night he told me, "Akiyoshi-san, what do you think of the idea of starting a Buddhist Church in Seattle when we get back there?" I thought the idea was great, and I told him so.[5]

After the salmon season, Akiyoshi and Hatano traveled to Seattle's Skid Road. Here they gathered signatures in support of a Buddhist mission. In Nihonmachi (Japantown), Akiyoshi and Hatano met Jiro Iwamura. These three recruited six young entrepreneurs: Chojiro Fujii, Mataichi Kinomoto, Yasutaro Masuda, Konai Miyamoto, Ushitaro Ota, and Toyojiro Otani. All nine were in their 20s; only Ota and Miyamoto were married. Akiyoshi, Hatano, and Otani worked as day laborers. Fujii and Ota were hoteliers, Masuda owned a restaurant, Miyamoto operated a bamboo-furniture store, and Kinomoto managed a confectionery. By this time Iwamura had switched jobs from selling rice cakes to owning a curio store in Seattle. The predominance of businessmen in this group established a pattern that continues to the present.

In February 1901 the nine founders sent a petition with 48 signatures to Kyoto asking that a permanent minister be sent to Seattle as soon as possible.[6] On November 1, 1901, the Reverend Kakuryo Nishijima, the cofounder of the San Francisco Buddhist Mission, came to Seattle to establish a YMBA branch. The Jodo Shinshu missionary knew there were co-religionists residing in and around Seattle who would help spread "the wonderful mysteries of Buddha."[7] The Seattle church would be the fourth Buddhist mission established by Nishijima since he had arrived in the United States. Nishijima spent his evenings in a room above Matajiro Tsukuno's Chinese noodle shop, conferring with the nine founders. They wasted little time. On November 15 this small group adopted a constitution, established bylaws, and elected officers. Toyojiro Otani was installed as acting YMBA president and Jiro Iwamura as secretary-treasurer. Chojiro Fujii, Mataichi Kinomoto, the Masuda brothers, and Konai Miyamoto were on the board of directors. During the next four weeks Nishijima accompanied the founders to the shops of local merchants, soliciting financial pledges for the support of a mission house and dormitory.[8]

On December 15, 1901, Nishijima presided over the first general session of the Seattle YMBA. The Jodo Shinshu minister announced that Shodo Hatano would serve as the acting director of the mission. During that same meeting more than 200 Issei signed financial pledges to support the proposed mission house, dormitory, and social center. Akiyoshi described the mood:

> Needless to say, our first meeting was a tremendous success. Everyone was enthusiastic. It was decided we would meet regularly on the second floor above the noodle shop on the corner of Main and Maynard.[9]

Hatano and Iwamura quickly rented a modest two-story frame house at 624 Main Street for $50 a month. It was conveniently located in the heart of Nihonmachi, but from the beginning the converted dwelling was inadequate. Upstairs, dormitory manager Iwamura strove to maintain "good conduct" in three rooms stuffed with 30 rack beds. Downstairs, Hatano delivered sermons in a small, bare living room used as the *Hondo* (worship hall). On three walls an artist member painted lotuses. On the fourth wall Hatano hung a picture scroll inscribed with the six characters that spelled out *Namo Amida Butsu* ("I take refuge in the Amida Buddha"). The cramped facilities spurred the membership to dream of something larger.[10]

Shodo Hatano, the acting mission director, adopted the Christian Sunday as the religious observance day. But to accommodate Issei merchants who closed their stores at 7:30 P.M., he delivered the *Bukkyo Kowa* (sermon) at 8 P.M. instead of 11 A.M. as the Christian churches did. The *Sangha* (congregation) began each service with the chanting of the *Shoshinge* sutra (The Hymn of Faith). Hatano also instituted *Doyo Kai*, the Saturday Club, which met once a month at 8:30 P.M. Members discussed the principles of Pure Land Buddhism, then reviewed current events. After several members gave self-improvement speeches, the agenda turned to en-

The original home of Buddhist services in Seattle, located in the heart of Nihonmachi, at 624 Main Street. The worship hall was on the main floor while dorm rooms upstairs housed 30 men. Courtesy of the Seattle Buddhist Temple.

tertainment. Members told jokes to vigorous applause from their peers. Others recited poems or sang old songs. Throughout the proceedings the men helped themselves to tea and confections.[11]

Seattle's first resident Buddhist missionary, the Reverend Gendo Nakai, arrived on July 2, 1902. A new graduate of the Buddhist University in Tokyo, the 28-year-old Nakai possessed "the character of uprightness and enthusiasm," though he suffered from constant head colds.[12] He could see substantial potential for growth. Two years before Nakai arrived, the federal census enumerators had counted 2,990 Japanese living in Seattle. Four huge hotels on Jackson Street sheltered 2,430 Issei railroad and sawmill workers. The remainder, scattered over 31 blocks south of Yesler Way in the area known as Chinatown, were an assortment of merchants and their wives, day laborers, gamblers, and prostitutes.[13] Between 1887 and 1902, the number of Japanese restaurants and hotels operating in Chinatown mushroomed from two to 162.[14] Japanese immigrants shared the district with hundreds of Black, Chinese, Greek, Italian, Russian, and Finnish bachelors.[15]

This diverse populace acquired a colorful reputation, given leeway by the inaction of Seattle police, who allowed opium dens, rough-hewn taverns, and houses of prostitution to operate brazenly day and night. For the Japanese community, that meant gang leaders such as George Gonda had a free hand. During the first decade of the 20th century, Gonda and his underlings extorted at will from drug peddlers, prostitutes, and honest merchants alike.[16]

Tatsujiro Akiyoshi, a YMBA founder, mounted an opposition to Gonda's depredations, as well as to the proliferation of saloons and prostitution houses. Akiyoshi was secretary of the anti-crime Humane Society, formed in 1907. The wider Japanese community—Baptist, Buddhist, Congregational, Methodist, and YMCA congregations, as well as businessmen in the newly formed Nihonjinkai (Seattle Japanese Association)—took to the streets in what then seemed a hopeless effort to dissuade sawmill hands and railroad section workers from "undesirable moral development." The religious groups wanted to offer wholesome alternatives, but their dormitories accommodated only 300, leaving approximately 2,100 men easy prey to the "dens of iniquity."[17]

From the day that he arrived until the day he left, Nakai was intensely active spiritually. His saddest duty was to preside over hundreds of Issei memorial services. Many were killed on the job, died from epidemics, or passed away during childbirth. The Japanese death rate in Seattle averaged 26 per 1,000 every year from 1903 through 1907.[18] Two doctors, Masahige Matsura and Naotoshi Fujimori, attended the townspeople.[19] No matter where a Buddhist immigrant expired—Idaho, Montana, British Columbia, Oregon, or Washington—Nakai went there to perform services. Once a year the Buddhist missionary and members of the Sangha made the rounds of Puget Sound cemeteries to perform memorial services and clean the grave-sites.[20]

Nakai's missionary effort into King County began in the White River Valley during 1902. He established *Howakai* (private home gatherings) in Kent, Orillia, O'Brien, and Thomas, towns in south King County. In 1900 there were 187 field hands, as well as a dozen prosperous Issei who rented land in the valley for dairies and vegetable farms.[21]

There was a great demand for English lessons when the Buddhist missionary visited the villages of Nagaya and Yama on Bainbridge Island on January 18, 1903. Japanese immigrants had been working as lumber handlers at the island's Port Blakely Mill Company since 1882. Nakai was surprised to find that 28 Japanese families lived there and that they had erected a recreational hall. After conducting the dedication of a *Nyubutsushiki* (Buddhist shrine), the Sangha asked Nakai to look for a bilingual teacher in Seattle. On Nakai's monthly visit to Bainbridge Island he carried English dictionaries and elementary readers.[22]

Nakai's greatest missionary success occurred in Oregon. On August 10, 1903, he traveled to Portland to give a Dharma talk (the teachings of the Buddha). After listening to Nakai, local Buddhists transformed a rented storefront overnight into the sixth Buddhist mission on the Pacific Coast. The first act of the Portland YMBA was to send a formal request to Bishop Kentoku Hori in San Francisco for a full-time missionary. Three months later the Reverend Shozui Wakabayashi was installed by Nakai as Portland's first Buddhist minister.[23]

In Seattle, Nakai found that he could operate an educational program with little overt opposition from the Caucasian community or city officials. He was able to do what he liked most: teach English to Japanese schoolboys in the afternoon and older immigrants in the night school. The education program was formalized on January 18, 1903, with the hiring of Selma Anderson. Born in Norway and educated in the eastern United States, she was fluent in six Asian and European languages. Anderson had taught English to Chinese and Japanese immigrants in a Portland Methodist church for two years before moving to Seattle. She had intended to convert her students to Christianity, but the peace of mind exhibited by students moved her to adopt Buddhism. A reporter once asked how she would answer the question, "Which one is the right faith?" She responded:

> When the question is put to me in that manner, I never say that one faith is superior to another. I would first teach them to be pure and clean. When they attain to that state they may select their own religion without danger of making an error.[24]

For his part Nakai emphasized in his monthly newsletter, *The Teachings of Buddha*, that history proved Christianity and Buddhism were compatible. For 1,900 years people of the two religions had exchanged ideas in ancient Persia as they traded with each other. The spirit of that religious exchange continued in full flower as the 20th century began:

> In recent years commerce and trade between the United States and our country have flourished. Seattle has made giant strides and is prospering as a center of trade . . . Especially now that the Orient has become peaceful, it is our national destiny that more and more people should emigrate and it is clearer than anything that this area is ideal as a colony for our countrymen.[25]

## THE CAMPAIGN TO BUILD A BUDDHIST TEMPLE

For two years and five days the dream of dedicating a Seattle mission building lay dormant, until December 20, 1903. On that auspicious day, the Reverend Nakai met with Seattle's two most prosperous Issei merchants, Masajiro Furuya and Kuranosuke Hirade. Accompanying the Buddhist minister were YMBA founders and members of the newly formed Building Committee, Chojiro Fujii, Jiro Iwamura, Yasutaro Masuda, Ushitaro Ota, and Toyojiro Otani. Four new YMBA members, businessmen Tomejiro Kaneko, "Joe" Kawano, Shu Sakamoto and Sensuke Shimomura, attended as alternate committee members. Nakai conducted a short service. Then the group discussed how to raise enough money to purchase land and erect a Jodo Shinshu mission and dormitory. All except Hirade agreed to serve on a fund-raising committee, with Yasutaro Masuda taking Hirade's place. Committee members set a goal of $10,000 to pay for the land and to construct the mission complex.[26] Three months later the YMBA membership authorized the formation of a Construction Committee. Masajiro Furuya, Toyojiro Otani, and Ushitaro Ota explored possible sites south of Yesler Way.

The outbreak of the war between Japan and Russia on February 8, 1904, forced postponement of the campaign to fund the mission. The merchants bought Imperial war bonds, donated cash to the Japanese Red Cross, and paid ship passage for young Issei called home to serve in the Imperial Army or Navy.[27] The Imperial Army drafted six YMBA members, including Jiro Iwamura. Following the Sunday sermon on October 9, 1904, there was a send-off party. [28]

Nakai thanked the six draftees for going to war to serve their homeland and expressed his devout wish that they would survive the struggle. One by one, the other YMBA members said goodbye to the draftees. Speaking on behalf of the conscripted, Iwamura said they had served in the military before and would do so again for Japan. Following Iwamura's speech, everyone stood and sang the Japanese national anthem, *Kimigayo*. J. Matsumi led banzai cheers for the emperor, the army, the navy, and the draftees. Iwamura offered banzai cheers for the Seattle Buddhist Mission. There was thunderous applause for the six war-heroes-to-be.[29]

Jiro Iwamura was embarrassed by being treated as a war hero before he had even boarded the ship to Japan. In Korea, Iwamura served in a reserve battalion behind the front lines. He wrote to the Seattle mission that he was "especially sorry" that he had not seen combat. Iwamura declared there was no need to give him a hero's welcome on his return to Seattle.[30] After the war ended on May 28, 1905, Iwamura stayed in Japan to court Chiyo, the woman who became his wife. In so doing, he missed the greatest Nihonmachi celebration in Seattle's history. Three thousand Seattle Japanese greeted Baron Jutaro Komura, the Japanese minister of foreign affairs, as he passed through Seattle on his way to the 1905 peace conference in Portsmouth, New Hampshire.[31]

In the days following the Portsmouth peace conference, Nakai and the solicitation committee renewed their campaign to erect a mission. The head minister turned over the afternoon English language sessions to Selma Anderson so that he could spend more time calling on Japanese workers in outlying areas.[32] Auburn, Fife, and Tacoma residents responded with donations ranging from $10 to $100. In Dawson City, Northwest Territories, Canada, Hisataro Kobayashi collected and sent $100. Seitaro Nonaka canvassed mill workers in Mukilteo and Shoichi Kawano solicited at Bellingham canneries. Small individual donations came from Startup, Skykomish, and Leavenworth.[33] By May 1, 1906, more than 400 subscriptions totaling $2,789 had been received for constructing the Seattle Buddhist Mission.[34]

As the money started coming in, the Reverend Nakai, hotelier Chojiro Fujii, and Selma Anderson met in the Mutual Life Building in Seattle to incorporate the Buddhist Mission Society. Charles P. Rowland provided legal advice. Rowland, a multi-talented attorney and carpenter, helped many immigrant groups over the years construct both the legal foundations and physical walls of community organizations. The Buddhist Mission Society was the first corporation ever organized on the West Coast for the purpose of founding Buddhist churches. For years Rowland had been the middleman in arranging leases for Japanese businessmen with downtown banks and mortgage companies. According to the articles of incorporation, the society's purpose was "to purchase, hold, mortgage, sell and convey real estate and personal property." Since Washington statutes forbade Japanese aliens from being the majority stockholders of an incorporated company, Rowland and Anderson held 120 shares worth $6,000. Nakai and Fujii owned 80 shares worth $4,000. The term of existence of the society was set at 50 years. Nakai was elected president and treasurer, Anderson vice-president, and Fujii secretary.[35]

## THE NEW CHURCH BECOMES A REALITY

The week after incorporation papers were filed on January 27, 1906, Toyojiro Otani, director of the construction committee, announced to the YMBA membership that his group had found a large vacant lot at 10th Avenue South and South Main Street priced at $4,500. The site was four blocks east of the center of Nihonmachi. The owner, William Holt, still owed $2,450. YMBA members agreed to assume Holt's mortgage and buy out his equity.[36] Seattle architects Saunders & Lawton entered a $280 contract to design a two-story building, 56 feet by 78 feet.[37]

The main floor would hold the minister's office, the Hondo, the library, and classrooms. On the second floor would be a 40-bed dormitory, four bathrooms, additional classroom space, and meeting rooms. The daylight basement would be divided into a kitchen, dining room, auditorium-gymnasium, and classrooms. Over the front entrance to the building, Saunders & Lawton conceived a sweeping Oriental arch supported by two large columns. The architects estimated the construction cost at $9,760.[38] Rowland signed a contract with the Buddhist Mission Society to supervise the building of the mission for 10 percent of the total cost of the labor, material, and fixtures.[39]

During a series of ceremonies in the spring of 1907, the solicitation committee collected enough cash and pledges to raise the building fund to $15,000. Benefactors were accorded "special status" for visits to the interior of the Kyoto Nishi Hongwanji temple.[40] Upon the assurance of the solicitation committee that its members could raise an additional $5,000, the construction committee directed the architects to finish the daylight basement with plastered partitions and bathroom facilities to accommodate 17 people.[41]

Sadly, Nakai, who had been suffering for months from chest colds, developed a serious eye infection. The Seattle Buddhist minister applied for and was granted an extended leave of absence. He returned to Japan for medical treatment on October 29, 1907. Doctors saved Nakai's vision, but his chest troubles continued. Assistant minister Ehan Fujiyeda took over the head minister's duties until the Nishi Hongwanji could dispatch Nakai's replacement.[42]

Although Nakai had labored to the point of exhaustion, many of his goals were

Buddhist ministers and supporters used Seattle as a base from which to serve Japanese American Buddhists throughout the Northwest. Courtesy of the Seattle Buddhist Temple.

unmet. The mission building was not finished. And he was frustrated in his efforts to organize a women's association, a Seattle *Fujinkai*. When the first minister asked all of the wives to meet, only the elderly Ichi Deguchi, Mary Hasegawa, Chiyo Iwami, and Momo Kawamura had responded. The four women faithfully spent hours preparing the weekly decorations and offerings for the front of the shrine.[43] And they frequently accompanied Nakai to hospitals to visit the sick.[44] Over time, other married women with children, notably Kana Fujii, Retsu Hotta, Chiyo Iwamura, Yoshiye Kinomoto, and Chiyo Shimomura, joined in working at the shrine.[45]

*Kaikyoshi* (missionary) Hoshin Fujii arrived in Seattle on May 28, 1908. The 30-year-old graduate of Takanawa Buddhist University was strong and energetic, spoke and wrote English fluently, and enjoyed teaching and working with people.[46] The Reverend Fujii would need all of these attributes because he faced incredible challenges. Delegations from two Buddhist colonies, one south of Seattle in the White River Valley and the other in Vancouver, British Columbia, called on him during his first week to ask for immediate help in raising funds to construct missions. Spokane, Pasco, and Yakima petitioners asked him to convey to the Nishi Hongwanji their urgent need for missionaries. Fujii also would have to teach the Dharma at a dozen private home gatherings in isolated areas around the state.[47]

Those demands became even more pressing when assistant minister Ehan Fujiyeda returned to Kyoto three days after Fujii arrived in Seattle. For the next four years Fujii was the only Buddhist clergyman to care for the religious welfare of about 2,000 active Buddhists in Washington State and British Columbia.[48]

As Fujii's Seattle ministry began, the nine wives who cared for the shrine formed a *Fujinbu* (women's section). Mesdames Fujii, Iwamura, and Kinomoto were the wives of YMBA founders. Mesdames Deguchi, Hasegawa, Hotta, Iwami, Kawamura, and Shimomura's husbands had joined the mission shortly after its establishment.[49] Fujii helped the Seattle Fujinbu write the request to Nishi Hongwanji asking for formal recognition. On August 22, 1908, the Fujinbu, which had been renamed the Fujinkai (Women's Association), received the *Obutsudan* (altar box containing a statue of the Buddha) from the *honzan* (mother temple) in Kyoto, Japan.[50]

Since 1903, more than 1,000 Issei had been settling annually in the Queen City, making it the largest Japanese population center in the Pacific Northwest. In the prosperous sections of both Main and Jackson streets, the number of businesses had nearly doubled in five years, from 223 in 1903 to 431 in 1908.[51] By mid-1910 the shops served 4,982 Issei bachelors, 409 couples, and 327 Nisei children. There now were 12 doctors along with four midwives, signaling that Nihonmachi was well under way in its transformation from a society of migratory single men to a stable community of families.[52]

After February 1908, the Japanese immigration wave ebbed as a result of the so-called Gentlemen's Agreement. In an exchange of diplomatic notes with the United States, Japan had agreed to voluntarily cease issuing passports to workers. Wives, students, and ministers would, as in the past, be allowed to immigrate.[53]

The Gentlemen's Agreement accelerated the number of "picture brides" disembarking at Washington State ports. During the Reverend Nakai's five years in Seattle he conducted 190 Buddhist weddings. During the Reverend Fujii's 14-year ministry he officiated at the weddings of more than 700 picture brides,[54] 195 of them in 1910 alone.[55]

Fujii's appointment books indicate he limited the amount of time spent on weddings. If there were more than two couples on a particular boat, the Buddhist minister took the brides and grooms to the ship's dining room or the U. S. Immigration Office for a group ceremony. In fact, from the beginning of his stay in Seattle he put the completion of the Seattle temple at the top of his responsibilities.[56] Little construction work on the new temple had been accomplished since Nakai had left. The $5,000 that had been pledged to finish the temple had not been collected. Fujii called on "100 valiant" members of the Sangha to help him complete the task. Over a period of four months the group gathered the $5,000. Construction resumed.[57]

On October 1, 1908, Reverend Fujii informed contract supervisor Rowland that the first and second floors of the new Seattle Buddhist Temple building had been completed to his satisfaction. Schoolboys moved into the new dormitory on the second floor and Fujii occupied quarters on the first floor. The Seattle Japanese Language School, which inculcated the mother tongue in the Nisei, moved into the new classrooms with the understanding that it would eventually construct its own building.[58]

The *Ijikai* (the temple board of directors) asked Fujii to schedule the formal dedication of the new building for Sunday, November 15, 1908, to commemorate the meeting exactly seven years before in Tsukuno's noodle shop. The new minister readily agreed to hold the dedication on founders' day.[59] He also announced that when he was leaving Japan in 1908, his friend and fellow minister Shaku Daishin had entrusted him with a very old statue of the baby Buddha, a gift to be placed in the *butsudan* (altar box) of the new temple. In his letter of conveyance, Daishin wrote:

> I hear that Buddhism has spread on the West Coast of the United States.
> Seattle has the strongest mission, and it is flourishing very vigorously. This
> reflects the trend of Buddhism to advance Eastward filling up America
> and then crossing the Atlantic Ocean.[60]

When dedication day dawned, Buddhist ministers Hoshin Fujii, Senju S. Sasaki of Vancouver, British Columbia, and Shozui Wakabayashi of Portland, Oregon, carried the gift of Shaku Daishin the four blocks from the old mission to the new temple. In front of and behind the ministers was an *ochigo* (a procession of children dressed as heavenly beings). In the Hondo the Women's Association had lit candles encased in lanterns that burned before a painting of Buddha. Large Japanese and U.S. flags were prominently displayed on both sides of the main hall. The women had also placed offerings of fruit and confections on the sides of the shrine. Garlands of ivy and chrysanthemums decorated the halls.'[61]

As the ministers placed the ancient Amida statue in the butsudan, the Sangha sang praises of the Buddha. Jiro Iwamura spoke for the seven founders who had lived long enough to see their dream come true.[62] There was ample evidence in the dedication proceedings of the Japanese community's eagerness to cement its connection to its adopted home. In his congratulatory address, the Reverend Fujii praised Issei success in building a new community that had adapted to American culture. Consul General Tokichi Tanaka spoke of Nihonmachi enhancing economic cooperation between Japan and America. The Sangha ended the program by offering incense. Afterward young Japanese girls served tea and cake to the hundreds of participants and visitors.[63]

Dormitory director Jiro Imada translated the entire dedication proceedings into English for the benefit of honored Caucasian women guests. The Seattle Japanese newspaper, *North American Times*, praised the women as "the flowers of gold who graced the occasion." For months these friends of Selma Anderson had voluntarily taught Issei women about buying groceries, clothes, and household items. As the months passed, the volunteers introduced the Issei wives to the complexities of childrearing in America.[64] The Reverend Fujii acknowledged later the role of Caucasian women in the development of the Japanese-American family:

Once a month at a meeting in the temple addresses of interest to the women are delivered. Last week a Seattle woman spoke on the subject of the care of babies in this country, and the means of preventing the large mortality among Japanese infants born in this city.[65]

The dedication of the Buddhist Temple marked the end of the missionary era in Seattle. On that special day, November 15, the official name of the church was changed from the Seattle Buddhist Mission to the Seattle Temple Branch of the Nishi Hongwanji.[66] Its new role was to pursue the development of missions in the hinterland. Nakai and Fujii had started the process, but after 1908 that would be the Seattle Temple Branch's major outreach objective.

## EXPANSION OF BUDDHISM

Ten years after Consul Miki Saito had declared Buddhism would never flourish in the Pacific Northwest, Portland and Seattle had established permanent temples with Japanese language schools for children and night English classes for adults. Seattle alone had more than 500 members in the Sangha. Moreover, Seattle ministers had developed, with the assistance of strong local leadership, Jodo Shinshu howakai everywhere in Washington State. In King and Kitsap counties, regular gatherings took place in private homes in Bellevue, Seattle's Green Lake and South Park neighborhoods, Port Blakely, and Winslow. South of Seattle howakai were held in Auburn, Kent, and small villages such as Christopher, O'Brien, Orillia and Thomas that disappeared during World War II. Although great rivalry existed between Tacoma townspeople and Pierce County farmers, they banded together to meet the Reverend Hoshin Fujii monthly in Soroku Kuramoto's grocery store in Fife. In central Washington, Pasco, Toppenish, Wapato, Yakima, and Spokane howakai were started by Seattle ministers Hoshin Fujii and Chosui Ike.[67]

From the beginning many areas where howakai met sought mission status so that they could have their own minister. In 1912 the Auburn, Christopher, Kent, Orillia, and Thomas Howakai merged into one Sangha. A building in Thomas was converted into a mission and language school. The Reverend Kozen Morita, who had transferred from the Seattle temple, was the first resident minister. On March 18, 1918, the White River Mission became a temple.[68] When Tacoma and Pierce County Buddhists outgrew Kuramoto's grocery store in 1918, the Sangha rented a large corner room in the Columbus Hotel in downtown Tacoma. The Reverend Danryo Motodani moved from Seattle to become its first minister.[69] In 1920 the Seattle Buddhist Church sent the Reverend Chosui Ike to assist the Yakima, Toppenish, and Wapato howakai. On May 16, 1928, the Reverend Ryujo Nagoya was transferred from Korea to serve as the first minister of the Yakima Buddhist Church.[70] The Reverend Eiyu Terao, who had served in Seattle before World War II, opened the Spokane mission in 1946.[71-]

The Seattle Buddhist Temple today at 1427 Main Street. Courtesy of the Seattle Buddhist Temple.

While the Buddhist outreach program was making steady progress, the young members of the Seattle Sangha were organized into youth groups. Fujii created the first Dharma School for elementary school children in 1912. The youngsters who attended Dharma School learned the basic teachings of the Buddha. At the age of 15 the boys and girls became members of the Lotus *Seinenkai*, the young Buddhist association. Lotus held oratorical contests, fielded sports teams, and offered annual entertainment programs that were renowned throughout Nihonmachi.[72] In 1932 Lotus boy and girl presidents Masasru Kumata and Kimi Tai invited youths from Portland, Tacoma, White River, and Yakima to Seattle to form the Northwest Young Buddhist Federation (NYBF).[73] At annual sessions the NYBF discussed Buddhism, held oratorical and sports contests, and sponsored roundtable discussions on Nisei problems. One NYBF president, Masaru Harada, participated in the creation of a national Buddhist movement among West Coast Nisei.[74]

All of the efforts of the ministers, Ijikai, Fujinkai, and Lotus Seinenkai to expand Buddhism received a severe shock on December 7, 1941. Fourteen of the leaders of the Seattle Ijikai were arrested and lodged in the Immigration Building on the afternoon of December 7.[75] Two subsequent arrest waves practically destroyed the Seattle Buddhist Church's board of directors. In April the Japanese-born ministers in Seattle, Tacoma, White River, and Yakima were taken into custody and evacuated to Missoula, Montana. Finally, during May 1942, all of Seattle's Japanese were interned at the Puyallup Assembly Center. But even under such adverse circumstances, Buddhism continued to be practiced by 1,409 displaced Seattle Buddhists.[76] After the war, 938 eventually returned to Seattle.[77] Most of those who did not come back were in their 20s. They had left camp for jobs or further education in the Midwest and East Coast or had enlisted in the Army.[78]

The story of the rebirth of the Seattle Buddhist Church is testimony to the resolve of the returnees and the leadership of Reverend Tatsuya Ichikawa. In 1945 it would have been hard to imagine that within 10 years the Seattle Buddhist Church would celebrate a golden age, but such was the case. On November 14, 1954, Nishi Hongwanji in Kyoto, Japan, elevated the Seattle Buddhist Church to *Betsuin* (special church) status and Reverend Tatsuya Ichikawa was accorded the title *Rinban* (honorific title). The prewar organizational structure had been rebuilt: The Dharma School for the preteens, the Young Buddhist Association for the teenagers, the Lotus *Shoyukai* for the young marrieds, the Fujinkai for the first generation women, and the *Gojikai* for the Issei men.[79] The new Lotus Central Religious Committee translated curriculum materials into the English language for Dharma schools throughout the nation. The Bon Odori celebration every July became a major all-Seattle event when the Betsuin joined with the annual Seattle Seafair festival.[80]

When Reverend Tatsuya Ichikawa retired after a brilliant career as Rinban in 1959, he was succeeded by Reverend Kenryo Kumata, who had been born and raised in Seattle. The appointment of Kumata was tacit recognition that control of the Church had passed from the Issei into the hands of the Nisei. Today, one hundred years after the founding of the Seattle Buddhist Mission, the third-generation *Sansei* are coming of age. Similar to the Issei who founded the Seattle YMBA in November 1901, and the Nisei who managed the Church for the past 40 years, the Sansei will carry on the objective of "experiencing and spreading the wonderful mysteries of Buddha."[81] The dream of the founders of Buddhism in Seattle that their religion would find a permanent home has been realized.

## NOTES

[1] *Buddhist Churches of America, 75-Year History 1899–1974*, Ryo Munekata, editor (Nobart, Inc. Publishers, 1974), vol. 1, 45. The main source for information on early Buddhist history in America is Kakuryo Nishijima, editor, *The Light of Dharma, A Religious Magazine Devoted to the Teachings of Buddha* (San Francisco: Buddhist Mission, April 1901–August 1906). For information on early Puget Sound–area Buddhist history, see Gendo Nakai, editor, *The Teachings of Buddha* (Seattle: Y.M.B.A., January 1906–September 1927), translated by John E. Hodge. A standard secondary account for American Buddhist history is Rick Fields, *How the Swans Came to the Lake: A Narrative History of Buddhism in America*, 3rd ed. (Boston and London: Shambhala, 1992), hereafter cited as Fields. All of the documents and interviews included in this essay have been deposited in the Seattle Buddhist Church archives. Sadie Yamasaki is the president of the Archives Committee and Ellen Hale is the

chief archivist. This article, "Buddhism Comes to Seattle," is based on *Mukashi Mukashi (Long, Long Ago)*, a Seattle Buddhist Archives book project that tells the 100-year history of the Seattle Buddhist Church. Ronald Magden is the author. The King County Landmarks & Heritage Commission and the Kawabe Foundation are partially funding the project.

[2] Fields, 143.

[3] For information on the life of Jiro Iwamura, see interview by Ellen Hale of Katsuzo Iwamura, on 4 February 1991, hereafter cited as K. Iwamura. Katsuzo was the son of Jiro Iwamura. Also see interview by Ronald E. Magden of Yoshiye Iwamura, 10 January 2000. Yoshiye Iwamura was the wife of Katsuzo.

[4] K. Iwamura.

[5] Rihei Akiyoshi, "My Life Story," interview by Takaye Tsurui, *Asian Resources*, vol. 1, No. 2, 1974, 27, hereafter cited as Akiyoshi.

[6] Akiyoshi, 27–28. Peggy M. Kinomoto Mitchell, interview by the Seattle Buddhist Church Archive Committee, 9 July 1990.

[7] Nakai, January 1906, 4.

[8] Nishijima, February 1902, 28. Anonymous, *Brief History of the Seattle Buddhist Church 1901–1951*, 1–2. Fields, 143-45.

[9] Akiyoshi, 28. Nishijima, June 1902, 73.

[10] Hokubei Kaikyo Enkakusha, *North American Mission History* (Seattle 1933), 5. Hereafter cited as Hokubei.

[11] Nakai, January 1906.

[12] Nishijima, August 1902, 108.

[13] Twelfth Census of the United States, Part of Seattle City, April 1910. Hereafter cited as 1910 Federal Census.

[14] *Seattle City Directory*, 1887. *Seattle City Directory*, 1902. Kazuo Ito, *Issei: A History of Japanese Immigrants to the United States, Section on Maps of Old Japanese Districts. Seattle, Washington*, translated by Shinichiro Nakamura and Jean S. Gerard. Hereafter cited as Ito. Yoshito Fujii, "Study of the Early Japanese Immigrants of the Seattle Area, Their Organizations and Businesses, 1890–1930." Subtitled section on "Successful, Outstanding Leaders in Seattle before 1905." Hereafter cited as Y. Fujii.

[15] 1910 Federal Census.

[16] *Seattle Times*, 9, 14, 17, 27, and 30 September 1902; 30 May and 11 September 1903; and 9 March 1904. Hereafter cited as *ST*. All newspaper citations are courtesy of John R. Litz.

[17] *ST*, 5 December 1907.

[18] John R. Litz, "Japanese Deaths Reported to King County Washington Health Department 1889–1907." John R. Litz, Publisher, 1999.

[19] Y. Fujii.

[20] *Seattle Betsuin 75th Anniversary 1901–1976*, 21. History Committee, Seattle Betsuin, 1976.

[21] 1900 Federal Census.

[22] Hokubei, 3. 1910 Federal Census. Andrew Price, Jr., *Port Blakely: The Community Captain Renton Built* (Port Blakely Books, 1989), 130–43.

[23] Jack Ouchida, *A History of Eighty Years of the Oregon Buddhist Church 1903–1983*, Oregon Buddhist Society, 1983. 19. Courtesy of Albert Abe.

[24] *Seattle Post-Intelligencer*, 29 March 1908. Hereafter cited as *PI*.

[25] Nakai, January 1906. Reverend Nakai delivered a revised version of the speech, "The Christianized Life of the Buddha," on 11 August 1906, to the Saturday Club.

26 Old Buddhist Mission Society Corporation Record Book, 20 December 1903. Hereafter cited as BMS Record Book. Also see *Seattle Post-Intelligencer*, 9 November 1905.

27 Nakai, May 1904.

28 Nakai, November 1904.

29 Nakai, November 1904.

30 Jiro Iwamura, "Letter from Japan after the Japanese-Russian War" in Nakai, March 1906.

31 *ST,* 9 July 1905.

32 Nakai, March 1906.

33 Nakai, March 1906.

34 Nakai, June 1906.

35 BMS, 27 January 1906.

36 BMS, Warranty Deed No. 379213.

37 BMS, 10 February 1908, trustee meeting minutes.

38 Saunders & Lawton, "Specification for A Two-Story and Basement Frame Building to be Erected at 1018 Main Street, Seattle, Washington, for the Buddhist Mission Society" (undated). Hereafter cited as Saunders & Lawton.

39 BMS Record Book, Contract between the Buddhist Mission Society and Charles P. Rowland, 1 October 1907.

40 Nakai, May 1906

41 Saunders & Lawton, Addendum

42 *Seattle Betsuin 75th Anniversary 1901-1976*, 23.

43 Nakai, May 1906.

44 Nakai, July 1906.

45 Nakai, May 1906.

46 *PI*, 13 June 1909.

47 Hoshin Fujii, 1908 appointment book.

48 Hokubei, 7.

49 Hokubei, 5.

50 Hokubei, 5

51 Japanese Association of the Pacific Northwest, *Japanese Immigration: An Exposition of Its Real Status*, 5–9.

52 1910 Federal Census.

53 *U. S. Foreign Relations*, 2 (1924): 338–73.

54 John R. Litz, "Index to Marriage Register, Volumes I–VII, 3 March 1889 to June 30, 1920 (King County), Japanese Names," John Litz, Publisher, 2000. Hereafter cited as Marriage Index.

55 Marriage Index.

56 Hoshin Fujii, 1908 appointment book.

57 Anonymous, An Outline of the Development of the Church. 2.

58 BMS, 1 October 1908.

59 Hoshin Fujii, 1908 appointment book.

60 1907 statement of donation to Seattle Buddhist Temple, one bronze statue, by Shaku Daishin.This letter is filed in the Seattle Buddhist Archives File Cabinet A.

61 *ST,* 19 November 1908.

62 *ST.*

63 *ST.*

[64] *PI*, 19 November 1908.

[65] *PI*, 13 June 1909.

[66] Hokubei, 6.

[67] Hokubei, 5. See also *Buddhist Churches of America. A Legacy of the First 100 Years*, 325–28, 341–43, 370–74. Hereafter cited as BCA.

[68] BCA, 370–71.

[69] Ronald E. Magden, *Furusato, Tacoma-Pierce County Japanese 1888-1988*, 53.

[70] BCA, 373–74.

[71] BCA, 334–35.

[72] Nakai, June 1922.

[73] *The Japanese American Courier*, 20 February 1932.

[74] Minute Book of the Northwest Young People's Buddhist Federation, 28 May 1932–26 March 1954 *passim*.

[75] J. Edgar Hoover, Director, Federal Bureau of Investigation, United States Department of Justice, Memorandum to Mr. L. M. C. Smith, Chief of Special Defense Unit, 8 December 1941.

[76] Masaru Harada counted Seattle Nishi Hongwanji Buddhists incarcerated at Minidoka during September and October 1942. His papers, filed under the title "Block 16," are located in the Seattle Buddhist Church Archives.

[77] "Summary of Minidoka Relocation Center Final Accountability Roster, October 28, 1945." A comparison was made between the government summary and the 1942 Harada census.

[78] Computer Disk A: "Seattle Buddhist Returnees and Non-Returnees 1942-1946. " Compiled by the author."

[79] Seattle Buddhist History Committee, *Seattle Betsuin 1954*, published by the Seattle Buddhist Church, unpaged. Hereafter cited as Betsuin.

[80] Betsuin.

[81] Nakai, January 1906, 10.

# "To Help Her Live the Right Kind of Life"

## Mothers' Pensions in King County, 1913-1937

### Michael Reese

Margaret O'Sullivan applied for a mothers' pension after her husband died of influenza in 1919. Like many counties at the time, King County provided a monthly stipend to some single mothers[1] so they would not have to send their children to an orphanage. The social worker who investigated O'Sullivan worried about granting her a pension because her "house was dirty" and "there was a half empty bottle of whisky in the cupboard." O'Sullivan did receive a pension, but the social worker resolved to "maintain careful supervision of her . . . to help her live the right kind of life." For the next 10 years caseworkers fought an unsuccessful battle to "reform her character." When she expected visits from social workers, "her house was very clean and . . . respectable." When they dropped by without advance warning, caseworkers found her "probably drunk," "pretending not to be home," or "listening to a phonograph . . . with a pile of dirty dishes lying out." O'Sullivan always placated the caseworkers by apologizing for such incidents, though she never seemed to change her behavior fundamentally, and a few months later she would once again be promising that "it will never happen again." But her promises, apologies, and evasions allowed her to retain her pension, and that pension enabled her to keep her family together and put all three of her children through high school.[2]

Unfortunately, historians have paid little attention to women like Margaret O'Sullivan even though interest in the history of the welfare state has increased in recent years. Scholars have examined the beliefs and actions of reformers, politicians, and administrators, but they have neglected welfare recipients. This neglect is because most historical studies of welfare have been national, rather than local, in scope—a rather surprising fact since virtually all public welfare programs before 1935 were run by local agencies.[3] Local-level studies can illuminate the perspectives, strategies, and agency of welfare recipients such as Margaret O'Sullivan.

In addition, local studies can help explain how mothers' pensions, one of the most popular reforms of the Progressive Era, evolved into one of today's most hated government programs, Aid to Families with Dependent Children. In 1913 women's groups in Washington State mobilized broad public support for a mothers' pension bill and steered the bill through the legislature. The question of pre-cisely which single mothers were entitled to pensions proved divisive after the bill's passage. Some wanted the program restricted to widows while others thought all single mothers were deserving. After some setbacks women's groups convinced the 1919 state legislature to allow divorced and abandoned women to receive pen-sions. But women's associations gradually drifted to the right, adopting a more restrictive view of mothers' pensions and helping professional social workers take over the administration of the pension program. Social workers made pensions more stigmatizing by increasing the surveillance of recipients and imposing mor-alistic regulations: they prohibited recipients from living in certain neighborhoods, required them to send their children to Sunday school, and restricted their ability to take in male boarders.

Nonetheless, it would be a mistake to view mothers' pensions primarily as "social control," as some historians have.[4] Administrators certainly did try to regu-late the behavior of pensioned families, but these efforts were remarkably unsuc-cessful. King County records show that Margaret O'Sullivan was hardly the only mother who successfully broke rules and evaded requirements. In addition, pen-sioners found ways to bend the system to their own advantage, and they often enlisted caseworkers' aid in disputes with landlords, doctors, and troublesome rela-tives. Single mothers turned pension administration into a series of negotiations—a sort of tug-of-war rather than a system of social control. Overall, these mothers acted on their own notions about what constituted "the right kind of life."

## "A Mother's Natural Right": Creating Mothers' Pensions

The number of single mothers increased as the U.S. industrialized during the late 19th century. High rates of industrial accidents produced many widows. Urbaniza-tion and geographic mobility fragmented many extended families, reducing their ability to support widowed kin. The number of husbands abandoning their fami-lies also rose during the late 19th century. In this era few single mothers could afford to keep their children, so they had to give them up to orphanages or foster care. Orphanages and foster care proliferated even though more than half the chil-dren in these institutions had a living parent.[5]

While industrialization fueled the growth of orphanages and foster care, cul-tural changes eroded popular support for these institutions. Many evangelical churches and women's clubs had long glorified the maternal role of nurturing and educating children. By 1890 most Americans accepted the notion that mothers—not fathers or schools—were the most important educators of children. This "maternalist" notion did not directly challenge traditional gender roles, but it did substantially raise the cultural status of motherhood. Changing ideas about moth-erhood made it seem logical that children without fathers should be raised by their mothers rather than institutions.[6]

Women's groups that promoted maternalist ideas grew stronger and became politically active during the early 20th century. In 1900 the U.S. led the world in providing women with access to a college education, but high-status professions such as law and medicine still refused to hire women. Finding the professions closed to them, thousands of educated and ambitious women instead joined reform agencies or settlement houses: they became professional reformers.[7] Middle-class married women who had not attended college also desired to increase their participation in the public sphere, and millions of them joined the growing number of women's clubs in the early 20th century. Many of these clubs became active in political and charitable ventures. Maternalist ideology united clubwomen and professional women; both groups argued that women possessed inherent capacities to nurture that made them more qualified than men to develop public policies for children and the poor. Tellingly, women's clubs and settlement houses often justified their reform activities as "civic housekeeping," an extension of women's domestic role into the public sphere.[8]

The politicization of women's clubs in Washington State became apparent in the first decade of the 20th century. Scores of women's groups, mostly literary and social clubs, affiliated to create the Washington State Federation of Women's Clubs (WSFWC) in 1896. The WSFWC initially served as a forum to discuss social issues, but it soon evolved into the political arm of the women's clubs. After 1901 clubwomen directed the WSFWC to lobby for a host of measures—increasing funding for the state library, forming local boards of health to fight tuberculosis, creating juvenile courts to reform juvenile delinquents rather than jailing them, and so forth.[9] A few dozen women established the Washington Congress of Mothers in 1906. The congress merged with the Federation of Parent-Teacher Associations in 1912, and the resulting Washington Congress of Mothers and Parent-Teacher Associations (WCOM-PTA) became the largest women's club in the state. Local chapters focused on the needs of individual schools, but the state-level organization publicized and promoted legislation.[10]

Although the WCOM-PTA and the WSFWC both held maternalist values, their emphases differed. The congress glorified motherhood even more than did the federation. The congress, which limited its membership exclusively to mothers, also tended to be a bit more conservative than the federation. (For example, the WSFWC persuaded the Legislature to liberalize Washington's divorce law in 1905. In 1911 the WCOM-PTA unsuccessfully promoted a bill to restrict somewhat the legal grounds for divorce.) In addition, the congress focused more exclusively on measures to promote children's education and health—the creation of public kindergartens, the free distribution of homogenized milk to needy children, and the addition of home economics course requirements to public school curricula. Despite their differences, the WSFWC and WCOM-PTA had an excellent relationship and often worked together.[11]

The congress and the federation resolved to lobby the state legislature for a mothers' pension act soon after they learned that Illinois had passed the nation's first mothers' pension law in 1911. They felt confident they would succeed. Washington voters had enfranchised women in 1910. In the 1912 elections the Progressive Party, which had endorsed mothers' pensions and many other reforms favored by clubwomen, won one-third of the seats in the state legislature. Mothers' pensions were just part of the legislative program that clubwomen presented to the 1913 legislature: other bills proposed restrictions on child labor, an eight-hour day for women and adolescents, a minimum wage for women, an expanded state library system, and tougher penalties for soliciting prostitution. Each of the largest women's groups agreed to steer one or two of these bills through the legislature. The WCOM-PTA volunteered to sponsor the mothers' pension act. Lucia Rae Bogardus, chair of the organization's legislative committee, spearheaded the effort on behalf of the pension bill.[12]

Bogardus and other WCOM-PTA leaders asserted that the state had a moral obligation to assist single mothers. Mothers' pensions were "not charity, but justice, a mother's natural right," according to Alice Yarnell, head of the Tacoma WCOM-PTA.[13] Single mothers had earned the right to receive aid because their work raising children substantially benefited society. Bogardus explained "these [single] mothers have a right to a pension. The term pension implies a payment for services of worth . . . America has always placed the highest estimation on the place of motherhood in society." Women's groups also argued that a mother's care was far superior to care by orphanages, "which grind out, not citizens, but public charges."[14] Mothers' pensions could thus reduce juvenile crime and produce better-educated and more productive citizens. But pension advocates' most common rhetorical strategy was to tell tear-jerking stories of heart broken single mothers who had to give up their children.[15]

Bogardus persuaded many organizations throughout the state to endorse mothers' pensions, but these groups often favored pensions for different reasons than did the clubwomen. The Washington State Federation of Labor and the Washington Grange echoed some maternalist arguments, but they also viewed mothers' pensions as a way to reduce child labor. Labor leaders frequently mentioned mothers' pensions in the same breath as child labor laws; both reforms would keep children "where they belong—in school."[16] Seattle Juvenile Court Judge Archibald Frater endorsed mothers' pensions as a way to curtail juvenile crime even though he explicitly rejected the notion that single mothers had a moral or legal right to public aid.[17] Bogardus even convinced Governor Marion Hay to endorse pensions in a speech to the Legislature. But Hay focused on the rights of children rather than the rights of mothers. He told the Legislature, "Every child born under the Stars and Stripes is entitled to be well fed, well clothed and well cared for in its tender years and to receive a fair education. If the parents cannot do this, then the state must, or else our boasted civilization is a failure."[18]

Mothers' pensions did attract some scattered opposition in Washington. Many private charities believed that pensions would "promote pauperism" by destroying single mothers' incentive to work and negating families' duty to support their destitute relatives. Charities also opposed pensions because "every social worker knows that there are many women utterly unfitted to be trusted with child raising without close and constant, personal, intelligent and sympathetic supervision." They doubted that public agencies would institute sufficient supervision. Some women's clubs with close ties to charities also opposed pensions. Adele Fielde, the president of the Women's Legislative Coalition of Washington (and a member of two charities' board of directors), declared that "until such time as women shall learn something of eugenics; marry only healthy, honest men; and acquire the sort of education that will enable them to raise more than half of the children they beget, there appears to be no sound reason why the rest of the community should be taxed for the support of child-bearing women who are poor."[19]   Not all of Washington's charity community opposed mothers' pensions. The issue deeply divided the Washington State Conference of Charities and Corrections. This group invited Bogardus to present her pension proposal to their annual meeting, which was held in Olympia just days before the opening of the 1913 Legislature. The minutes note a "spirited debate" after Bogardus's talk. The executive committee resolved the debate by deciding that the conference would not take formal positions on any pending legislation since the delegates were divided on too many issues.[20]

When the conference ended, Bogardus stayed in Olympia to cajole legislators, and her lobbying proved effective. Bogardus persuaded the house judiciary committee to scrap its original mothers' pension proposal in favor of a more liberal bill. The revised bill also raised the amount of the pension. Possibly to mollify skeptical legislators, Bogardus and her allies allowed the bill to be amended on the floor of the house; the amendment required that a "probation officer, charity commissioner, or any person having knowledge of the facts shall . . . [be appointed to] carefully investigate the merits of every application to the end that . . . no person be granted relief hereunder except those justly entitled thereto." Pension supporters then defeated several attempts to table the bill, and when the measure finally reached a roll-call vote, it passed the house 87 to 4 and the senate 34 to 3.[21] As historian Mark Leff aptly observed, "Mothers' pension provisions often carried by near-unanimous tallies; opposition successes depended on preventing the bills from coming to a vote."[22] Many legislators may have disliked mothers' pensions, but few were willing to risk the wrath of newly enfranchised female voters at the next election.[23]

When Governor Hay signed the bill, Washington gained one of the most liberal mothers' pension laws in the nation, but the law still fell far short of providing full financial support to all single mothers. The law directed county juvenile courts to administer the pension program. Though many states merely allowed counties to create pension programs, Washington's law required counties "to provide . . . [funds] sufficient to meet the purposes of this law." The law limited payments to each family to a maximum of $15 per month for the first child and $5 for each additional child age 14 or younger. (This amount was obviously insufficient to support a family. Researchers in the early 1910s generally estimated that a family of four required $40 per month just to meet its minimum subsistence needs.[24] To obtain the additional income they required, pensioned mothers would have to work for wages or rely on aid from relatives. The law specified that only three categories of single mothers could obtain pensions: widows, women whose husbands had abandoned them over a year earlier, and women whose husbands were "totally disabled" or in an insane asylum or penal institution. Furthermore, applicants had to be "destitute," and they had to have lived in Washington for at least a year. Mothers also had to be, "in the judgement of the court, . . . a proper person morally, physically, and mentally for the bringing up of her child or children."[25]

Placing mothers' pensions in the juvenile courts was a logical step because it built on clubwomen's earlier legislative successes. Although the idea of establishing juvenile courts originated with judges, the WSFWC strongly endorsed the notion and guided a bill creating juvenile courts through the 1905 legislature.[26] The WSFWC and WCOM-PTA followed up with successful campaigns in 1911 and 1913 to "remove . . . juvenile court[s] from politics" that by requiring juvenile court judges be elected on a nonpartisan basis, which eliminated political parties' ability to nominate these judges.[27] The pension law's requirement that counties provide the courts with whatever funds were needed to administer the program also sustained the courts' independence. Women's clubs thus helped create an institutional framework that granted juvenile courts a good deal of autonomy.

## "THERE ARE NO ILLEGITIMATE CHILDREN, ONLY ILLEGITIMATE PARENTS": REGULATING ACCESS TO MOTHERS' PENSIONS

Disappointing the clubwomen, the King County Juvenile Court chose to interpret the mothers' pension statute in a restrictive manner. The passage of the pension law sent the court scurrying to create rules and procedures for this new welfare program for which "no blanks, books, or precedent existed."[28] Judge Frater named probation officer J. A. Sigurdsson to head the court's new Mothers' Pension Department. The department had only one other employee, Josephine Stuff, who worked part-time as Sigurdsson's assistant. While Judge Frater was a liberal Republican on good terms with Seattle's clubwomen, Sigurdsson proved to be a conservative administrator. Judge Frater initially felt that the court's "humanitarian standpoint" dictated that divorced women should be allowed to receive pensions even though the law did not specifically mandate this. Sigurdsson strongly disagreed; he decided that only those divorcées who had been abandoned before their divorce were eligible for pensions.[29] The court also restricted access to the program by adopting a narrow interpretation of the law's stipulation that only "destitute" mothers could receive pensions. The court defined "destitution" not simply as poverty, but as a complete lack of financial assets of any type. This definition required single mothers to sell their homes and exhaust their savings before they could get a pension. These restrictive policies caused the court to reject more than 40 percent of applications for pensions and kept the program quite small. A scant 160 mothers in King County were receiving aid at the end of 1914.[30]

The court's decision to restrict access to the program was driven by a desire to keep costs to an absolute minimum. Significantly, the court decided to exclude divorcées and women with property only after more than 100 mothers applied for pensions in the first three days of the program. Even though the court had a measure of autonomy, it decided not to antagonize the taxpayers and county commissioners with large expenditures on mothers' pensions. The conservative *Seattle Post-Intelligencer* explained, "The county commissioners are instructed to provide funds for the payment of the pensions, but as no such funds have been provided by tax levy, the law having passed since the levy was made, the county may be somewhat embarrassed if the demands for pensions by mothers are very numerous." In his 1913 report to the county commissioners, Judge Frater stressed that the program's cost of $2,000 to $3,000 per month was "extremely economical." The court's restrictive policies mollified fiscal conservatives. By 1914 the initially skeptical *Post-Intelligencer* was convinced that, "considering the service extended, the amount expended [on mothers' pensions] is not unreasonable."[31]

Fiscal conservatism came naturally to Sigurdsson, who feared that mothers' pensions could breed dependency and sap the work ethic. "Too much generosity" could "pauperize" pension recipients, he argued. Sigurdsson believed that all able-bodied single mothers had an obligation to work, even if it reduced the time they could spend with their children. Pensions were meant to be "a help, not the sole source of support" for mothers.[32] In 1916 Sigurdsson was pleased to announce that 72 percent of mothers' pension recipients in King County worked outside the home, while 17 percent did sewing, laundry, or other paid work at home. At this time, only about 5 percent of mothers in two-parent families worked for wages. Sigurdsson and other administrators clearly expected single mothers to become breadwinners, as well as maintaining their maternal and domestic roles.[33]

Sigurdsson also thought that the relatives of a single mother had an obligation to help support her. The department's application forms inquired at length about the occupations of an applicant's parents, siblings, and older children. If an applicant was not being assisted by relatives who lived in the area, Sigurdsson or Josephine Stuff interviewed those relatives to see why they were not giving aid (which was most often because they had no money to spare). Sigurdsson and Stuff denied pensions to women who "could be adequately supported by their relations," whether or not these relatives were actually providing this support.[34] In addition, they frequently granted only small pensions to mothers who had children age 16 or older, believing that these children should work full-time to help support their mothers and younger siblings.[35]

In general, Sigurdsson sought to keep each pension as small as possible. When investigating applications, he and Stuff spent most of their time researching the family's financial status. They awarded only partial pensions to mothers who received insurance money or who held relatively well-paying jobs. For example, Stuff found that Ruth Swan had worked incredibly hard to support her four children after her husband's death. She planted a large garden. She also plucked chickens, accepting hens in lieu of wages; she then made a fair profit selling eggs. Stuff thus reported, "Taking into consideration the natural fiscal capacity of this mother, I feel that with an allowance of $20 per month [$10 less than the legal maximum], she and her children could be made comfortable."[36] After their initial investigation, families on pensions received very little supervision during the first years of the program; the limited supervision the court did impose focused on family finances. In the fall of 1914 Sigurdsson briefly reexamined the financial situation of most mothers collecting pensions. He then increased the amount of 9 pensions, decreased 34, and revoked 8 because the families had become "self-supporting." Sigurdsson proudly announced that his "readjustment" had reduced the average pension by $2 per month[37] (see figure 1).

Furthermore, Sigurdsson argued that Washington's pension law was too inclusive. "It is well to remember," he explained, "especially in connection with divorced mothers . . . and even in some cases of abandonment, that Seattle is a favored city, in the eyes of many a 'city of refuge.'" To stave off a mass migration of single mothers, he suggested increasing the length of time a mother had to live in the state before she was eligible for a pension. He also believed that excluding divorced and abandoned mothers from the program would discourage divorce and abandonment.[38] Judge Frater held more liberal views than Sigurdsson, but he moved up to the King County Superior Court in 1914 and was replaced by Judge King Dykeman, who concurred with Sigurdsson. Dykeman thus endorsed the efforts of charity groups that sought to scale back the pension law during the 1915 legislative session.[39]

The 1915 legislature proved to be a receptive audience for pension opponents. Without Theodore Roosevelt at the top of the ticket, the Progressive Party had been trounced by the Republicans in the 1914 elections, producing a more conservative legislature.[40] Though women's groups defeated a measure to repeal the mothers' pension law, the Seattle Charity Organization Society marshaled support for a bill to restrict access to pensions. This act denied pensions to abandoned wives and extended the residency requirement from one to three years. (However, the act did liberalize the pension law in one respect: it removed the requirement that an applicant be "destitute" and only required her to have "insufficient property or income, or lack of earning capacity."[41]) The WSFWC and the Washington Federation of Labor lobbied vigorously, but unsuccessfully, to defeat or amend the bill.[42] The WCOM-PTA was conspicuously silent during these legislative battles. It appears that the organization was divided on the merits of allowing abandoned women to receive pensions. After the bill passed, the WCOM-PTA's newsletter declared it to be "an improvement over the 1913 law."[43]

Most single mothers, on the other hand, probably did not think the new law was an improvement. Although a dozen women who had initially been denied aid

**Figure 1:**
**Average Pension Amount in King County**

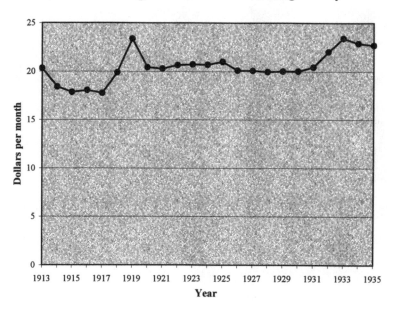

because they owned a house were now given pensions, fully one-third of the mothers in the program had their pensions canceled when the new rules took effect in June 1915. The number of women receiving pensions in King County dropped from 174 to 117[44] (see figure 2).

Personnel changes in two organizations during 1916 strengthened the hand of those who favored broader access to mothers' pensions. The WCOM-PTA selected more liberal leaders at its 1916 convention, and Bogardus, architect of the original pension law, became vice-president of the group.[45] In addition, Sigurdsson retired as head of the Mothers' Pension Department and was replaced by his assistant, Josephine Stuff, who was not nearly as fiscally conservative. When inflation drove up the cost of living during World War I, Stuff increased the amount of the average pension[46] (see figure 1). She also endorsed a 1917 bill, sponsored by the new leaders of the WCOM-PTA, granting pensions to abandoned and divorced women. This bill passed the state senate, but conservatives prevented it from coming to a vote in the house.[47]

After disappointments in 1915 and 1917, pension advocates put together an impressive coalition in 1919. They sought a "child maintenance act" to increase pensions by $5 per month and make all single mothers—including divorced, abandoned, and never-married women—eligible for pensions. The act would also transfer the administration of mothers' pensions to school boards. Women's clubs, led by the WCOM-PTA and WSFWC, spearheaded the lobbying effort. The Seattle

### Figure 2:
### Number of Families Receiving Pensions in King County

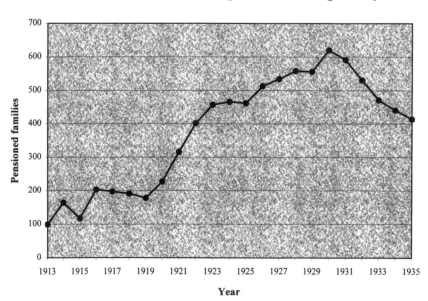

Women's Label League, a working-class women's group, convinced the Washington Federation of Labor to endorse the proposal.[48]

Clubwomen's arguments on behalf of the 1919 measure focused on the needs of children rather than the rights of mothers. Significantly, clubwomen called their proposal a child maintenance act rather than a mothers' pension bill. In 1913 women's groups had stressed the inherent nurturing capacities common to all mothers and had depicted pensions as "a mother's natural right," but they jettisoned these themes in 1919. Children now became the primary object of concern. Instead of recounting tragic tales about suffering single mothers, clubwomen recounted heart-rending stories about hungry children. They argued that the existing pension law wrongly "discriminate[d] against needy children" by excluding some types of single mothers; this discrimination "deprive[d] needy children of their rights to decent living conditions."[49] The focus on children helped pension advocates defend the controversial proposal to grant aid to women who had children out of wedlock. "There are no 'illegitimate' children," the WCOM-PTA proclaimed, "only illegitimate parents . . . We must stop judging the child by the status of his parents, over which he has no control."[50]

The focus on the needs of children was more than a rhetorical ploy; it sprang from conviction as well as political expediency. By 1919 most clubwomen had forsaken the notion of pensions as an entitlement owed to poor mothers. Few would have objected to WSFWC leader Edna Boag's claim that "the object of a mothers pension is primarily for the children and not the mothers."[51] The First World War had made most Washington women's clubs more conservative. Concerned about the loyalty of immigrants, the clubs embraced immigration restrictions and promoted Americanization programs for immigrant mothers and their children during the war. The "problem of the immigrant mother" led women's groups to abandon rhetoric that proclaimed the rights of all mothers or glorified the bonds between all mothers.[52] But women's groups continued to idealize children, even immigrant children, depicting them as "helpless angels . . . who need the protection of laws like the Child Maintenance Act."[53]

The advocates of mothers' pensions were even more powerful in 1919 than they had been in 1913. The membership of the WCOM-PTA had more than doubled during this period as mothers organized PTAs in virtually every public school. Given the growth of the PTA movement, it is not surprising that the WCOM-PTA wanted to move the administration of mothers' pensions: the group would have far more influence over policies made by school boards than policies made in courts. While the WCOM-PTA convinced virtually every women's club in the state to endorse the Child Maintenance Act, charities were divided. The Washington Council of Charities and Corrections took no formal position on the bill. Some charities strongly opposed the measure, a small handful endorsed it, and many remained neutral.[54]

Nonetheless, pension advocates achieved only partial success. The 1919 legislature was dominated by Republicans, but the GOP had moved to the left somewhat due to its reabsorption of the Progressive Party and the election of liberal Republicans in some districts.[55] The senate judiciary committee approved the Child Maintenance Act but deleted the section that increased pensions by $5 per month. The bill stalled on the floor of the senate after officials from several school boards claimed they could not take on the responsibility of administering mothers' pensions. Legislators and lobbyists from women's clubs then agreed to amend the bill to resolve the impasse. The amended bill left juvenile courts in charge of pension administration but allowed all types of single mothers to receive pensions. (Of course, applicants still had to comply with restrictions set by previous legislation—the lengthy residency requirement and the stipulation that they be a "proper person morally, physically, and mentally.") Once amended, the Child Maintenance Act passed by wide margins.[56]

Although the act did not liberalize mothers' pensions as much as clubwomen had hoped, it did set the stage for a massive expansion of the pension program. Scores of previously ineligible mothers now applied for pensions. Although Josephine Stuff ruled that the "moral fitness" requirement disqualified never-married mothers, she freely pensioned divorced and abandoned women. As early as 1920, more divorced mothers than widows were receiving pensions in King County. The number of pensioned mothers more than tripled in the four years after the passage of the Child Maintenance Act. The program continued to grow, though at a slower rate, for the rest of the 1920s[57] (see figure 2).

The autonomy of the juvenile court facilitated the growth of the pension program. The court had the legal authority to set its own budget, and this authority helped insulate it from political pressure. The county commissioners appropriated a fixed amount for mothers' pensions at the start of every fiscal year, but the court frequently spent more than this amount, and the commissioners had no choice but to pick up the tab. The Mothers' Pension Department exceeded its appropriation eight times between 1919 and 1931. In a way, pension advocates may have been fortunate that they failed to transfer the program to school boards. Schools boards could not exceed their appropriations, and their budgets had to be approved by voters. While women's groups would have had substantial influence over the policies adopted by school boards, the fiscal constraints faced by school boards would probably have slowed the expansion of the pension program.

Women's clubs continued to fight to liberalize mothers' pension laws during the 1920s, but their efforts were unsuccessful. The legislature rejected several bills to increase the size of pensions, and Governor Roland Hartley vetoed a measure to allow mothers of 15- and 16-year-old children to receive pensions. However, pension advocates did defeat proposals to grant pensions only to mothers who were U.S. citizens and to lengthen the residency requirement to five years. The legislative fight over access to mothers' pensions thus resulted in stalemate during the 1920s.[58]

The legislative deadlock left administrators squarely in charge of determining who was or was not entitled to a pension. In 1926 the King County Juvenile Court granted pensions to two never-married mothers, although it continued to deny most such applications.[59] On the whole, however, the administration of pensions became more moralistic and invasive over time.

## "THERE IS AN UNWRITTEN LAW THAT MOTHERS MUST KEEP THEMSELVES, THEIR CHILDREN AND THEIR HOME CLEAN": ADMINISTERING MOTHERS' PENSIONS

As the Mothers' Pension Department hired and promoted employees who had been trained by charities, pension administration became more moralistic. Charities feared that cash aid could pauperize and corrupt recipients: such aid could destroy the work ethic, weaken family obligations, and promote lax morality. Preventing pauperization required supervision by "friendly visitors" who would improve recipients' morals, hygiene, and money management skills.[60] Many charities had opposed mothers' pensions because they believed government agencies would not adequately supervise recipients. It is therefore not surprising that pension officials who used to work for charities sought to increase the supervision and regulation of pensioned families. Nevertheless, supervisory and regulatory policies evolved slowly in King County.

J. A. Sigurdsson, who headed the Pension Department from 1913 to 1916, certainly worried about pauperization, but his philosophy differed from that of the charity administrators' in several ways. Sigurdsson, a former schoolteacher, thought it was more important to keep costs down than to supervise pensioned families stringently. He refused to hire additional staff to monitor recipients; he and Josephine Stuff simply did not have time to supervise families after their application for a pension had been approved. While charities such as Goodwill Industries and the Seattle Social Welfare League typically spent more than half their budgets on investigators' and administrators' salaries, Sigurdsson spent only 10 percent of the department's funds on payroll.[61] In addition, even though Sigurdsson exhaustively investigated the finances of applicants' families, he did not share charities' concern with determining the "moral fitness" of applicants. I found only one instance when Sigurdsson denied an application because he thought the mother was morally unfit. He granted pensions to women whom many charities would have refused to aid. For instance, he evinced little concern when Stuff reported that one applicant lived "in a miserable shack . . . There was an empty whiskey bottle under the kitchen table and a quart beer bottle on a table stacked with dirty dishes . . . The neighbors say she is frequently profane. Her children are neglected in that they are left alone a great deal." Despite this report, Sigurdsson approved the application.[62]

The department's policies changed when Sigurdsson resigned and Stuff took over. Stuff had received her social work training at the Seattle Children's Aid Society, an organization that ran foster care programs. Although Stuff was more willing than Sigurdsson to pension abandoned women and divorcées, she brought a moralistic style to the administration of mothers' pensions in many ways. She denied pensions to about 3 percent of applicants on the grounds of "moral unfitness."[63] She also instituted policies to help pensioned families live the "right kind of life." Worried about sexual impropriety, she banned mothers from taking in a solitary male boarder who was not a relative. (Since some mothers operated boardinghouses, she did not prohibit them from taking in multiple male boarders.) Furthermore, Stuff required pensioned families "to make their homes in the outlying parts of the city, which furnish wholesome associations for both mother and children." She threatened to revoke the pensions of women who refused to move out of Seattle's "disreputable downtown district," which contained several illegal bars and card rooms.[64] After America's entry into the First World War, she encouraged foreign-born mothers to attend housekeeping and Americanization classes offered by the Women's Christian Temperance Union.[65] Initially, however, these new rules went largely unenforced because Stuff waited until 1919 to employ more staff to supervise pensioned families.

The court increased its supervisory capacities by hiring three new staff members in 1919. Lena Hemphill, a graduate of Geneva College in upstate New York, was the court's first college-trained social worker. She served as chief investigator from 1919 to 1921 when she replaced Stuff as head of the Mothers' Pension Department. Two other women, one of whom had been trained by Seattle's largest private charity, were hired to serve as field visitors. The court hired two additional visitors in the latter part of the decade. Hemphill painted a rosy picture of the visitors' function:

> The visitor is a friendly counselor in the home-life who devises ways and means for the betterment of a family, rendering countless services to its members, and linking them up with social opportunities furnished by the community. A plan has been adopted in this Department whereby the visitor calls at each home once a month to ascertain if the children are given proper care. A close check is kept on their attendance in school.[66]

Hemphill also brought greater scrutiny to the application process. She introduced a new application form that required much more information, and she deemed that 5 percent of applicants were morally unfit to raise their children and thus ineligible for pensions.[67]

Hemphill and other administrators frequently ordered extra supervision of racial and ethnic minorities. Department officials were clearly suspicious of these women even though they did not often deny their applications for pensions. In general, the pension rolls accurately reflected the ethnic diversity of King County,[68] but this did not mean that all pensioned families received equal treatment. Hemphill revealed her biases when she investigated Belle Greenburg and reported that "she is entirely illiterate and there is a strong suggestion that she is partly of negro blood . . . Her home was apparently clean but had the noticeable smell of bad housekeeping . . . [A] close check on this home might be advisable . . . every few weeks." Immigrants and African-Americans were often singled out for additional surveillance in this manner.[69]

Furthermore, the staff's presumption of the superiority of Anglo-American culture led to occasional conflict with foreign-born mothers. Like many middle-class white Protestants, pension officials viewed the consumption of alcohol as immoral (not to mention illegal—Washington voters had passed a dry law in 1914). Caseworkers threatened to revoke the pensions of mothers who drank, and they occasionally made good on their threats.[70] In addition, officials and pensioners sometimes fought over the proper way to care for children. Stuff and Hemphill argued with Ella Johanssen when they visited her house after hearing that her daughter was ill. They were horrified that she was feeding her sick daughter "chiefly bread and coffee, as is common among the Scandinavian people." They told her to take the child to the hospital. Johanssen refused; the last time her daughter had visited the hospital, the child only became sicker and caught pneumonia. When Johanssen persisted in her defiance, the administrators revoked her pension and refused to reinstate it after her daughter recovered.[71]

When Hemphill became head of the department in 1921, she imposed additional regulations designed to improve the hygiene and morals of pensioned families. Virtually all of Hemphill's case files commented on the tidiness of the mother's house. She believed that a dirty or cluttered home indicated that an applicant was a poor—and possibly unfit—mother. She usually approved pension applications even when a mother's "house was exceptionally dirty," but the applicant "was advised that she would be required to clean up if taken on the Pension List."[72] Indeed, Hemphill informed all applicants that "there is an unwritten law that the mother must keep herself, her children and her home clean."[73] Mothers found it difficult to meet this ideal because most of them had jobs outside the home as well as their household and child-rearing work. Hemphill tried to promote godliness as well as cleanliness. She declared that recipients' children were expected "to be regular in attendance at day and Sunday school." If she found "the children were not in any Sunday School, . . . [t]he mother was informed that such attendance would be required of them."[74] Jewish children had to attend Sabbath school.

The increasing supervision and regulation of pension recipients in King County reflected a national trend: pension administration became more invasive as professional social workers began to run the programs. Social work educators such as Mary Richmond sought to standardize the management of charity and public welfare. Richmond's books *Friendly Visiting Among the Poor: A Handbook for Charity Workers* (1914) and *Social Diagnosis* (1917) were the most commonly assigned textbooks in social work courses, and they shaped the emerging profession. Richmond argued that casework—the "expert collection and interpretation of social evidence"—was a social worker's most important skill. Her books provided elaborate instructions on how to gather, record, and interpret "social evidence" such as medical and financial records, employment histories, and interviews with relatives and neighbors. Even though Richmond believed that most poverty was caused by economic factors beyond a family's control, she was steeped in the Protestant charity tradition and claimed that cash aid could pauperize and corrupt a family. She therefore urged caseworkers to monitor their clients carefully for signs of fiscal or moral laxity.[75] The leaders of the U.S. Children's Bureau, while more liberal than Richmond in many ways, also urged mothers' pension agencies to hire trained social workers and supervise their clients closely.[76]

The professionalization of social work proceeded a bit more slowly in Seattle than in many other big cities. Although the University of Washington offered social work classes during the 1920s, it did not create its School of Social Work until 1935. The King County Mothers' Pension Department didn't hire a second college-trained social worker until 1928. These factors may help explain why pension recipients in Seattle received a slightly lower level of supervision than those in other big cities. A 1927 Children's Bureau study of pension programs in 10 large cities found an average of 80 families per caseworker, while each caseworker in King County had to supervise 110 families.[77]

Many historians have depicted social workers' "capture" of pension administration in large cities as something that happened against the wishes of the women's clubs who had lobbied for pension laws, but evidence from King County challenges this assertion. King County women's clubs moved substantially to the right during the First World War and the postwar labor unrest. As previously noted, the clubs abandoned the maternalist notion of pensions as a "mother's natural right," and they advocated programs to Americanize foreign-born mothers. In addition, during the 1920s they became increasingly concerned with the activities of adolescents, urging girls to dress modestly and calling for government regulation of motion pictures and dance halls.[78] The moralistic policies imposed by Lena Hemphill and her staff were fundamentally congruent with clubwomen's desire to improve public morals. Furthermore, Washington women's groups, even though they were mostly composed of housewives, had long supported the cause of professional women.[79] When social workers began to think of themselves as professionals, clubwomen supported the aims of this new, female-dominated profession.

The cooperation between women's associations and the Washington State Conference of Social Work (WSCSW) demonstrated the growing ties between clubwomen and social workers. Organized in 1923 as the successor of the moribund Washington State Conference of Charities and Corrections, the WSCSW was composed of social workers from all types of public and private agencies. Mothers' pensions administrators from all parts of the state held their own discussion group at the annual meeting of the WSCSW. These administrators decided to ally with women's clubs to fight for legislation increasing the dollar amount of mothers' pensions. The WSCSW also convinced clubwomen to help lobby for the creation of a state-level department of child welfare. The proposed agency would have several functions: licensing and inspecting orphanages, conducting research, and coordinating the administration of mothers' pensions in different counties to "promote improved and more uniform standards."[80] The agency would train officials in rural counties so they could better supervise pensioned families. The WCOM-PTA and other women's clubs played a prominent role in persuading the Legislature to pass bills establishing a department of child welfare in 1925, 1927, and 1929; however, Governor Roland Hartley vetoed all these bills.[81]

Social workers discovered that it was even harder to control pensioned families than it was to enact legislation. Some historians have called mothers' pensions a form of social control, but this implies that mothers were in fact controlled. Although pension officials undoubtedly did try to regulate mothers' conduct, King County's records indicate that these efforts were exceptionally unsuccessful. These records are littered with visitors' reports lamenting mothers' poor housekeeping and alleging that children were not attending Sunday school. Lena Hemphill acknowledged her failure to impose social control in an annual report: "We urge and encourage all mothers who are not citizens to become naturalized as soon as possible. We have not been very successful, however, in this . . . Many mothers show no desire to take out citizenship papers."[82] Mothers did, however, show a desire to maintain control over their own lives, and they found many ways to frustrate the designs of the Mothers' Pension Department.

Several mothers proved quite skilled at evading the department's rules. The department caught virtually no mothers engaged in "sexual misconduct." (I found only two cases where women lost their pensions due to sexual misconduct; these single mothers had become pregnant, which was obviously difficult to conceal.) Yet we must figure that a fair number of recipients were violating the department's moral standards because nearly one-quarter of them remarried before their children were fully-grown. Furthermore, the department's files contained numerous reports alleging that some mothers were "not faithful to the memory of [their] husband[s]."[83] Visitors, however, were unable to confirm these reports and rumors. When some neighbors impugned the conduct of pensioners, others often denied the accusations. For example, although some people told Josephine Stuff that widow Edith Stockton was "not a chaste woman," others claimed there was nothing improper in Karl Baum's frequent visits, explaining that "the relations between Mrs. [Stockton] and Mr. [Baum] are those of friendship, only." Unable to determine the truth of the matter, Stuff approved Stockton's application for a pension. She continued to receive the pension until she married Baum 15 months later.[84] Many accusations followed the same pattern: when some alleged that a woman "hit the sauce too hard," others claimed she was a "decent, clean and sober mother."[85] As long as a mother did not alienate the vast majority of her neighbors, she was unlikely to get caught violating the department's policies. Caseworkers sometimes visited homes in the early morning or late evening in an effort to catch pensioners breaking the rules, but many mothers simply refused to answer the door. One visitor reported that she "knocked and knocked on the door for 10 minutes . . . [The mother] must have been home because I heard noises and the light was on. She later said she took the family over to a friend's house but I do not believe her."[86] There was little visitors could do in these instances because they rarely had proof that a family had refused to answer the door.

Even when their rule breaking was detected, many mothers succeeded in keeping their pensions by telling administrators what they wanted to hear. As described earlier, Ella Johanssen lost her pension when she refused to take her daughter to the hospital; however, she had sidestepped trouble on several previous occasions. In 1917 Stuff had granted a pension to Johanssen on the condition that she move out of her "disreputable" downtown apartment building. Johanssen said she was already looking for an apartment north of the city. In 1918 Stuff's assistant described an early-morning investigation of Johanssen, who was still living in the same downtown apartment

> I called but was not admitted to the room as Mrs. [Johanssen] replied to my knock by opening the door a few inches and saying that she was too busy to receive me. A man was in the room at this time and Mrs. [Johanssen] later explained his presence to me by saying that he was her pastor. I found this hard to believe since she had earlier said she was [C]atholic . . . It was clear that Mrs. [Johanssen] was not living the right kind of life.

Johanssen mollified her caseworker by promising to move to a better neighborhood soon and by sticking to her story that the man in her apartment was her pastor. She also vowed "not to do anything that could possibly be seen as dubious behaviour." She then irritated caseworkers by moving to an apartment on Capitol Hill, just a few blocks away from downtown. But it was only when she refused to hospitalize her daughter in 1920 that she finally lost her pension.[87] As Johanssen's case illustrates, the department rarely revoked a pension for a first offense, and most cancellations came at the end of a series of confrontations with officials. Most mothers could obtain a second—or a third or fourth—chance by seeming contrite and promising to reform their behavior in the future. Caseworkers accepted these promises because they honestly believed they could improve the morals of these mothers and their children.

After a quarrel with pension officials, many mothers played along by keeping their houses spotlessly clean and by inviting the department's visitors over for tea. Margaret O'Sullivan, who was described in the first paragraph of this essay, was a master at this game. In the 11 years that she received a pension, O'Sullivan had no fewer than 13 confrontations with caseworkers about her drinking, poor housekeeping, and failure to send her children to church. But she kept her pension because she always told administrators what they wanted to hear: she appreciated the staff's efforts to show her the right way to live, she was making progress, she was sorry she had "backslid," and it would "never happen again."[88] This strategy proved quite successful.

The history of mothers' pensions in King County contradicts the notion that pensions "enforced domesticity."[89] Administrators expected all able-bodied mothers to work for wages, a violation of typical standards of domesticity. Hemphill defended this policy, claiming, "The growing tendency of housewives to enter the business world has a broadening effect on the mothers. The mothers generally realize that the aid is not primarily for them, but know that the state is interested in her only as a guardian for her children, and they appreciate the aid and are anxious to do their part . . . by working [for wages]."[90] In actuality, however, most single mothers disliked having to work. A great many of them had never previously worked outside the home, and almost all had quit working once they had children. Nonetheless, the inadequacy of a $20 to $30 monthly pension compelled most of them into the labor market. One mother objected that working "ruins the point of a pension, . . . bringing the kids up right with a mother at home."[91] Pensioned mothers didn't complain about "enforced domesticity"; they resented being forced to abandon domesticity.

Furthermore, scholars who label pensions as social control have focused exclusively on the program's regulation of mothers, but King County officials tried to control the behavior of children too. Given that pension advocates came to view assisting children as the primary goal of the program, it is not surprising that caseworkers spent a great deal of effort trying to monitor and regulate children's behavior. Children were obligated to attend Sunday school even though mothers were not required to go to church. The department's visitors periodically checked the children's school records and interviewed their teachers and principals. Though some mothers disliked this scrutiny of their children, others appreciated the information that visitors gleaned. One mother told her caseworker, "I try to keep up on how they are doing in class but some times I can't . . . Thank you for . . . telling me about my daughter's [problems] at school." (One imagines that the daughter was less thankful for the visitor's diligence.) A few mothers even asked pension officials to keep close tabs on their children in order to keep them from playing hooky.[92]

The relationship between pension administrators and single mothers was more a negotiation than a top-down system of social control.[93] While the balance of power in this negotiation was not equal, mothers were far from powerless. They found ways to use the system to obtain things their families needed. If they or their children needed medical care, mothers begged the pension department for help; the department often convinced doctors, dentists, and optometrists to donate their services. Mothers also asked caseworkers to plead with their landlords when they were behind on their rent; this almost always prevented an eviction.[94] After several mothers complained that their apartments were "drafty and led to frequent illness among the children," pension officials persuaded the Modern Woodworkers of America to build some houses and sell them very cheaply to pensioned mothers.[95]

In addition, pension recipients enlisted caseworkers' help in family disputes. Some women used mothers' pensions to escape the control of relatives who were even more meddlesome than social workers. Lydia Jackson moved in with her husband's parents after her husband died in a logging accident. After several quarrels with her in-laws, Jackson applied for a pension so she and her children could move into their own apartment. She told Lena Hemphill that "her husband's parents were cross, disagreeable people that thought they knew how to raise the children better than she did." Hemphill agreed that "a pension will allow her to keep the children away from their grandparents who are a bad influence."[96] Elizabeth Dibble convinced the department to have her violent brother evicted from his apartment, which was across the hall from hers. Mothers also used caseworkers to speak with estranged children and ask recalcitrant relatives for money.[97] The term "social control" simply cannot describe these complex negotiations and interactions between social workers and single mothers.

## "MOTHERS' PENSIONS ARE DEAD": MOVING FROM MOTHERS' PENSIONS TO AID TO DEPENDENT CHILDREN

The Great Depression undermined political support for mothers' pensions. As the skyrocketing unemployment rate became the main political issue, public concern for the plight of single mothers diminished. When a reporter asked Governor-elect Clarence Martin about mothers' pensions and women's unemployment, Martin replied, "These are important issues, but they are not at the top of our list right now . . . [U]nemployed men are our first priority."[98] Indeed, labor groups, social work organizations, and even women's clubs placed their efforts to liberalize mothers' pension laws on the back burner during the first years of the Depression.

This loss of political support led to the contraction of the mothers' pension program. During 1929 and 1930, however, the number of women receiving pensions increased as economic stresses drove up the rates of divorce and abandonment (see figure 2). To slow the growth of the program, administrators began denying pensions to mothers with only one child in 1931.[99] This measure failed to satisfy the King County commissioners, who worried about the county's falling tax revenues and its spiraling debts; the commissioners directed pension administrators to cut expenditures. Although pension officials did not legally have to comply, they chose to avoid a confrontation. The Mothers' Pension Department stopped processing applications and instituted a waiting list in 1932. It also canceled the pensions of many mothers with only one child. The number of women on pensions decreased dramatically (see figure 2), and the waiting list grew longer. By 1934, when the department once again began processing a substantial number of applications, the waiting list for pensions was nearly a year long.[100]

As the relief programs of the New Deal began to reduce male unemployment, interest in reforming mothers' pensions waxed once again. The passage of the Social Security Act of 1935 accelerated this process by creating and partially funding the Aid to Dependent Children (ADC) program, which was designed to replace mothers' pensions. The Washington State Conference of Social Work noted that the new law ensured that "mothers' pensions are dead . . . The only question is what form [ADC] . . . will take in this state."[101]

Although the history of ADC is beyond the scope of this essay, it is worth noting that social workers, especially the staff of the King County Mothers' Pension Department, took the lead role in shaping Washington's ADC policies. However, single mothers held some influence in this process as well. The leftist Washington Old Age Pension Union had organized many single mothers into a branch of their organization and lobbied for a liberal ADC program. Washington's 1937 ADC law increased funding, but not as much as the pension union had hoped: the maximum mothers' pension for a woman with two children had been $20 per month, and the maximum ADC grant was $30. The legislation also broadened eligibility for aid by, among other changes, removing the requirement that a recipient be a "proper person morally, physically, and mentally." However, caseworkers could still cancel the pensions of those who failed to "provide a suitable home for the children."[102] Though the administration of ADC was less moralistic than the management of mothers' pensions, many policies remained in place. ADC officials did not require Sunday school attendance or prohibit recipients from drinking, but they continued to visit the homes of recipients and to monitor children's school attendance and mothers' sexual behavior. ADC clearly inherited many of the invasive and stigmatizing aspects of mothers' pensions.

Unfortunately, the idea that single mothers are morally dubious people who need to be investigated has persisted, and this idea continues to shape the politics and administration of welfare. Nevertheless, it is important to remember that welfare programs were not always unpopular. Women's clubs built a tremendous amount of public support for the concept of mothers' pensions during the Progressive Era. Women's associations also succeeded in broadening the program to accept divorced and abandoned mothers. In today's era of "welfare reform," when advocates of welfare spending are continually on the defensive, it is perhaps heartening to recall that some movements to expand welfare elicited broad popular support and were successful.

Unfortunately, these successes were partially undermined by administrators who imposed moralistic regulations and monitored pensioned families. The same women's groups that had built public support for mothers' pensions had a hand in these developments: they grew increasingly suspicious of immigrant mothers; they jettisoned the notion of pensions as a mother's right; and they cooperated with the professional social workers who were gaining control of pension administration. Beginning with Josephine Stuff, pension officials steadily added regulations and hired more supervisory staff. Regulations and surveillance grew hand in hand with the professionalization of social work.

Despite the efforts to regulate their behavior, single mothers in King County retained a good deal of control over their lives. These women did have to work long hours and deal with vexing caseworkers, but they were not victims of social control. Mothers turned pension administration into a series of negotiations. They broke rules, hid from investigators, and deceived officials quite successfully. They used pension administrators to get access to health care, to monitor their children, and to deal with troublesome relatives. These single mothers found ways to keep their families together and hold on to their own ideas about what was "the right kind of life."

## NOTES

[1] I use the term "single mothers" in its broadest sense, to denote all mothers without an employable male breadwinner. My definition includes widows, women whose husbands were totally disabled or in jail, divorced women, and women who had been abandoned by their husbands, as well as never-married mothers. For a useful discussion of the changing meaning of the terms *welfare* and *single mothers*, see Linda Gordon, *Pitied but Not Entitled: Single Mothers and the History of Welfare* (Cambridge, Mass.: Harvard University Press, 1994), 1–3, 19–22.

[2] Case 988, mothers' pension records, King County Juvenile Court, Clerk's Office, Seattle. Throughout this essay I use pseudonyms to preserve the privacy of pension recipients.

[3] The most important recent works on the history of welfare in the U.S. are Gordon, *Pitied*

*but Not Entitled,* and Theda Skocpol, *Protecting Soldiers and Mothers: The Political Origins of Social Policy in the United States* (Cambridge, Mass.: Harvard University Press, 1992).

[4] See, for example, Mimi Abramovitz, *Regulating the Lives of Women: Social Welfare Policy from Colonial Times to the Present* (Boston: South End Press, 1988); Frances Fox Piven and Richard Cloward, *Regulating the Poor: The Functions of Public Welfare* (New York: Random House, 1971); Barbara Nelson's and Gwendolyn Mink's essays in *Women, the State, and Welfare,* ed. Linda Gordon (Madison: University of Wisconsin Press, 1990).

[5] Gordon, *Pitied but Not Entitled,* 20–24; Ann Vandepol, "Dependent Children, Child Custody, and the Mothers' Pensions: The Transformation of State-Family Relations in the Early Twentieth Century," *Social Problems* 29 (1982): 223–26.

[6] Paula Baker, "The Domestication of Politics: Women and American Political Society, 1780–1920," *American Historical Review* 89 (1984): 630–35; Kathryn Kish Sklar, "The Historical Foundations of Women's Power in the Creation of the American Welfare State" in *Mothers of a New World: Maternalist Politics and the Origins of Welfare States,* ed. Seth Koven and Sonya Michel (New York: Routledge, 1993), 40–46; Molly Ladd-Taylor, *Mother-Work: Women, Child Welfare, and the State, 1890–1930* (Urbana: University of Illinois Press, 1994), 135–41; Skocpol, 321–28.

[7] Robyn Muncy, *Creating a Female Dominion in American Reform, 1890–1935* (New York: Oxford University Press, 1991), 3–12; Ellen Fitzpatrick, *Endless Crusade: Women Social Scientists and Progressive Reform* (New York: Oxford University Press, 1990), xi–xiii; Skocpol, 340–50.

[8] Mary Ritter Beard, *Woman's Work in Municipalities* (New York: D. Appleman, 1915), vi–vii, 45–46, 259; Sklar, 46–52; Anne Firor Scott, *Natural Allies: Women's Associations in American History* (Urbana: University of Illinois Press, 1991), 12–44; Baker, 632–37; Ladd-Taylor, 1–11, 43–46; Skocpol, 350–68.

[9] Resolutions book, 1900–1912, and Serena Matthews, "The History of the Washington State Federation of Women's Clubs," [circa 1950], box 1, Washington State Federation of Women's Clubs records, accession 3463-11, Manuscripts and Special Collections, University of Washington Libraries, Seattle [hereafter, WSFWC records].

[10] Convention programs, 1907–1913, box 4, Washington State Branch of the National Congress of Mothers and Parent-Teacher Associations records, Accession 2226, Manuscripts and Special Collections, UW libraries [hereafter, WCOM-PTA records] and *Parent-Teacher Associations of Washington,* WCOM-PTA Bulletin 13 (1914), box 6, WCOM-PTA records.

[11] Convention programs, box 4, WCOM-PTA records; resolutions book, box 1, WSFWC records.

[12] [Seattle] *Western Woman's Outlook,* 14 November 1912, 19 December 1912, 16 January 1913, 30 January 1913; resolutions book, 1912, box 1, WSFWC records; minute book, 11 December 1912, box 2, records of Seattle branch of the WCOM-PTA, accession 3421, Manuscripts and Special Collections, UW libraries; Robert Saltvig, "The Progressive Movement in Washington" (University of Washington Ph.D. dissertation, 1966), 310–11.

[13] *Western Woman's Outlook,* 19 December 1912.

[14] *Western Woman's Outlook,* 12 December 1912.

[15] *Seattle Star,* 15 June 1913; *Western Woman's Outlook,* 12 December 1912, 19 December 1912, 30 January 1913, 6 February 1913, 13 February 1913.

[16] *Seattle Union-Record,* 15 March 1913. See also *Proceedings of the Annual Convention of the Washington State Federation of Labor,* 1912, 85, 112; and ibid., 1913, 37, 44, 47.

[17] *Seattle Juvenile Court's Annual Report*, 1914, 63. See also ibid., 1912, 7–9, 11–13, 16–17.

[18] "Third Message of Governor M. E. Hay to the State Legislature, 1913" in *Washington Public Documents, 1911–1913*, vol. 1, 40–41.

[19] *Western Woman's Outlook*, 28 November 1912. 9 January 1913, See also ibid., 16 January 1913, 30 January 1913, 3 February 1913; *Proceedings of the National Conference of Charities and Corrections at the Annual Session Held in Seattle, Washington, July 5–12, 1913* (Fort Wayne, Ind.: Fort Wayne Printing, 1913), 306–8.

[20] Minutes of annual conferences, 1913, box 3, Washington State Council of Social Work records, accession 3882, Manuscripts and Special Collections, UW libraries [hereafter, WSCSW records]. See also *Morning Olympian*, 22 January 1913.

[21] *House Journal of the State of Washington*, 1913, 297. See also ibid., 54–55, 129–30, 356–57; *Senate Journal of the State of Washington*, 1913, 1095–96; C. E. Bogardus to state senator Ralph Nichols, 30 December 1912, Ralph Nichols papers, Manuscripts and Special Collections, UW libraries; *Western Woman's Outlook*, 13 February 1913; and *Seattle Star*, 13 March 1913.

[22] Leff, 400–1.

[23] Legislators' fear of women's newly acquired ballots and the Progressive Party's strong support of clubwomen's agenda made a potent combination. While unions, farm groups, and other reformers were mostly disappointed by the 1913 legislature, clubwomen got virtually every major piece of legislation they sought. See Saltvig, 310–12.

[24] U.S. Bureau of Labor Statistics, *Summary of the Report on Condition of Woman and Child Wage-Earners in the United States*, Bureau of Labor Statistics Bulletin 175 (1915), describes several cost-of-living studies.

[25] *Laws of the State of Washington*, 1913, 644–46.

[26] *Laws of Washington*, 1905, 331–33; resolutions book, 1904, box 1, WSFWC records; *Seattle Post-Intelligencer*, 14 January 1905; [Seattle] *The Patriarch*, 22 October 1910; Ellen Ryerson, *The Best Laid Plans: America's Juvenile Court Experiment* (New York: Hill and Wang, 1979), 2–12.

[27] Resolutions book, 1910, box 1, WSFWC records. See also *WSFWC Year Book, 1910–1911*, box 1, WSFWC records; *Laws of Washington*, 1911, 189–90; and *Laws of Washington*, 1913, 64–68. Clubwomen later tried to extend juvenile courts' power even further by turning them into "courts of domestic relations" with control of divorce, alimony, and abandonment proceedings. Established courts blocked these efforts.

[28] *Seattle Juvenile Court's Annual Message to the Community*, 1914, 57–58.

[29] Judge Frater quoted in *Seattle Star*, 20 June 1913. See also *Seattle Post-Intelligencer*, 20 June 1913, and *Seattle Juvenile Court's Annual Message to the Community*, 1914, 58–59, 64.

[30] Case 3, mothers' pension records and *Seattle Juvenile Court's Annual Message to the Community*, 1914, 59–60. *Annual Report of the Seattle Juvenile Court for 1913*, 8–9, and *Seattle Juvenile Court's Annual Message to the Community*, 1914, 56.

[31] *Seattle Post-Intelligencer*, 14 June 1913. See also ibid., 20 June 1913; *Seattle Star*, 15 June 1913, 20 June 1913. *Annual Report of the Seattle Juvenile Court for 1913*, 8–9. *Seattle Post-Intelligencer*, 30 August 1914.

[32] *Seattle Juvenile Court's Annual Message to the Community*, 1914, 62–64.

[33] *Seattle Juvenile Court Report for the Year 1916*, 26–27; Gordon, *Pitied but Not Entitled*, 17–23; Goodwin, "Employable Mothers," 253–58.

[34] Case 1, mothers' pension records.

[35] Cases 97, 174, 725, ibid.; *Journal of Proceedings of the King County Commissioners*, vol. 20 (1917): 425.

[36] Case 695, mothers' pension records. See also cases 751 and 816.

[37] *Seattle Juvenile Court's Annual Message to the Community*, 1914, 56–57.

[38] Ibid., 58–65; quotations are from 59, 63.

[39] Ibid., 9–10. See also *Proceedings of the Washington State Conference of Charities and Corrections, Held in Centralia, Washington, June 2–4, 1914* (Centralia Commercial Club, 1914), 37–40 and [Centralia] *Daily Chronicle-Examiner*, 4 June 1914.

[40] Saltvig, 304, 348–52; Keith Murray, *Republican Party Politics in Washington During the Progressive Era* (University of Washington Ph.D. dissertation, 1946), 160–64, 223–24. The Democratic Party was a virtual nonentity in Washington State politics at this time.

[41] *Laws of the State of Washington*, 1915, 364.

[42] *Senate Journal of the State of Washington*, 1915, 54–55, 618–19, 676, 1088; *House Journal of the State of Washington*, 1915, 570, 881–82, 1027, 1033, 1042; *Seattle Star*, 2 March 1915, 11 March 1915; *Proceedings of the Annual Convention of the Washington State Federation of Labor*, 1915, 134, and 1916, 88–89.

[43] *Washington Parent-Teacher*, June 1916. See also minute book, 1915, box 3, WCOM-PTA records.

[44] *Seattle Juvenile Court Report for the Year 1915*, 24–25; *Seattle Star*, 30 June 1915.

[45] Convention minutes, 1916, box 2, WCOM-PTA records; *Washington Parent-Teacher*, June 1916.

[46] *Seattle Juvenile Court Report for the Year 1919*, 14, 16.

[47] *House Journal of the State of Washington*, 1917, 986; *Seattle Juvenile Court Report for the Year 1916*, 21; *Seattle Star*, 9 February 1917; *Washington Parent-Teacher*, June 1917; "Second Inaugural Message of Governor Ernest Lister" in *Washington Public Documents, 1915–1916*, vol. 1, 37; *Proceedings of the Annual Convention of the Washington State Federation of Labor*, 1916, 88–89.

[48] *Legislative Counselor*, January 1919, January extra 1919, February 1919; *Proceedings of the Annual Convention of the Washington State Federation of Labor*, 1918, 135, and 1920 supplement, 9; *Seattle Union-Record*, 13 March 1919; resolution book, 1918, box 1, WSFWC records; *Yearbook of the Washington State Federation of Women's Clubs, 1919–20*, box 2, WSFWC records; *Washington Parent-Teacher*, December 1918.

[49] *Proceedings of the Annual Convention of the Washington State Federation of Labor*, 1918, 135.

[50] *Washington Parent-Teacher*, December 1918. See also *Legislative Counselor*, January extra 1919; and *Seattle Star*, 11 March 1919. This shift in rhetoric away from the mother and to the child had begun a few years earlier: see resolutions book, 1917–18, box 1, WSFWC records; *Seattle Star*, 11 March 1915, 9 February 1917.

[51] *Seattle Post-Intelligencer*, 11 March 1919.

[52] Leona Burke McCulloch, "Condensed History of the Washington State Federation of Women's Clubs," n.d. [circa 1955], 54, box 1, accession 3463-10, WSFWC records. See also ibid., 49–56; resolutions book, 1917–1923, box 1, WSFWC records; convention records, 1918–1922, box 4, WCOM-PTA records.

[53] *Washington Parent-Teacher*, December 1918.

[54] *Parent-Teacher Associations of Washington*, WCOM-PTA Bulletin 31 (1917), box 6, WCOM-PTA records; *Washington Parent-Teacher*, December 1918; *Seattle Post-Intelligencer*, 11 March 1919; *Seattle Star*, 11 March 1919; *Legislative Counselor*, March 1919.

⁵⁵ Murray, 272–78.

⁵⁶ *Senate Journal of the State of Washington*, 1919, 322–23, 407, 533–34; *House Journal of the State of Washington*, 1919, 528; *Laws of the State of Washington*, 1919, 254; *Seattle Post-Intelligencer*, 11 March 1919; *Legislative Counselor*, March 1919.

⁵⁷ *Annual Report of the Seattle Juvenile Court*, 1918–1929.

⁵⁸ *House Journal of the State of Washington*, 1925, 86, 150, 190; ibid., 1927, 638, 712, 732, 859; ibid., 1929, 355, 435, 667; Senate Journal of the State of Washington, 1925, 385–86; ibid., 1927, 117, 418, 465, 693–94; ibid., 1929, 150, 270, 479, 632, 658.

⁵⁹ *Annual Report of the Seattle Juvenile Court*, 1926, 18.

⁶⁰ Roy Lubove, *Professional Altruist: The Emergence of Social Work as a Career, 1880–1930* (Cambridge, Mass.: Harvard University Press, 1965), 1–11, 40–47; Ladd-Taylor, 146–47; Gordon, *Pitied but Not Entitled*, 41–45.

⁶¹ *Seattle Juvenile Court's Annual Message to the Community*, 1914, inside cover, 56; [Seattle] Social Welfare League, *Yearbook*, 1920/1921, 23–24.

⁶² Case 7, mothers' pension records.

⁶³ This statistic is based on an analysis of reels 5 and 7, mothers' pension records.

⁶⁴ Cases 515, 683, ibid.; *Seattle Juvenile Court Report for the Year 1916*, 16. *Seattle Juvenile Court Annual Report for the Year 1917*, 18. See also cases 480, 515, mothers' pension records; and Mary Bogue, *Administration of Mothers' Aid in Ten Localities*, Children's Bureau Publication 184 (1928), 129, 136.

⁶⁵ Bogue, *Administration of Mothers' Aid*, 140–41; *Seattle Juvenile Court Report for the Year 1917*, 16.

⁶⁶ *Seattle Juvenile Court Report for the Year 1919*, 14–15.

⁶⁷ This figure is based on an analysis of reels 9 and 11, mothers' pension records.

⁶⁸ During the 1920s roughly 1 percent of pensioners were African-American, and African-Americans constituted 0.85 percent of the population of King County. Approximately 4 percent of pensioned mothers were Jewish, and about 3 percent of the county's residents were Jewish. Mothers of Asian descent were, however, underrepresented on the pension rolls: less than 0.5 percent of recipients were Asian, but Asians constituted about 4 percent of King County's population.

⁶⁹ Case 900, mothers' pension records. See also cases 1001, 1264, 1682, and 1856.

⁷⁰ Cases 7, 704, 988, 1219, 1856, 2284, 2467, ibid.

⁷¹ Case 515, ibid.

⁷² Case 1124, ibid.

⁷³ *Seattle Juvenile Court Report for the Years 1920 and 1921*, 19.

⁷⁴ Case 452, mothers' pension records. See also case 1219.

⁷⁵ Mary Richmond, *Social Diagnosis* (New York: Russell Sage Foundation, 1917); quotation is from page 7. See also Lubove, *Professional Altruist*, 9–11, 40–54, 80–84; Gordon, *Pitied but Not Entitled*, 76–88; and Daniel Walkowitz, "The Making of a Feminine Professional Identity: Social Workers in the 1920s," *American Historical Review* 95 (1990): 1051–75.

⁷⁶ Gordon, *Pitied but Not Entitled*, 88–106; Barbara Nelson, "Origins of the Two-Channel Welfare State: Workmen's Compensation and Mothers' Aid," in *Women, the State, and Welfare*, 142–45; Muncy, chapters 2 and 3.

⁷⁷ Bogue, *Administration of Mothers' Aid*, 9, 26. In the rest of Washington State, only Spokane County's pension administration was as professionalized as King County's. Medium-size counties like Pierce and Snohomish had no college-trained administrators and about

150 families per caseworker. Some rural counties, such as Pacific and Island, had no case-workers at all. See Ruth Bloodgood et al., *Child Welfare in Selected Counties of Washington*, Children's Bureau Publication 206 (1931), 20–25, 83.

[78] Resolutions book, 1917–1925, and McCulloch, "Condensed History of the Washington State Federation of Women's Clubs," 49–56, box 1, WSFWC records; convention records, 1918–22, box 4, WCOM-PTA records.

[79] The clubs had demanded equal pay for male and female teachers and had lobbied to get professional women appointed to many government positions. Resolutions book, 1903, 1907, 1914, 1919, box 1, WSFWC records.

[80] *Washington State Conference of Social Work Newsletter*, July 1928.

[81] Ibid., November 1925, November 1928, March 1929, July 1929, January 1930, April 1931; resolution book, 1928–1931, box 1, WSFWC records; *Washington Parent-Teacher*, June 1929, December 1930, December 1931.

[82] *Seattle Juvenile Court Report for the Year 1922*, 24.

[83] Case 2979, mothers' pension records.

[84] Case 98, ibid.

[85] Case 1341, ibid.

[86] Case 823, ibid.

[87] Case 515, ibid.

[88] Case 988, ibid.

[89] Abramovitz, 6. Mink, Moore, and Wedel hold this interpretation as well.

[90] *Seattle Juvenile Court Report for the Year 1922*, 22.

[91] Case 1169, mothers' pension records. See also cases 138, 454, 1683, 2851.

[92] Case 429, ibid. See also cases 1150 and 2583.

[93] Linda Gordon makes a similar point about social workers and their clients in *Heroes of Their Own Lives: The Politics and History of Family Violence: Boston, 1880–1960* (New York: Viking, 1988).

[94] Cases 47, 298, 490, 630, 1038, 1727, 2075, 2079, 2111, mothers' pension records.

[95] *Seattle Post-Intelligencer*, 30 August 1914. See also Bogue, *Administration of Mothers' Aid*, 11–14, 117.

[96] Case 1825, mothers' pension records.

[97] Cases 23, 419, 839, 1305, ibid.

[98] *Seattle Times*, 6 December 1932.

[99] *Annual Report of the Seattle Juvenile Court for the Year 1931*, 22.

[100] Mothers' Pension Department Supervisor Martha Castenburg to Juvenile Court Judge Michael Holmes, 2 February 1934, Juvenile Court financial records, King County Archives, Seattle.

[101] *Washington State Conference of Social Work Newsletter*, June 1936.

[102] *Laws of the State of Washington*, 1937, 718–31.

# MEXICAN-AMERICAN WOMEN POLITICIANS IN SEATTLE

## Elizabeth Salas

Imagine being a Mexican-American woman politician trying to get elected in the city of Seattle where there are no Mexican-American enclaves or viable ethnic political organizations to sponsor your candidacy. Nonetheless two Mexican-American women tried and failed to get on the Seattle City Council as radical Chicana politicians while two liberal Democratic Mexican-American women ran for the posts of state senator and state representative and won.

This essay examines Mexican-American women political candidates through a biographical lens, taking into consideration Chicana radical leftist politics and Mexican-American mainstream liberal politics in the evolution of successful Mexican-American women politicians in Seattle.

Stella Ortega wanted to be appointed to the Seattle City Council in 1989 after Norm Rice had vacated the post as mayor while Yolanda Alaniz, a member of the Freedom Socialist Party, was defeated after running for a seat on the Seattle City Council in 1991. Margarita Lopez Prentice, a Democrat, currently serves as a state senator for the 11th District (West Seattle, the International District, Beacon Hill, White Center, South Park, Harbor Island, and parts of Renton, Tukwila, and the Boeing Industrial Park). Phyllis Gutierrez Kenney, a Democrat, was appointed as a state representative for the 46th District (Pinehurst, Lake City, Northgate, Greenwood, Green Lake, Ravenna, View Ridge, and Hawthorne Hills) in 1997 and was elected in 2000. This article will evaluate to what extent these politicians highlight or mute their ethnic identities as part of their campaigns for office and their political concerns while serving their Seattle constituents, who for the most part are not Mexican-Americans.[1]

## MEXICAN-AMERICANS IN WASHINGTON

Many people in Seattle and the state of Washington know little about Mexican-Americans or their history in the Pacific Northwest. In general there is a misguided belief that Mexican-Americans are recent arrivals or are mostly "illegal aliens." Historically, Mexican-Americans represent both one of the oldest founding groups in the area as well as many of the latest immigrant arrivals to Seattle. As Spanish colonials, Mexican men were part of the expeditions sent to the Pacific Northwest by the empire of New Spain in the 1790s. The settlement at Neah Bay in 1792 consisted of 200 men. No women were among the colonists. The settlement lasted only two years before being dismantled. By 1818, Spain had ceded its holdings in the Pacific Northwest to the United States. As of 1848, the United States had waged a brutal war against Mexico to gain ownership of Texas, New Mexico, California, Arizona, and parts of Colorado, Utah, and Kansas. When these areas became part of the United States, about 80,000 to 100,000 Mexicans who remained on these lands became Americans as stipulated in the 1848 Treaty of Guadalupe Hidalgo. From the 1840s to the 1860s a few of these new American citizens began a northward trek to what would later become Washington State as muleteers and miners. Some families settled in Washington for brief periods and then moved either back to the U.S. Southwest or farther northward to Canada. It wasn't until the 1920s through 1940s that Mexican-Americans and Mexicans began to lay down permanent roots in Washington State. Many of them were migrant farm workers from Texas, California, New Mexico, or Mexico. During World War II, male Mexican workers known as *braceros* were contracted from Mexico to work in the Southwest as well as the Pacific Northwest as agricultural or railroad workers. Between 1942 and 1947 about 47,000 braceros worked in Washington, Idaho and Oregon. Many of the braceros liked the Pacific Northwest and returned to the area with their families. Immigration from the Southwest and Mexico has been constant since then and the number of people of Mexican ancestry in Washington has increased as jobs in agriculture and related industries have developed in the state. It has been difficult for Mexican and Mexican-American women to move into politics because of limited education and the traditional duties they had as mothers of large numbers of children. Yet Mexican-American women politicians tend to cite the importance of their mothers as role models.[2]

According to the 2000 U.S. census, there are 35.3 million Latinos in the United States. People of Mexican origin represent 20.6 million, or 58.5 percent, of these Latinos. An estimated 7 million "illegal aliens" live in the United States. Probably a significant number of them are from Mexico. In the state of Washington, the 2000 census counted 5,894,121 residents, of whom 441,509, or 7.5 percent, are Latinos. About 113,667 Latinos are registered voters. Most of Washington's Latino population is Mexican-American or Mexican. A considerable number of Mexicans in Washington are described as'"indigenous" peoples who speak in native dialects rather than Spanish or English.

In 1990, Latinos were evenly divided between eastern and western Washington. But according to the 2000 census, about 54 percent of Latinos live in western Washington and 46 percent live in eastern Washington. Yakima County, which is about 35 percent Latino, has been replaced by King County as the county having the largest number of Latinos. The Latino population in King County more than doubled (115 percent) between 1990 and 2000. King County has 95,242 Latinos, and they represent 5.5 percent of the county population. Seattle has about 29,719 Latinos. Other cities have considerably fewer Latinos, with 6,486 in Kent, 5,827 in Bellevue, 3,818 in Renton, 2,538 in Redmond, and 2,320 in Tukwila. Barrios are emerging in Bellevue, with the Latino population representing 16 percent of the city's new residents in the last 10 years.[3]

One of the problems affecting Mexican-American politicians trying to establish an ethnic voting base in Seattle has to do with the age of the population. Statewide, the Latino population is young, with about 40 percent under age 18 and unable to vote. Several other factors hinder effective Latino efforts to get elected to office. Although the majority of Latino voters tend to vote Democratic, both the Democratic and Republican parties are thought to ignore Latino voters and do not focus on issues of importance to Latinos, such as education, farm worker housing, and immigration amnesty. Organizers who work for voter registration note that volunteers need to go "door-to-door" to encourage Latinos to register and vote. Outreach efforts to the Latino population need to include recruiting individuals with bilingual skills in both Spanish and English, spreading information about the process of voting for first-time voters to dispel the idea that any connection with the government is bad, and promoting the use of absentee ballots for migratory farm workers. The lack of U.S. citizenship also makes it hard to integrate the Mexican community into American political participation. Mexico now allows its citizens to have the right of dual citizenship in both Mexico and the United States, and this change in Mexico's policy is considered an important boost to U.S. citizenship efforts.[4]

In Seattle, most Mexican-Americans do not live together in identifiable neighborhoods and do not have local organizations that evolved from ethnic neighborhood consciousness of problems. Rather, El Centro de la Raza has emerged as an institution that Latinos go to for help, services, and various kinds of political activism. It is a nonprofit organization that was established in 1972 to provide social, community, civic, and cultural services to Chicano/Latino low-income residents from its location on the former Beacon Hill Elementary School property.

There is not an ethnic Mexican-American statewide agenda, something political observers think is caused by "the Cascade Curtain." Another factor is the "turf mentality" of grassroots leaders who work in isolation from each other and find it hard to support Latino issues and needs.[5]

## MEXICAN-AMERICAN WOMEN IN WASHINGTON STATE POLITICS

The three top Mexican-American office holders in the state of Washington are women, two of whom are based in Seattle: state Senator Margarita Lopez Prentice, who represents the 11th District, and state Representative Phyllis Gutierrez Kenney, who represents the 46th District. Their political careers are considered later in this essay. A third Mexican–American woman, state Representative Mary Skinner (a Republican) represents Position 1 of the 14th District in Yakima. In the 2000 election Skinner got 15,401, or 66 percent of the vote. The main industries in the 14th District involve agriculture, tree fruits, grapes, wineries, tourism, fruit packaging and processing, and light manufacturing. As of 2000 Skinner is serving her fourth term as state representative for the 14th District. Previously Skinner, who worked as a junior high school teacher and community volunteer, served as the 3rd Congressional District member of the Washington State Board of Education.

The fact that the three highest Mexican-American office holders in the state of Washington in 2002 are women is unusual. Mexican-American men have held office at the local and state levels in the past, but there seems to be no good explanation why they do not hold high office at this time. Possible explanations for the low numbers of Mexican-American men running and getting elected to office might include a lack of effective grassroots organizing due to the fact that women are the workhorses for campaigns, a perceived "negative" view of politics as a good and consistent employment opportunity, and more opportunities for influence and prestige in the economic rather than the political arena. Meanwhile, in the Southwest, Mexican-American men politicians have held local, state, and national offices and continue to seek higher office. In March 2002, Tony Sanchez, an oilman who traces his ethnic roots to the 18th century, defeated Dan Morales, a third-generation Mexican-American former state attorney general, to win the Democratic gubernatorial nomination in Texas.[6]

Mexican-American women politicians such as Ortega, Alaniz, Prentice, Kenney, and Skinner come from a generation of activism by Mexican-American women all over the state of Washington. Among the Mexican-American women politicians who have been influenced by the Seattle politicians are Luisa Torres, Clara Jimenez, and Becky Diaz. These three Mexican-American women politicians fit the political profile of successful Latina office holders. Predictors for Latina political participation include financial status, civic skills, and an involvement in organizations especially related to education.

Luisa Torres, director of the Department of Health and Social Services in Pasco, was appointed to that town's city council in 1989. When she ran for the city council in 1990, however, she was soundly defeated. Her appointment has been explained as maximizing the large Latino voting age population through voter registration drives conducted by the Northwest Community Projects and the Southwest Voter Research Institute of San Antonio, Texas, in 1988. A local activist, Luz Bazan Gutierrez, director of the Northwest Community Projects, is also cited as an important woman activist who helped promote Torres's appointment to the city council.[7]

Clara Jimenez and Becky Diaz are among the Mexican-American women who have also been elected to local offices in Washington. In 1997 Jimenez, 38, ran for the Toppenish City Council and won. She grew up a farm worker with a strong desire to become a history teacher and run for office. Her self-determination led her to say, "I just decided I was going to be a councilwoman and showed them I could do it running a good, clean campaign."[8] She ran on the issues of paying increased attention to young people's needs and encouraging business development in Toppenish. Her campaign was featured in a local Spanish-language newspaper and resulted in a very high voter turnout in the predominantly Mexican-American east precinct of Toppenish. She combined advocacy of non-ethnic issues with a pronounced specific interest in issues relevant to a large number of Mexican-American voters in her area. Jimenez is a Mexican-American woman politician who maximized her political strength by using an ethnic voter base of support.

Becky Diaz, on the other hand, was elected to the Bellingham school board in 1997 in what is described as a mostly Euro-American community of northwest Washington. Diaz, a homemaker, had been active in the Whatcom Hispanic Organization for the previous 10 years. She focuses on education with the view that Latino children without education do not have a chance to compete in American society. Diaz considers her move into elected office as "natural" for Latinas, equating taking care of a household with taking care of the community through politics.

These three politicians show the beginning of a trend toward the mainstreaming of Mexican-American politics. All three had to diversify their political portfolios to either galvanize their ethnic enclaves or expand their electoral bases by focusing on general issues such as education and labor rather than on issues that impact only Mexican-Americans. The political experiences of these politicians helped to formulate how candidates in Seattle would successfully run and win elections.[9]

## CHICANA RADICAL POLITICS AND THE SEATTLE CITY COUNCIL

Two Chicana activists sought to either get appointed to the Seattle City Council or win a seat by defeating another candidate. Both women, Stella Ortega and Yolanda Alaniz, were greatly influenced by the Chicano Movement and the creation of Chicano studies programs in the 1960s. El Movimiento (the Movement) promoted change in the United States for Mexican-Americans by the creation of a new and aggressive identity as Chicanos and Chicanas and a very progressive agenda that included the rights of working-class Mexicans and Mexican-Americans to obtain better jobs, higher wages, bilingual education, and an end to discrimination based on racial profiling in all areas of life in the United States.

The Seattle City Council has nine members who are elected at large to four-year terms through citywide elections held in odd-numbered years. When Norm Rice, an African American, left the Seattle City Council in 1989, Stella Ortega wanted to be appointed to replace him. She received the recommendation of Rodrigo Barron, president of a Seattle Latino organization known as Concilio. Ortega was born into a farm worker family in Texas in the 1950s. As a young adult she was an advocate for farm worker rights as well as student rights when she attended the University of Houston. She participated in the American Indian Movement for treaty rights on the Nisqually River in Washington State and at Wounded Knee, South Dakota. She had worked at El Centro de la Raza for seven years and was noted for developing one of the best and most comprehensive social delivery systems in the city according to *La Voz*, the local Mexican-American newspaper. She did not get the appointment.[10]

Yolanda Alaniz, dubbed by admirers and critics alike as "Seattle's favorite fire-brand and organizer," ran for the Seattle City Council in 1991. Alaniz sought to combine her radicalized ethnicity as a Chicana with concerns about gender and world politics, not through mainstream politics but through third-party radical politics. She believed in organizational development through demand-protest behavior. However, running a third-party political campaign made her task harder.

Alaniz was born in the early 1950s in Texas. Her family came from Brownsville, Texas, and in 1956 moved to Sunnyside in the Yakima Valley in eastern Washington. Yakima is known as the "Little Mississippi" of the Northwest. This is a very negative designation as life for African-American farm workers in Mississippi is extremely difficult. The Yakima Valley is also considered the "Fruit Bowl of the Nation." It is 60 miles long and about 15 to 20 miles wide. Intensive irrigation and the Yakima River supply water to the dry but rich land for labor-intensive crops such as fruit orchards, grapes, hops, asparagus, mint, and sugar beets. Alaniz's parents, Ninfa and Ramon, had seven children. She was the oldest. Farm work is dangerous for children. Alaniz and her sister Louise barely saved their brother Ramon Junior from drowning after he fell into an irrigation ditch. By the age of 6, Alaniz was on the picket line at the local Safeway store alongside her mother.[11]

Alaniz knew that school was important because her parents had only completed the second grade. She would study after working in the fields. One of her sisters remembered her burning the midnight oil studying her books. In the late 1960s she attended the University of Washington when the Chicano Movement developed in the midst of the civil rights and anti-war protests. While there she became a member of a radical organization called the Brown Berets. The paramilitary group considered themselves combatants for El Movimiento and promoted militant action to address social injustices against Chicanos. Alaniz also joined another ethnic organization, called MEChA (Chicano Student Movement of Aztlan). She recalled having to fight the "machismo" of MEChA. Alaniz was one of many college-educated feminists during the 1960s. These Chicanas, according to Alaniz, "were strikingly militant, courageous, dedicated, and verbal" in their demands to college administrators for "bilingual and multicultural childcare for Chicana students and staff, Chicana curriculum and Chicana instructors." But, according to Alaniz, Chicanas "were often ordered back to the kitchen, the bedroom, and the typewriter, and told to leave politics to the men."[12]

She wrote a pamphlet called "In Defense of Adultery," because MEChA denounced Chicanas who had "affairs." Her struggle against MEChA was fairly typical of the bias that Chicanas encountered with this organization throughout the Southwest. Chicanas in the Southwest challenged MEChA's "machos" in conventional protest of exclusion from leadership positions while doing the bulk of the

Yolanda Alaniz during her City Council campaign, speaking at the 1991 Lesbian/Gay/Bisexual/Transgender Pride Parade and Freedom Rally in Seattle. Courtesy of Kathleen Merrigan / Freedom Socialist Party.

busywork of the organization. Alaniz went a step further in her challenge against the double standard practiced by MEChAistas (followers of MEChA) by confronting them in public spaces, something most Chicanas did not want to do. Most Chicanas considered it more important to subsume gender protest than to challenge solidarity with Chicano men based on ethnicity and class.

Alaniz's struggles with sexist and nationalistic Chicano men on the University of Washington campus as well as organizing a campus union of low-paid service workers led her to join the Freedom Socialist Party (FSP) in 1976. The FSP started in Seattle in 1966 as a political party where women, people of color, and lesbians and gays were considered to be the movers and shakers in working-class struggle for change. An offshoot of the FSP was a sister organization known as Radical Women. This women's group, which Alaniz also joined, was described as a socialist, feminist, Trotskyist, internationalist organization "standing in the front lines of the fight for indigenous peoples' struggles against racism, sexism, anti-gay bigotry, and labor exploitation."[13] In her personal life, Alaniz came out as a lesbian. She raised her daughter in a communal house in accordance with her socialist beliefs.

Alaniz spent more than 30 years as one of the most radical activists in Seattle's history. She supported most causes calling for loud protest and militant demonstrations. While Alaniz supported Chicano causes, she strongly believed in the political integration of all movements for social and economic change. She changed from identifying herself as a "Chicana" to calling herself a "Chicana socialist feminist." In 1989 she coauthored, with Megan Cornish, a series of newspaper articles that turned into a book, *The Chicano Struggle: A Racial or a National Movement*. On the political front, Alaniz ran for a seat on the Seattle City Council in 1991. She netted 18 percent of the vote, but her opponent, Sue Donaldson, who had been appointed to Norm Rice's seat, won the race.

In 1995 Alaniz decided to move to Los Angeles and agitate for radical causes there. She continues to be part of ethnic struggle in Los Angeles and co-edited with Nellie Wong a book called *Voices of Color* in 1999. She continues to be a member of the Freedom Socialist Party and Radical Women. Alaniz describes the political party as "integrationist, internationalist, feminist, and multi-issue." She maintains that people of color will spearhead the coming American revolution. Her move to Los Angeles may have been partly based on the fact that her socialist message could be addressed to the large number of people of color who live in California as opposed to remaining in Washington State, where people of color are a minority.[14]

The political experiences of Ortega and Alaniz show that the Seattle City Council was not ready for militant Chicana activists who placed ethnic and working-class issues high on their political agendas. These two organizers were known and admired in the Chicano and radical political communities as fiery activists but were unable to convince Seattle decision makers and voters that they would represent all constituents.

## Margarita Lopez Prentice and the State Senate

Margarita Prentice is a Democrat who has done well in advocating education and labor reforms. Born in the early 1930s, she grew up as Margarita Lopez in California, the daughter of Mexican immigrants. Her schooling includes Phoenix College, Youngstown University in Ohio, St. Joseph's Hospital School of Nursing in Phoenix, and the University of Washington. Prentice worked as a registered nurse for 46 years and was director of the Mount St. Vincent nursing home in Seattle. She lives in Skyway with her husband of 42 years, Bill Prentice, and has three children and five grandchildren.

Like many politically active Mexican-American women, Prentice ran for her local school board (in Renton). She was very active in the Democratic Party, serving as vice-chairperson of the King County Democratic Central Committee. She ran for the state House of Representatives and served four years, from 1988 to 1992.[15] As a state representative Prentice drew praise from health-care and labor

Margarita Prentice (D), Washington State Senator for
the 11th District. Courtesy of Washington State.

groups for sponsoring legislation on their behalf. She was for improved health care
for Hispanics, stating her concerns about "maternal care for our women, particularly women who don't have access [to health care] in any other way than through
state-funded programs." But she was also aware that health programs often run
out of money in the fall and must ask a reluctant Legislature for more funds. In
1991 she introduced a bill that would raise the state's minimum wage by 50 cents,
to $4.75 an hour. Prentice's reason for raising the minimum wage was to counter
the "skyrocketing housing costs and a higher cost of living than many other re-
gions of the country." Prentice also sponsored House Bill 1567, which would force
employers to provide protective clothing or equipment at no cost to workers who
were exposed to pesticides on the job. In sponsoring the bill, in 1991, Prentice
remarked that "farm workers put in long hours under exhausting conditions for
low pay, and the least we can do is protect them from harm."[16]

In 1992, Prentice decided to run for the state senate in the 11th District and
won. The greater Seattle area that she represents tends to lean liberal. Part of her
campaign contained an appeal to Latino voters. She said,

> Hispanics in Washington State must unify and become more politically
> active to ensure that gains already made will not be taken away and that
> Hispanic issues will be addressed in the Legislature. We really need to

educate ourselves about the necessity of running for office. If we hang back and don't become involved, then anything can be done to us.

Prentice's four issues of concern were worker protection and safety, transportation planning, crime prevention, and education reform.[17]

While Prentice sponsored positive farm worker legislation that was affirmed by the Mexican-American community in 1991, since that year she has continually sponsored legislation that the Mexican-American community interested in farm worker rights regards as highly negative. In 1997 Prentice sponsored a bill, Senate Bill 5668, that dealt with temporary farm worker housing. The bill allowed agricultural growers to build housing for farm workers without heat, electricity, insulation, or toilet or kitchen facilities. Prentice, as the highest-ranking Mexican-American in the state legislature, was thought of by local Chicano leaders as a "credible voice for farm workers, due to her past advocacy of farm worker rights" and therefore the bill unanimously passed the state legislature. It was suggested that Prentice "is not acting alone" and is the "point person, once again, for those who seek only a narrow and questionable solution in the form of substandard housing."[18] Activists from the Mexican-American community found the bill unacceptable because requirements for constructing farm-worker housing were eliminated by exempting employer-provided worker housing from the state building code. The bill authorized the widespread use of tents and other substandard housing with seven-foot ceilings and 3,000-square-foot barracks for up to 60 people. Newly appointed state Representative Phyllis Gutierrez Kenney was said to have remarked that, as a child who had to sleep in labor camps and work in the fields, she found the bill unacceptable and the legislation a "giant step backwards."[19]

The legislation, according to Kenney, made farm workers "feel and live like they are lesser beings." The opposition to the legislation was so strong that Governor Gary Locke vetoed the bill.[20] Providing migrants with temporary and permanent housing continues to be a very knotty issue for Washington State. During the 2002 legislative session, Prentice once again sponsored bills relating to agricultural workers. Senate Bill 6680 exempts agricultural workers who are paid on a piece-rate basis from minimum-wage laws.[21]

Prentice began her political career by acknowledging her own ethnicity as well as fighting for issues of concern to Mexican-Americans involving worker rights, especially for farm workers. But by 1997 Prentice had clearly decided to sponsor legislation that would negatively affect farm workers in relation to housing. Prentice believes that the issue of farm worker housing is a very difficult one, especially if the rights of all sides—farm-workers and farmers—are to be addressed. Her stance on the issue of farm workers is at odds with most elements of the Mexican-American political community.

# PHYLLIS GUTIERREZ KENNEY IN THE STATE HOUSE OF REPRESENTATIVES

Phyllis Gutierrez Kenney is a Democrat who has done very well in combining civic activism while remaining a strong advocate for Mexican-American rural and urban communities. She has been characterized by local Mexican-American leaders as a "leader and she happens to be Latina." Her parents emigrated from Mexico in 1919 and worked as migrant farm workers. Felipa, as she was known then, was born in Hardin, Montana, in 1936, the sixth of eight children. Her father organized the first beet workers in Montana during 1936–1937, while her mother sold sandwiches and sodas for additional money. By 1942 the family moved to Washington State. Kenney grew up in the Yakima Valley, in Wapato and Toppenish.

In Wapato she entered the first grade knowing only Spanish. The family picked potatoes by hand. At the early age of 5, Kenney's job was to shake the vines free of potatoes so that the older children could pick them up and put them in heavy sacks that they dragged behind them. Kenney is allergic to pesticides and could not work in the hop fields. She remembers the lack of bathrooms in the fields while she was picking asparagus for 75 cents an hour. She recalls the death of a friend who fell off a plank and into an irrigation ditch, as well as the brother who died of pneumonia caused by poor housing. Snow would come into the cracks, the windows would break, and the family would struggle to close the cracks by putting blankets over the windows. It was from these beginnings that Kenney became a strong advocate for farm workers.

Kenney's father died at an early age, so her mother set out to establish a restaurant. While many thought she would not succeed in starting a business, she persisted. It took her a long time to learn English. Kenney's mother was fond of saying, "I can do it. I'm going to do it." Kenney regarded her mother as her mentor and role model for determination and will power in accomplishing what she wanted to do. Kenney recognized the challenge of being both a woman and an ethnic minority, but noted that there is a challenge in being a Hispanic woman in many professions, whether it's in higher education or in medicine.

Kenney later moved to the Tri-Cities and lived there for 21 years. She worked in the fields for the full nine months of her first pregnancy. Her family would pick grapes, prunes, and other fruit in the Tri-Cities on weekends to make extra money. She went through a divorce from her first husband and recalled the difficulties of being a single parent of 10 children. Kenney's second husband, Larry Kenney, was the former president of the Washington Labor Council. The couple moved to north Seattle and has lived in the 46th District since 1976. Kenney beams with pride when she talks about her 10 children and her 18 grandchildren.

Her first major stint at organizing began when she co-founded the Daycare Aid Program in the Tri-Cities that trained migrant mothers. The women worked to get their high school diplomas through the GED program and were then encouraged to seek higher education at colleges. Many of the graduates of this pro-

Phyllis G. Kenney (D), Representative from the 46th District to the Washington State House of Representative. Courtesy of Phyllis Kenney.

gram became educators at Central Washington University. Kenney likes the idea of helping migrant mothers to enter the education field at all levels, from K–12 to the universities. She also co-founded the Educational Institute for Rural Families in Pasco. Her commitment to Latinos and women in education has seen her call for a Latino to be appointed to the Board of Regents at the University of Washington and to say that, "before she dies," she hopes that a woman will be appointed president at the University of Washington.

Health care is another concern for Kenney. She is a founder of the Farm Workers' Clinics in eastern Washington. She is concerned that people are not receiving the medical care they require at affordable prices. She thinks that many insurance companies like to take the premiums but don't like to pay for health-care services. Like her mother, who owned a business, Kenney started a small consignment shop for women's fashions, called Felipa's. She remains a strong advocate of labor union activism due to her former membership in the Tri-Cities Culinary Union and the Washington Federation of State Employees, AFSCME (American Federation of State, County and Municipal Employees).[22]

Kenney made the move from activist to politician in 1996, at the age of 60, when she ran for secretary of state. The Washington secretary of state oversees elections, corporate registrations, and state records. Many Mexican-American women have held the secretary of state position in New Mexico since 1922. In New Mexico, this position is considered the niche that Mexican-American women have created for themselves in state politics. Kenney's opponent was the incumbent, Ralph Munro, who had held the office for the last 16 years. She characterized herself as "very energetic" and believed new management was needed at the secretary of state level, especially in relation to bringing in new technological approaches to the position. Kenney stated that the reason she moved from civic activist to public elected official was because her parents had instilled in her a desire to give back to the community and move up in society.

She believed that limited representation of Latinos in state politics was due to many factors. She cited the community's "lack of self-assurance," and the fact that Latinos were not concentrated in urban areas like other minority groups. "We don't have barrios, or our own International District, or our own Central District," she said. "We are scattered throughout. This produces both positive and negative consequences: It's good and it's bad. It's good that we are going out into the community and living where we want to live. It's not so good because we really don't have a forum to come together to unite and be strong." Kenney also noted that there was no one on the mayor's staff to serve as an advocate for Latinos.[23]

Kenney believed her experiences as an administrator, educator, businesswoman, parent, and community volunteer made her an excellent candidate for the position of secretary of state. She believed that the only way upward mobility in a minority community can be established is to gain power within the state and society. She put forth an A-C-T-I-O-N agenda: "Advocacy" for jobs, "Change" to increase the vote by mail, "Teaching" children to be excited about voting, "Interaction" through improved Internet access to the secretary of state's office, "Opportunity" to make Washington a leader in voter participation, and "New leadership" and vision in the office. Kenney noted that the secretary of state's office was in charge of the state archives. According to Kenney, the five major state archives in Washington were "pretty antiquated," and she wanted to put the archives in an electronic retrieval and storage system. She lost the election to Munro.[24]

Although Kenney lost the election, in 1997 she was sworn in as a member of the state Legislature representing the 46th District. This occurred when state Senator Nita Rinehart left the Legislature to direct the Senate Democratic Caucus, leaving room for state Representative Ken Jacobsen to move into the Senate and for Kenney to be appointed to the Representative position. For her first legislative session, Kenney was assigned to the Law and Justice, Appropriations, and Higher Education committees.

Kenney is a strong supporter of social justice for women and Mexican Americans and Mexicans. She is very good at linking gender and ethnicity issues in her political concerns. Such is the case with trafficking of women and children legislation proposed in the 2002 legislative session. At a 2001 conference on the subject held at the University of Washington, Kenney commented that "prostitution is alive and well" in the state and explained how Mexican women and girls were impacted by this trafficking. She talked about "Rosa," a 14-year-old Mexicana from Vera Cruz who ended up in the United States where she thought she was getting a respectable job. Instead she was told to have sex with men for money. One of her bosses raped her; she got pregnant and had an abortion. Rosa felt ashamed and thought life was not worth living. Kenney said that just as there were laws against children working in the fields, there should be laws protecting children like Rosa from the sex trade.[25]

## MEXICAN-AMERICAN WOMEN POLITICIANS AND EDUCATION

The issue that concerns elected Mexican-American officeholders the most is education from K–12 to the university level. The issue is vital to Mexican-Americans because between 1986 and 2000 the number of Latino children in Washington in K–12 increased by 173 percent, compared to Asian/Pacific Island student growth of 99 percent, African-American student growth of 80 percent, and Euro-American student growth of 13 percent. While the number of Latino students increases, academic-achievement indicators remain low. Over the last two decades Latino children have consistently scored last or next to last on statewide assessments. There is also a need for Latino teachers. In the year 2000, the Latino teacher-to-student ratio was the worst in the state. The ratio of Latino teachers to Latino students was 1:100, compared to 1:66 for African-Americans and Native Americans, 1:63 for Asian/Pacific Island–Americans and 1:16 for Euro-Americans.[26]

Both Prentice and Kenney have a strong commitment to providing access to the universities and to providing labor rights for professors and teaching assistants. They both support legislation to provide Hispanics with scholarship funds. In February 2002, both Prentice and Kenney had the honor, as primary sponsors of Senate Bill 6440 and House Bill 2403 (collective bargaining rights for college faculty), of presenting these bills before the Senate and House. The collective bargaining bill passed the Legislature and was signed into law by Governor Locke. While the collective bargaining bill is considered a historical event in the state of Washington, it also serves as a historical first in that two Mexican-American women politicians were prominent in securing the passage of this legislation, which combines both higher education and labor rights for residents of Washington.

## CONCLUSION

Mexican-Americans are under-represented in political office in King County, Seattle, and the state of Washington. Barriers to political participation include problems of citizenship, the young age of the Mexican-American population, language skills, low levels of registered voters, and the lack of well-defined neighborhoods and community political organizations. Mexican-Americans who are in office in Seattle and the state of Washington at the highest levels are women. This success can be attributed to a democratic leveling process alive and well in the United States, where women as individuals can aspire to participate as leaders at both the local and state level. While Alaniz's core constituency was Chicanas and radicals, the more successful candidates for office in Seattle have been Prentice and Kenney, who are not seen as "ethnic" politicians. This success shows that in a largely Euro-American state like Washington, to win elections, "it pays to be race neutral."[27] Yet Alaniz, Prentice, and Kenney have addressed the major issues that profoundly impact the Mexican-American community. Elected officeholders, Prentice and Kenney emphasize the importance of labor in their political and legislative agendas. But while Kenney is a strong advocate of all workers, including farm workers, Prentice is strongly committed to labor rights for all workers, but doesn't meet the standards of some regarding farm workers. Better education for Mexican-Americans remains a clear, constant, and ethnic theme for Seattle's Mexican-American women politicians.

## NOTES

[1] Mexican American, Hispanic, Chicana/o and Latina/o are terms that refer to U.S. born or naturalized citizens while the term "Mexican" refers to persons born in Mexico. The term "Chicana" can also reflect a belief in radical third-party politics that emerged in the leftist ideology of the Chicano Movement of the 1960s.

[2] Erasmo Gamboa, "Washington's Mexican Heritage: A View Into the Spanish Explorations, 1774–1792." *Columbia*, vol. 3 (Fall 1989). Erasmo Gamboa, *Mexican Labor and World War II: Braceros in the Pacific Northwest, 1942–1947* (Austin: University of Texas Press, 1990).

[3] *The Seattle Times*, 26 March 2001.

[4] *The Seattle Times*, 30 November 1997. *Seattle Post-Intelligencer*, 1 November 2000.

[5] *Ibid.*

[6] In New Mexico, hundreds of Mexican-American men have held political office, ranging from territorial governor to the state legislature; see Maurilio Vigil, *Los Patrones: Profiles of Hispanic Political Leaders in New Mexico History* (Washington, D.C.: University Press of America, 1980). *Los Angeles Times*, 17 March 2002.

[7] *The Spokesman Review*, 14 November 1993.

[8] *The Seattle Times*, 30 November 1997.

[9] *Ibid.* Pei-te Lien, "Ethnicity and Political Parties: A Comparison Between Asian and Mexican Americans," *Political Behavior*, vol. 16, no. 2, 237–40.

[10] *La Voz*, December 1989.

[11] *Freedom Socialist*, September–November 1986, 14–16. Flyer about Alaniz dated 4 July 1995. Interview with Alaniz, 4 July 1995.

[12] *Ibid.*

[13] Yolanda Alaniz and Nellie Wong, editors, *Voices of Color* (Seattle: Red Letter Press, 1999).

[14] *Ibid.*

[15] *La Voz*, April 1992 and December 1994.

[16] *Ibid.*, March 1991.

[17] *Ibid.*, April, 1992.

[18] *Ibid.*, May 1997.

[19] *Ibid.*, December 1997.

[20] *Ibid.*

[21] Washington State Legislature/All Bills by Sponsor/Prentice.

[22] Washington State Hispanic Chamber of Commerce Newsletter, 1994. Kenney campaign materials for secretary of state position, 1996. *Yakima Herald-Republic*, 16 March 1996. The *Seattle Times*, 20 March 1996. *La Voz*, September 1996 and February–March 1997. Interview, 7 November 2001.

[23] *Ibid.*

[24] Kenney campaign materials for Secretary of State, 1996.

[25] "Labor Workshop," Trafficking in Women and Children conference, University of Washington, Seattle, November 3, 2001.

[26] La Voz, vol. 23, no. 1, January-February 2001.

[27] Nhien Nguyen, "Double Duty: The Rough Road for Northwest Politicians of Color," *ColorsNW Magazine*, April 2001, 19.

# BUILDING A VIETNAMESE COMMUNITY FROM SCRATCH

## THE FIRST FIFTEEN YEARS IN KING COUNTY

Nhien T. Nguyen

My father is a man of few words. When I was growing up, the only story he told our family was the one about nearly losing me in the ocean the day we fled from Vietnam. At 6 months old, I was strapped to my father's back, with my brother hanging for dear life on his front. As my father ran to the boat, his foot slipped along the dock, knocking him off balance. I teetered on his back with the waves snapping underneath me as he struggled to regain his composure.

It wasn't until I was in college, preparing an assignment on family history, that I learned of stories about other precarious moments that ensued after my near mishap while coming to America. I asked my father question after question about his struggles and achievements resettling our family of six—first in Spokane, Washington, then Portland, Oregon. I realized then that his years of silence were not because he did not want to tell the stories, but because I had never asked the questions.

Part of the excitement of this particular project was having the opportunity to ask Vietnamese-Americans in King County about their experiences of resettlement. As I embarked on the research process, I initially planned to interview a random selection of Vietnamese-Americans, from average working-class individuals to professionals. During the initial stage of identifying subjects to interview, I discovered that the handful of Vietnamese community leaders and activists who would provide me with resources had rarely, if ever, been asked to share their personal stories.

The individuals interviewed were specifically targeted for their ability to analyze their experiences in relation to the wider Vietnamese immigration experience in this area. They were also chosen to discuss their motivation for, and the process of, helping to build the Vietnamese-American community. The six individuals interviewed share the common traits of being educated and having a high level of English fluency, though they differ in when they arrived in the Pacific Northwest and their age at arrival. The following are the names of the subjects, the year and their age when they came to America, and their current occupation.

- Loan Nguyen:[1] Arrived in 1975 at age 12; former associate director of the Washington Commission on Asian Pacific American Affairs.
- Sinh Nguyen:[2] Arrived in 1978 at age 23; public affairs director for the Center for Career Alternatives.
- Van Diep:[3] Arrived in 1978 at age 1; public relations manager at Wing Luke Asian Museum
- Tuan (pseudonym):[4] Arrived in 1980 at age 34; restaurant owner and business leader.
- Thao Tran:[5] Arrived in 1982 at age 6; executive director of Vietnamese American Business Development of South Seattle (VABDOSS).
- Nhan Thai:[6] Arrived in 1983 at age 8; health educator for International District Community Health Services.

The Vietnamese community came together and built a strong network out of necessity to address their needs as recent immigrants in King County. Though the area provided government aid and social services, it was the grassroots work of Vietnamese leaders that made major impacts on the advancement of the Vietnamese community. The road to becoming a leader and activist, however, was not an easy one. Early adjustment obstacles, political disputes carried over from the homeland, and economic issues prevented individuals from taking action. Generational gaps that continue today greatly affected the development of the community.

This essay focuses on the first 15 years of the Vietnamese resettlement in King County, from 1975 to 1990. Generally, the Vietnamese arrived in two periods: the first wave from April 1975 to 1977 and the second wave from 1977 to 1982.[7] This project intended to compare the experiences of the immigrants from the two waves. The six interviews showed that there were fewer distinctions in resettlement issues with each wave than originally believed. In King County, these immigrants shared similar issues in their first few years of adjustment, regardless of which wave they arrived in.

By way of background, as a result of the Federal Government Refugee Dispersion Policy, 4,182 Vietnamese refugees of the first wave were resettled, 3.22 percent of whom were resettled in Washington between 1975 and 1982.[8] By 1977, 6,000 Vietnamese were living in Washington, 2,500 in King County.[9] In 1980, Washington State had the fifth-highest population of Vietnamese in the country.[10] The Vietnamese population grew steadily in the area for the first 15 years. According to the 2000 U.S. Census, the population of Vietnamese residents in Washington was 46,149, or 0.8 percent of the state population.

As the region was already a home to Asian immigrants for at least two generations, businesses and social service agencies had been established that made the transition for the Vietnamese easier in King County than in other, more homogeneous areas in the country. Markets serving the Asian community, such as Uwajimaya and other small grocery stores in Seattle's Chinatown/International District, were able to help the Vietnamese retain their culinary culture. The Asian Counseling &

Referral Service was called on to help the refugees receive psychological counseling and adjust to their new home.[11] The Employment Opportunities Center helped the newcomers find jobs.[12]

## EARLY OBSTACLES

Unlike the other Asian groups already in King County, the first wave of Vietnamese migrants did not choose to come there.[13] A 1977 study conducted by the Council of Planning Affiliates, an organization sponsored by the United Way of King County, found that many of the refugees "have a pervading sense of rootlessness" and that "depression and anxiety are common."[14] These mental issues helped to postpone the notion of community development, for the refugees were preoccupied with their individual immediate needs for emotional and physical survival.

The first obstacle to adjustment was to recover from the harrowing journeys of escape, the specific details of which are too rich and traumatic to fit within the scope of this essay. In general, the first wave of refugees had to deal with a sudden, chaotic rush to flee with hundreds of other people trying to do the same thing. As one brief example, Loan's family, who left during the fall of Saigon, attempted to escape several times within the span of a few weeks. Describing the experience of finally traveling by water, Loan said, "There was this big naval ship. They boarded everybody and they kept picking up people. It was a cargo ship full of people. They were not prepared for people. There was no food or water. They did fly in bread, water, and food a couple of days out at sea. They passed out a slice of Wonder Bread, your ration for the day."

Most refugees had to leave behind their belongings and build their new life in America from scratch. This was not only because of a lack of room to carry the items, but because the immigrants feared the newly established Vietnamese government and the unknown American officials. Loan said, "My grandfather ordered us to dump everything in the river to destroy our identity. I remember my brother dumping photographs into the river, and I remember thinking, 'I don't think this is right.' I just remember all the photos floating in the river, dumping it. It was a suitcase full."

Besides leaving memories behind, many families had to leave loved ones behind. Thao, at the tender age of 6, found himself suddenly on a boat to America without his mother and four sisters. Thao's father chose to take his three boys away from Vietnam so that they would not be drafted to fight in the war that continued between Vietnam and Laos. The escape was kept secret from the family due to several previous failed attempts. Thao said, "America to me begins one afternoon when my family was having a lunch and then I just heard my dad say to my mom, 'Honey, I'm going to take the boys,' to see my uncle. I remember what we were eating. We were having soup—catfish soup—and rice. We got onto a bicycle—two bicycles—and rode out to the main road, towards the water. The next thing I knew we were loaded onto a boat, and it wasn't long before we were out in the ocean." Thao, half naked because his boxers had blown away when they were hanging up to dry, was at sea for 12 days before a ship finally came and took them to the refugee camp in Hong Kong.

Though the Vietnamese arrived in their new home in America carrying few items, their emotional baggage weighed heavily on their shoulders. The second wave of immigrants, those unable to escape immediately after the fall of Saigon, had survived under a new regime in Vietnam for two to seven years. Many people who had collaborated with the South Vietnamese were put in reeducation camps— described by many as prison—that affected not only their mental state but also their economic status and that of their families. Tuan said, "When the Communists come, I spent three years in the camps. It changed me so much, after I get out of the camps." Nhan's grandmother, through selling food at the market, supported Nhan's family of seven while his father was detained at reeducation camp and his mother was banned from employment.

The Vietnamese who arrived in King County also had to adjust to a loss of status in the community.[15] Many refugees, including the people interviewed, came from middle-class backgrounds in Vietnam before the Communist government took over. By age 8, Nhan had developed a strong sense of himself in Vietnam that was taken away from him when he arrived in the United States. He said, "When I was in Vietnam, I had my little gangster group that I was leading . . . I had control over my world . . . I didn't understand at that age why we had to leave Vietnam. When I was in Vietnam, I had a very happy life. I didn't feel any kind of burden, any kind of restraint, anything like that at all. Looking back, I understand [that] at the time I was very bitter and I didn't like being here at all."

Arriving in the King County area was a major change for the refugees, not only because of the difference in climate and culture, but also because of its size. For some, the image of America was as a bustling, cosmopolitan metropolis like New York City. Tuan, who first went to France after leaving Vietnam, was surprised, and disappointed, by how small Seattle was compared to what he was used to. "Seattle is quiet," he said. "I have a feeling it just like a big village—quite separate, quite backwater. Not a metropolitan city compared to other cities, because I had lived in Paris and Toulouse. It's quiet and just like big village." For the next five years Tuan traveled to France, as he was fluent in the language and preferred the French lifestyle of leisure and socializing. He also preferred the nightlife in France versus the inactivity of Seattle after dark. About living in America, Tuan said, "When I first came here in 1980, the first couple of years were so tough, because I *live* here. But at the same time, I feel like I don't *belong* here."

Similarly, Sinh made a conscious decision to leave Vietnam to pursue the greater opportunities he had heard of in America. Saigon, though underdeveloped compared to Seattle, was crowded with lots of activity. Sinh said, "When I came to Federal Way I was surprised a little bit. What I thought about America was a big city. When I came to Federal Way, it was like countryside to me."

Compared to other areas around the country, King County and Washington State were receptive to the notion of accepting the refugees. The general attitude of the American public at the end of the war was unaccepting of the Vietnamese immigrating into the country. In May 1975, a Gallup poll showed more than half of the Americans were opposed to admitting Vietnamese refugees.[16] Washington State, showing its acceptance of refugees, officially sponsored the first group of Vietnamese to emigrate from the evacuation holding station in Guam.[17]

After the fall of Saigon on April 30, 1975, Washington prepared itself for the first wave of refugees. For example, a group of about 200 Puget Sound families came together to form the Vietnamese-American Association. Their mission was to help Vietnamese refugees adapt to American society. The group included military men and civilians who had married Vietnamese women while on duty during the war. Members of the association had about 1,500 relatives in Vietnam, about 250 of who were expected to be able to come to America. The members advocated for the Vietnamese, trying to dispel fears of refugees spending taxpayers' dollars and stealing jobs. They met with community college and vocational schools to develop ways to best aid the refugees.[18]

Overall, the churches and social service agencies that sponsored Vietnamese in King County were helpful in assisting with the resettlement process. Sinh's sponsor was a member of the Lutheran church in Des Moines with whom he lived for a month. Sinh, who came to America with his wife, said, "They were very good to me. They took time to show me around just like when I told them I want to go to school first. I didn't know much about the country, and they took time to take me around and introduce me to other members of the church, particularly young members, so I would be more comfortable hanging around younger people."

Loan's family was one of the last to leave Camp Murray, the refugee camp near Tacoma that processed about 1,650 refugees. People could not leave the camp until they were sponsored, so it took a long time before an organization would sponsor Loan's large family, who refused to be split up. Loan said, "The churches were really nice. They temporarily put us down in the basement of the church. It was a nice big Presbyterian church. They helped us rent the house—it was a modest home, but we were so used to living in cramped quarters. We were there for about a year before we moved to a three-bedroom apartment."

With the second wave of refugees, Vietnamese in America were sponsoring relatives to come to the States. Though their sponsors shared the same language and were either immediate or extended family, the new arrivals could not depend too much on their sponsors since they were still relatively new themselves. Thao lived with his uncle in Ballard for a year. Thao said, "They did what they could, but they were busy themselves. They had kids going to college. Their family was older. They were helpful when we really needed them, but they weren't hovering over us, taking us everywhere. My dad had to get a car and do everything by himself."

Tuan was sponsored by his brother and lived with him until he was able to afford his own home in preparation to receive his wife and children, whom he left behind in Vietnam. Though his brother's house was large and located in the nice Seattle neighborhood of Magnolia, Tuan was still not comfortable. Tuan said, "The first year was so terrible, I never have feeling that I sleep in my house. I feel so alien, so—I don't know—so temporary. I never had a feeling that it was my house, but after a while, it's my home."

The later portion of the second wave of refugees had to deal with Vietnamese who had already adjusted to American life for about seven years. Though they were relatives and family members, a growing cultural gap made living together a source of conflict. Nhan was sponsored by his mother's older sister, who had two daughters born on American soil. Though his cousins were younger than he was, he had to address them with the Vietnamese term of respect "*chi*," which means sisters of a higher rank. Nhan said, "I remember I didn't like them very much because they were really stuck up, I thought. They didn't speak much Vietnamese, and I didn't speak English at all, and so they always would have attitudes, saying things [in English] purposely so I wouldn't understand . . . When I first came over I didn't dress the way they did, and when we go grocery shopping they would stay as far away from me as possible."

Communication, both with Vietnamese immigrants and the wider American public, was critical in the period of early adjustment. Knowing English prior to coming to America was a tremendous benefit. Tuan said, "I learn English by reading when I was young because French and English are very similar. When I was young, I liked to read. In Vietnam, there is a market for old books. I like to read *National Geographic*, so I learned to read that way. And after this I learned English by watching television. And I would go to school learn English."

In Vietnam, Sinh studied English in high school, college, and private school. His interest in community building began early when he organized and taught English to refugees in camps. Sinh knew that in order to achieve success and further help his people, he had to learn more English. But finding time and money to take English classes took a strong commitment and willingness to work harder. Sinh said, "The first question my sponsor ask me is what kind of job I want. I said, 'I'm young, I'd like to study English.' He said, 'Sinh, you can't go to school because you don't have money.' I said, 'That would be fine. Get me a job in the evening, so I can go to school.' I told him my life would not be interesting if I don't understand the life, the culture, the community. So he hesitantly agreed that I can do it."

For younger refugees, education was a source of culture shock. Thrown into American schools, they found that language barriers prohibited communication between teachers and students. Still dealing with his new home, Thao, then 6, was put in first grade just two months after he arrived. Thao said, "My whole world was turned upside down. My mom wasn't there. Everything was unfamiliar. I had to learn English. I was going to school separated from my father. I went to school not knowing where the bathroom was. I had to point to my teacher . . . It sped up my growth, coming to America."

Minh, Cuc and Muoi Nguyen arrive at SeaTac Airport. Note "Inter-governmental Commission for Migration" bag. Photograph appeared in *Pacific Magazine*, June 29, 1986, *Seattle Times*. Courtesy of the *Seattle Times*, Matt McVay, Staff photographer.

Making friends and feeling comfortable in the education system was difficult, not only because of language barriers but also because of age. Vietnamese parents often changed the age of their children on paper in order to fit the grade level they believed would be most appropriate for them. Loan, at the preadolescent age of 12, was put in a younger class because her father wanted to give her a couple more years to learn English. Her Vietnamese friends were her age, but they were in older classes. Loan said, "I ended up in the fifth grade. Looking back, suddenly you're in class and you're with babies. I'm supposed to be in junior high school and I'm sitting here with babies. The whole environment, the whole way it was set up, was uncomfortable . . . Group eating was very strange. That first year I starved myself. I didn't eat. They would line you up at lunchtime. It was chaotic with a bunch of screaming kids."

Nhan, unlike Loan, was put one grade higher than he had been in Vietnam. His aunt registered him for the fourth grade because she believed the American education system was very far behind that of Vietnam. Nhan, in third grade in

Vietnam, had learned a lot of the multiplication that American children were only just beginning to learn in fourth grade. Nhan, agreeing with his aunt, said, "So I was ahead of everybody except for the language . . . I felt very vulnerable again. I was the second Asian kid in school. The first Asian kid was Vietnamese, but he was very stuck up too."

In the early 1980s, Vietnamese immigrants remained a mystery for both students and teachers, especially in areas outside Seattle. The result of the ignorance was sometimes discrimination, both subtle and direct. Nhan, who never misbehaved in school, told a story about his first teacher in Federal Way, who blamed him for a mess made in the cafeteria. Though the other children validated Nhan's innocence and another student even admitted to spilling the juice, the teacher insisted on calling his parents and making Nhan stay after school—a big deal for a normally well-behaved child. Later in the year, Nhan's teacher commented "foreign food stinks" when Nhan brought a Vietnamese dish to a school picnic. Nhan said, "I didn't know discrimination at that time. Looking back now, my fourth-grade teacher was extremely racist. The other kids were so supportive of me . . . I didn't know I was different at all except for the language thing. The whole racial difference wasn't there for me at all . . . I wasn't aware of the racial issues enough at that age. I just know it didn't feel good."

## GRASSROOTS COMMUNITY DEVELOPMENT

Slowly, Vietnamese families began to gather with each other as they settled into their new surroundings. Working through initial individual adjustment issues, the community began to develop. Tuan said, "In the '80s, we had lots of programs for welfare, for the newcomer. We don't have to work much, so we have a lot of spare time, free time, time to socialize and get together a lot."

Families who were in the refugee camp at Camp Murray and resettled throughout Pierce and King counties became friends. Cultural necessities such as having a place to worship and buying Vietnamese groceries were discussed at social gatherings. Loan said, "In the beginning, people really reached out to each other. The community was really tight. The first person who died, the funeral was so big, I think everybody in town went to the funeral—hundreds and hundreds of people. Everybody then knew each other from camp, and on the weekend people would be at my parents' house, having huge community get-togethers. They cooked and we had to clean the house, cater to all the guests, with men smoking up the house. They were talking about community, creating temples, grocery stores—you know, things to organize ourselves."

Seattle, with its thriving Chinatown, was a destination for cultural necessities. Vietnamese-Americans from all parts of King County and beyond would travel to Seattle to get groceries. Loan, living in Tacoma, said, "That was a big event for us. On the weekends, we would pile into the big station wagon because there was a bunch of us . . . This was pre–child seat belt laws: four of us would be in [the back]. I don't know how they managed to pack the groceries with us, on top of us . . . Everybody would shop there."

Social services also connected the community. English as a Second Language (ESL) classes offered by colleges, schools, and agencies became a place to befriend other Vietnamese in the area. Adults attended community colleges, such as Highline Community College, for ESL classes on top of their full-time jobs. Youths and children would be taken out of school for a couple of hours each day for ESL classes that often took place in another separate school. Sinh said, "At Highline [Community College] I met some Vietnamese there. The first time I met Vietnamese, I was like, 'Oh wow, there's another Vietnamese here.' They took me to the Vietnamese market at the time—there was only one in town here. We shopped for some Vietnamese food. That was very exciting."

Van, though she came to America as a baby, needed to take ESL classes when it was time for her to start school. Sponsored by the Lutheran church in Ballard, Van's family lived in Blue Ridge, a very good Seattle neighborhood. Most of the people living there at the time, according to Van, were white and elderly, with very few other children her age. Though she lived in a homogeneous neighborhood, Van became friends with other Vietnamese through ESL classes. She even spoke Vietnamese at school. Asian culture was celebrated in her school, including assemblies for the Lunar New Year, where there would be dancing, singing and *li xi*—red envelopes stuffed with dollar bills. Van said, "Living in Seattle during that time, we really did experience a really supportive immigrant community because there were so many refugees by the mid-'80s that the ESL programs were really large. There were a lot of Vietnamese, Southeast Asian kids in the programs."

As Vietnamese began to gather with each other, they were able to build establishments that they needed. Grocery stores that sold authentic Vietnamese food and tailor shops that made *ao dai*, traditional Vietnamese dresses, were started in homes, basements, and garages. Within their first couple years of living in America, a few Vietnamese families were able to begin small businesses in Seattle. For example, Broadway Cleaners and Dryers on Capitol Hill was opened by a Vietnamese couple who borrowed money from parishioners of their sponsor church.[19] The Mekong, a shop featuring Oriental foods and gifts, was established in the Chinatown–International District in April 1977.[20] In the early 1980s, Vietnamese opened the Asia BBQ and Fast Food on Jackson Street, in the same neighborhood.[21] Before long, Vietnamese businesses, travel agencies, jewelry stores, and hair salons dominated Jackson from Fifth to Twelfth avenues, creating a new four-block area called "Little Saigon."[22]

Many Vietnamese people in America were sending a large portion of their income back to their families in Vietnam, which delayed their ability to build up capital and open businesses. After a couple of years in America, Tuan and his brother made a decision to do something together. With $30,000 in capital they had built up from refinancing their house, they opened a market in Little Saigon. Though

Vietnamese green grocer in the International District, one of many small businesses opened by Vietnamese-Americans. Courtesy of the *International Examiner*.

Tuan was able to make a living, he closed the store down after two years when he realized the grocery business was not for him. Tuan moved on to the restaurant business, where he now has several successful establishments.

Little Saigon and Vietnamese establishments around the county offered opportunities for local Vietnamese to remain connected to their culture. In 1979, the Vietnamese Buddhist Congregation was able to throw a large celebration for Buddha's birthday that brought 340 Vietnamese Buddhists to the temple.[23] The ceremony also marked the grand opening of the temple, a two-story house at 1651 S. King Street that the congregation had bought two years before.[24] Vietnamese re-created nightlife in Vietnam through Vietnamese pop-music dances that started in people's homes. The first larger dance was held in 1978 at a Filipino church. Every year, the dances were held at various locations, such as Seattle's Doubletree Inn and Seattle University, and were put on by an enterprising Vietnamese refugee, Minh Huong Nguyen. The music presented pre-1975 songs from Saigon and more modern Vietnamese songs. By 1986, the dances had become elaborate dress-up affairs with a ballroom-type atmosphere.[25]

With the pervasiveness of Vietnamese culture, King County residents became more acquainted with their new immigrant neighbors. Vietnamese eateries became exotic places for the wider public to frequent. People ventured into Little Saigon, known for its inexpensive businesses, to try French-influenced Vietnamese sandwiches—fresh baguettes with special ham, peppers, pickles and carrots, paté, and soy sauce.[26] Non-Vietnamese could be spotted in windows fogged by steaming bowls of *pho*, Vietnamese beef noodle soup. Over time, Vietnamese food and restaurants have become mainstream staples of King County culture.

## NEW CHALLENGES

Vietnamese who settled in King County were fortunate in many ways to have a previously developed pan-Asian community. However, the mix of Asian groups was not always advantageous. Vietnamese immigrants encountered misunderstanding and discrimination from within the Asian community. In finding a location for his first business, Tuan had to forge through regulations in Chinatown. The landlord renting out the space, a Japanese-American, was at first reluctant to have a Vietnamese immigrant as a tenant. Tuan said, "[The landlord asked] 'What are you?' We say that we are Vietnamese. He said, 'No! No! No Vietnamese!'" The next day, however, the landlord called him back and accepted Tuan's business proposal.

Tuan attributed the landlord's hesitation to the fact that Americans, Asian and otherwise, did not know the Vietnamese community. During the first and second waves of Vietnamese refugees, the other incoming and recent Asian immigration was from Korea. Though both groups were recent settlers in the area, they arrived under very different circumstances. Koreans often arrived in America as professionals or with economic capital. They weren't fleeing from their home country and were able to obtain assets such as cars and nice houses. Living in Federal Way in the early 1980s, Nhan encountered only two groups of Asians: Vietnamese and Koreans. Nhan said, "We both had our pride. The teachers would separate us, with the Korean students over here and the Vietnamese over there, because you couldn't mix us. We'd always get into fights. At that age, looking back, I think it was about being boat people. So we're like the lower class . . . The other kids looked down on us. We have our pride and we have to stand up for ourselves and who we are; without thinking about it, we do it automatically."

In Washington State, political coalitions of Asian Americans had grown by the early 1970s. Chinese- and Japanese-Americans had long-established associations; Filipinos had organized into unions. The Asian-American community worked to establish the Commission on Asian Pacific American Affairs (CAPAA) in the governor's office.[27] Though the political and social organization of Asian Americans ultimately benefited Vietnamese immigrants, on some levels the successful organization and activism of other Asian groups was frustrating for the Vietnamese. Loan, who advanced to become associate director of CAPAA in 1990, said, "For the Vietnamese group, I had to remind myself that we're a young group because when you work side by side with a group that has been here longer, their infrastructure is much more developed because they have been here longer. We had some patience, but there was always this anxiousness, why can't we do this, you know? I guess you're going to have to accept that the other groups had the same growing-pains process and you can't skip it. You have to accept that it is the nature of the community at the time, when people are more concerned with economic survival and they don't have a whole lot of time for political involvement."

As the Vietnamese and Asian community developed, they learned, and continue to learn, about each other's culture and how to work together. Tuan said, "I think there is more mixing now, after a while; we are more accepting, more understanding. It take a while to build a relationship; even in our association, a lot of people don't like Chinese, they mistrust the other side. But I still believe we got to work together because we try to put people together, not divide them. I think that take a while. I believe we got to work with everybody."

The great melting pot of America was a new world of diversity different from the relative homogeneity of Vietnam. King County, in particular, though predominantly Euro-American, offered a mix of cultures from Scandinavian to African-American. This diversity became a source of learning and an impetus to community activism. Living in Seattle, Van found her early days at school were very comfortable. Van said, "I didn't feel like there was anything against me because I was an immigrant or because my family didn't have much, because everybody else didn't have much either." It wasn't until she moved to the homogenous suburb of Shoreline, where the median income at the time was about $60,000, that she came to appreciate diversity. While she was attending high school in Shoreline, Van said, "I was made fun of for being poor, I couldn't talk about my culture at school. In Seattle you could do that, you could talk about [Lunar] New Years. You could talk on a personal level about different culture." Angry about living in Shoreline, Van later harnessed that energy to raise issues of race as editor of the school newspaper.

Similarly, Thao's activism was sparked by his experience with moving around Seattle. Thao's family went from living in Greenwood to Ballard to a housing project in Rainier Vista, a neighborhood in south Seattle that was mainly African-American at that time, interspersed with a handful of Filipino, Chinese, and Caucasian families. Thao said, "I was friendly with everybody. That played a big role in me appreciating diversity . . . I had a very rich history and I was different than everybody else; that's what I always knew, and I always lived with that." After living in Rainier Valley for three years, Thao's family moved back to Ballard, right across the street from the Nordic Heritage Museum. Thao said, "It lacked diversity. It was like two [polar opposites] . . . We didn't really fit in."

The diversity of cultures, though beneficial in ways, also contributed to a common feeling of isolation for Vietnamese-Americans. Loan said, "You never feel like you are hooked into anything. Even though my parents were grounded, I never felt like I was part of any sort of community. I never felt like I was connected. Outside of a few friends you have from school, you're just out there. It is an isolated, awful feeling, growing up that way. Friends that you get to see on the weekend—everything is so cut up. We'd have so many different roles and different lives. You'd have your white friends at school and you'd have your Vietnamese friends [at home]."

One of the things that made Vietnamese such as Loan feel less isolated was working together and building a support system. The Vietnamese student associations at community colleges and the University of Washington were places to begin activism and also foster educational peer support. Sinh became president of the Vietnamese student group at Highline Community College and then was active in the Vietnamese Student Association (VSA) at the University of Washington, where he later transferred in 1979. Through the VSA, Sinh organized annual summer camps for young adults along with the Vietnamese Buddhist temple and the Catholic Church. The retreats were places to begin community development among Vietnamese from Oregon, Washington, and Idaho. It was one of the first opportunities for Vietnamese in the Northwest community to talk to each other and discuss the issues. Advocating for Vietnamese to work together, Sinh said, "Vietnamese at college should be going out and help other Vietnamese refugees in the community. In a way, we are more fortunate. We know the language. We know the culture—[although] not as much as we wanted. At least we know more than a lot of other people."

Vietnamese immigrants, through organized grassroots efforts and informal social assistance, found ways to reach out to the community. They tried to help each other find jobs, learn English, and buy houses, all during their own personal time. As a business owner in Little Saigon, Tuan began to feel the need to officially form a network for Vietnamese businesses. In the mid-1980s, as Little Saigon began to grow, burglaries and break-ins increased. Tuan resorted to his own means of controlling crime, including owning a gun, until he decided to network with other Vietnamese businesses. After a meeting with the police, the community of Vietnamese business owners discovered that they shared similar problems. The Little Saigon Business Development Association was formed shortly after that. Tuan said, "At that time, I see nobody do anything. And myself, I like social, I like to talk, share my ideas with other people, spend time together, and share problems . . . I think that maybe that's why I like to work with the community. To have something for ourself, build a home for us, to feel that we belong here."

In the mid-1980s, however, Vietnamese immigrants were still trying to become grounded with their own lives before they could move on to helping others. Despite coming from middle-class backgrounds in Vietnam, the jobs they found were often menial. Many of the jobs available were with government agencies in positions such as laundry, cleaning, or maintenance. Though they may have disliked what they were doing, many of the immigrant adults with families kept their jobs up until retirement.

The older generation remained closely tied to the homeland and its values, so much so that it perhaps hindered their progress in America. Van's father, a very traditional man and proud of his own culture, was stubborn about holding on to Vietnamese tradition. Because of his tight grip on his culture, he made a conscious effort not to learn English. With residual sentiments from the war, Van's father disliked Americans. Because of his unwillingness to assimilate, he never got a job outside of his janitorial work. Staying within his community, doing charitable work for newcomers and being active politically, was a way for him to keep his self-esteem. Van said, "A lot of people say if he doesn't like it here why doesn't he just leave? Well, he really doesn't have anywhere else to go. He really can't go where he wants to go, which is home."

Van's father, like some other older Vietnamese, was more interested in the politics back home than in his new home in America. For those who retain a strong connection to their homeland, the struggle to continue the battle against the Communist government in Vietnam remains at the forefront of their political agenda. At times, disagreement about this priority has caused extremists to label opposition as "Communists." In a *Seattle Times* newspaper article on August 31, 1978, a Vietnamese musician reported death threats that he received from other Vietnamese after he performed at the Paramount Northwest Theater on September 2—Vietnamese Independence Day. The musician was labeled a Communist and the show was boycotted by the "Provisional Anti-Communist Committee."[28]

For Vietnamese immigrants attempting to take leadership roles in the Vietnamese-American community, overseas politics became a barrier to community development. It wasn't necessarily the nature of the anti-Communist movements that prevented community progress but the ongoing disagreements about the direction of the community. As a group just forming, it had no process for addressing disagreements and opposition to leadership. At a community event, Sinh voiced his opposition for singing the former Vietnamese national anthem. He argued that the song was out of date and no longer necessary. His opinion resulted in some Vietnamese later calling him a Communist for not supporting their tradition. Discussing the issue of disputes over homeland politics, Sinh said, "We need to focus on the issues here in America . . . But other people took that opportunity to undermine my leadership in the community. There are some power players in the community. They don't want another person [to be a leader]. If you challenge that, you are in big trouble."

The ongoing clash between differing Vietnamese-American political groups is one reason why Tuan requested a pseudonym for this project. As his hope is to continue working in the community, he prefers not to stand out. His wish is to be part of the community in a way that makes everyone comfortable. In response to the homeland politics, Tuan quoted a phrase in Vietnamese: "*De la nha minh. Do la que minh.*" (Translation: "This is our home. That is our homeland.")

The more settled the Vietnamese became in America, the farther the old life in Vietnam drifted away. Though the culture of Vietnam—its food and festivals—was being preserved in King County, the values of Vietnamese tradition were harder to maintain. Family members in Vietnam were reunited with settlers in America, reminding assimilated Vietnamese-Americans of their roots. Thao, who had been living in Seattle with just his father during the formative years of ages 5 to 8, was reunited with his mother and sisters. Suddenly, he had a mother from Vietnam telling him what to do. Thao said, "I prayed every day for my mother to come, and when your mom comes off the ramp at Sea-Tac, you thought, that was your mom and that was your sisters." Thao, who had lost some of the traditional rules of family respect through growing up in Seattle, would say things to his mother that she mistook to be rude or curt. Thao said, "I had to learn to be quiet . . . The relationship was tough. Being so far from each other, we had to be reacquainted."

The tension between traditional Vietnamese culture and modern American values grew steadily as the younger generation attended school. The culture clash played a significant role in the development of young community activists, such as Loan, Thao, Nhan, and Van. Fighting Confucian gender roles and responsibilities that carried over to America became fuel for their fire. Growing up, Loan took on the responsibility of cooking for her six siblings while her mother was at work. Her brothers, meanwhile, were encouraged to play chess or music and take tae kwon do classes. Loan resented her role as a female and became quite rebellious. Loan said, "I didn't have that time to be a child. It's just that everybody was so busy—busy adjusting, working, raising kids, living in culture with different values." When it came time for Loan to attend college, she made a bold decision to go to the University of New Orleans. At the time, in keeping with Vietnamese tradition, a daughter or son moving out of the house was considered disrespectful and showed a lack of gratitude to the parents. Loan said, "My mom felt uncomfortable telling their friends that their daughter had moved away to college, so they would tell people I was at the [University of Washington]."

Like Loan, Van grew up with issues concerning gender. Her half-Chinese, half-Vietnamese father, true to traditional values, wished his first child had been a boy and thus treated Van as a son. A tomboy when she started school, it wasn't until she hit puberty that her father expected her to be more like a girl—less aggressive and more demure. The confusion in gender expectations became a source of major strife between her and her father. Now Van has come to understand that her father suffered from his own issues of identity. Not only was he doing janitorial work that was considered lower-skilled than what he had done in Vietnam, but his wife was making more money in her jobs as a garment worker and a cook. To compensate for his lowered status as an Asian man, he used traditional disciplinary actions on his wife and children in the form of abuse that was no longer acceptable in America. As a result, he alienated his family and lost his role as the revered head of household. Van said, "I hated him for many, many years. I understand now, because all of his self-esteem was taken away from him and that kind of emasculated his role in the family."

The loss of the traditional filial hierarchical structure was difficult for older Vietnamese to deal with in the new country. Parents, holding on to the values they grew up with in Vietnam, could not control their children in familiar ways. In Nhan's family, power struggles built up over the years, and Nhan's father, after waiting for Nhan to reach the American legal age of adulthood kicked him out of the house at age 18. Nhan said, "I was the only child in the family who didn't accept what he put out. By high school, I was old enough to rebel. I knew what was good for me." Being told to leave the house was a big deal in the Vietnamese community. Other families passed judgment on Nhan since, back in Vietnam, parents did not kick out sons or daughters unless they had been extremely bad. As a result, Nhan, unable to ask for support from his community, moved to Seattle and built a life of his own.

As the younger generation attended college and embarked on their careers, their pursuits became less about survival and more about emotional fulfillment. Parents, still enmeshed in the immigrant mentality, encouraged their children to choose traditional and prosperous professions, such as medicine and engineering. The lack of encouragement for social and political careers hindered the development of community activists and leaders. Van, who now works at a nonprofit Asian-American arts organization, struggled to obtain her parents' approval for her choice to work in the community versus at a corporation where she could earn a higher income. Her parents, after living in America for only 10 years, owned a nice house in Shoreline and had paid off more than two-thirds of the mortgage. Van said, "They look down on me for not being as careful with money as them, [for not] being as frugal. Up until recently, they have not been understanding of what I'm shooting for, what my goals are in life."

Thao, now executive director of the nonprofit organization Vietnamese American Business Development of South Seattle (VABDOSS), has taken a lower salary than what he could be making had he followed his parents' wishes for him to become a doctor or businessman. Thao started his political activity early, as freshman class president in high school. Back then, his parents argued for him to stop his extracurricular activities and focus on his studies. Thao said, "I just like contributing, doing things that are meaningful . . . I wasn't the model child. I wanted to do things in social service, be in law. They didn't see where the money was coming from. In a way it was bad for me because I didn't get their support."

For a brief period, after obtaining a degree in political science at the University of Washington, Thao did heed his father's hopes and went into financial and estate planning. He didn't like the clients or the people he was working for. He now finds satisfaction at VABDOSS. Thao said, "It's been very rewarding. It's very fitting for me, my personality, my background, the vision that I have for the Vietnamese community. It's a good place for me to be."

The sense of building community was critical in having a satisfying life. For community leaders, this satisfaction took priority over wealth. Loan, like Thao, worked unhappily in the corporate world. Though working at CAPAA was the lowest-paying job she had ever had, Loan was happy. Loan said, "It wasn't until I started working in the community here when I felt grounded, connected to a community. I think deep inside I wanted to belong somewhere . . . so I can make sense of my environment and my role in it. I was working at those other places, and I still felt that sense of isolation. The sense of purpose was totally missing in my life."

The driving force for young community activists has slowly become more about the nature of the work and not necessarily about their ethnicity. Early on, Nhan was a volunteer at Harborview as a patient liaison and he always wanted to help others. He said, "I don't think it's being Vietnamese that makes me interested in social work. I don't think the war affected me that much. I think it was the way I was raised." Back in Vietnam, Nhan's mother would have her children give money to a homeless person, teaching them to love all people. The value of social work was instilled in Nhan's family so much that Nhan is a health educator, one brother is a social worker, his older sister is doing home-care coordination, and his other brother is a Buddhist monk.

As the Vietnamese-American community grows, its members' lives become more and more anchored in America. The Vietnamese language is getting lost, even among those who were once fluent. The question arises as to what will happen to the community as Vietnamese culture becomes but family folklore. In King County, as Vietnamese achieve well-paying jobs and move out to the suburbs, will they want to work at their family's grocery store or restaurant in Little Saigon? As isolation becomes less prevalent, will there be a strong desire and need to build community?

The contributions of Vietnamese can be found all over the area, from businesses to social work and community services. The overall welcoming of Vietnamese immigration is important to remember as King County residents and Vietnamese-Americans continue to build the community. As early as 1977, the Reverend John Huston, an Episcopal priest with the Washington Association of Churches, said, "I think it is time to stop calling them 'refugees' and start calling them 'new Americans.' They are now, to all intents and purposes, permanent residents of our state and community."[29] The words remain true today.

## NOTES

[1] Loan Nguyen, interview with author, 13 December 2001.

[2] Sinh Nguyen, interview with author, 10 December 2001.

[3] Van Diep, interview with author, 14 December 2001.

[4] Tuan, interview with author, 11 December 2001.

[5] Thao Tran, interview with author, 10 December 2001.

[6] Nhan Thai, interview with author, 11 December 2001.

[7] Hien Duc Do, *The Vietnamese Americans* (Connecticut: Greenwood Press, 1999), 25.

[8] *Ibid.*

[9] Matt Miletich, "How Vietnamese refugees are doing," The *Seattle Times*, 21 August 1977, Pacific Magazine, 4.

[10] Do, *The Vietnamese Americans*, 42.

[11] Miletich, "How Vietnamese refugees are doing," 4.

[12] *Ibid.*

[13] Ronald Takaki, *Strangers From a Different Shore: A History of Asian Americans* (New York: Penguin Books, 1989), 448.

[14] Miletich, "How Vietnamese refugees are doing," 4.

[15] Gail Nomura, "The Asian American Community," in *Peoples of Washington: Perspectives on Cultural Diversity*, edited by Sid White & S. E. Solberg (Pullman: Washington State University Press, 1989), 152.

[16] Do, *The Vietnamese Americans*, 29.

[17] Nomura, "The Asian American Community," 149.

[18] "Local group wants to help," The *Seattle Times*, 2 May 1975, A9.

[19] Miletich, "How Vietnamese refugees are doing," 4.

[20] *Ibid.*

[21] Doug Chin, *Seattle's International District: The Making of a Pan-Asian American Community* (Seattle: International District Press, 2001), 100.

[22] *Ibid.*

[23] "Vietnamese mark Buddha's birthday," The *Seattle Times*, 14 May 1979, B8.

[24] *Ibid.*

[25] Paul de Barros, "Echoes of Saigon," The *Seattle Times*, 19 January 1986, L1.

[26] Carey Quan Gelernter, "Taste of Saigon awaits the visitor," The *Seattle Times*, 15 March 1986, G2.

[27] Gail Nomura, "The Asian American Community," 152.

[28] Timothy Eagan, "Vietnamese community split by political strife," The *Seattle Times*, 31 August 1978, B10.

[29] Miletich, "How Vietnamese refugees are doing," 4.

# CONTRIBUTORS

ED DIAZ, born in New York City, has made Seattle, Washington his home. His career in the United States Navy and extensive travel fueled his love of history. Diaz is the founder of the Association for African American Historical Research and Preservation. He has completed and released a compilation of fiction (*Stories by Cayton: Short Stories by Susie Revels Cayton*) and has compiled and edited *Horace Roscoe Cayton: Selected Writings*, two volumes of articles by Horace Roscoe Cayton, publisher of the *Seattle Republican* (1892-1913) and *Cayton's Weekly* (1916-1920). Diaz is in the process of editing a new release of the 1926 African American Achievement publication *Who's Who in Religious, Fraternal, Social, Civic and Commercial Life in Washington State.*

ROBERT S. FISHER was a professional restaurant cook for twenty years. His interests include local and culinary history. He has a Bachelors and a Masters degree in history and is currently the Collections Manager at the Wing Luke Asian Museum. He lives with his wife on a small farm in Kitsap County.

ERIC L. FLOM is a 1991 graduate of the University of Washington, where he majored in political science and history. From 1992 to 1995, he reviewed film for the *Enterprise*, a weekly newspaper in south Snohomish County. In 1997 he published *Chaplin in the Sound Era* (McFarland & Company, Inc.), an analysis of Charlie Chaplin's final seven motion pictures. Flom has contributed to www.historylink.org (an online encyclopedia of Seattle and King County history) and the *Seattle Times* on film and theatre related topics. He is in the process of completing a book on the Seattle theatrical appearances of several well-known silent film stars.

MARIANNE FORSSBLAD is the Director of the Nordic Heritage Museum in Seattle. Born in Sweden, Forssblad came to Seattle in 1964. She holds Masters in Library Science and Scandinavian Language and Literature, both from the University of Washington. Forssblad continues her studies as a Ph.C. in Scandinavian Studies. Scandinavian immigration is a focus of Forssblad's writings, and she keeps current with annual study trips to Scandinavia.

CHARLES P. LEWARNE. A King County native, Charles P. LeWarne has written elsewhere about the small town of his childhood, Bellevue in the 1930s and 40s. He has a Ph.D. in history from the University of Washington. He was an early president of the Pacific Northwest Historians Guild and is also active in other historical and heritage groups. His publications include *Utopias on Puget Sound, 1885-1915; Washington State,* a secondary school textbook; *Washington: A Centennial History,* co-authored with Robert Ficken; and numerous articles. A retired high school teacher living in Edmonds, he is married to Pauline LeWarne.

RONALD E. MAGDEN is currently writing a book on the history of the Seattle Buddhist Temple. Other publications include *Furusato: Tacoma-Pierce County Japanese, 1888-1998* (1998); *A History of Seattle Waterfront Workers, 1884-1934* (1991); *The Working Longshoreman* (1991); and, *The Working Waterfront: The Story of Tacoma's Ships and Men* (1982). Magden received his Ph.D. from the University of Washington in 1964.

NHIEN T. NGUYEN is currently Editor of Seattle's *International Examiner,* an Asian American news journal. Previous to this, Nhien was Development Director at the Wing Luke Asian Museum, participating in program development and outreach to the Southeast Asian community in the region. Her freelance writing includes articles in *Colors Northwest Magazine* and *A.Magazine.* She earned her Bachelors degree at Macalester College, St. Paul, Minnesota in political science and philosophy. A recipient of the Seattle Arts Commission 2002 Literary Artist Award, Nhien has completed her first novel based on her life experiences as a Vietnamese American.

MICHAEL REESE is a native Northwesterner. Born and raised in Portland, Michael earned his B.A. from Reed College. He currently lives in Seattle, where he is a Ph.D. candidate in history at the University of Washington. His essay in this volume was drawn from his dissertation, "Welfare States, Border States: Welfare in Washington State and British Columbia, 1910-1960."

KAY F. REINARTZ approaches Pacific Northwest history "from the bottom up," by studying the community and people who are the lifeblood of the community. Her community history books including "*Passport to Ballard* (1988), *Tukwila, Community at the Crossroads* (1990), *Queen Anne Community on the Hill* (1992) and, *Home Away from Home, The Renton Senior Center* (1993) have received national and regional awards. Reinartz's most recent Northwest history book, *The Inland Northwest, 1940-2000, A Dynamic Region in Transition,* is slated for publication late in 2002. Reinartz holds advanced degrees from the University of Minnesota, the University of New Mexico and Texas A & M University. Her doctorate is from the University of New Mexico in American Studies. A native of Minnesota, she lives in the Ballard district of Seattle with her husband Richard Frith.

ELIZABETH SALAS is Associate Professor in the Department of American Ethnic Studies at the University of Washington. Salas was graduated from UCLA with a Ph.D. in American History in 1987. Her book *Soldaderas in the Mexican Military: Myth and History* (1990) has gone into four printings and is available in both English and Spanish editions. She has written several articles about Mexican American women politicians in New Mexico.

COLL-PETER THRUSH is a doctoral candidate in history at the University of Washington, where he is completing a dissertation entitled "The Crossing-Over Place: Urban and Indian Histories in Seattle." Thrush's work has appeared in the *Western Historical Quarterly, Pacific Northwest Forum*, and anthologies of Native American, women's, and Asian-American history. He was co-curator of the award-winning exhibit *A Change of Worlds: Photographs and Artifacts from Puget Sound Native Americans* at the Museum of History & Industry in Seattle, and he was also a contributor to the Library of Congress's *American Indians of the Pacific Northwest* web site. He has served as visiting faculty at the University of Washington's Bothell campus and at Pacific Lutheran University in Parkland, Washington.

JACQUELINE B. WILLIAMS is an award-winning author of numerous historical essays and books including *Family of Strangers: Building a Jewish Community in Washington State*, co-authored with Molly Cone and Howard Droker (forthcoming, 2003); *Hill With a Future: Seattle's Capitol Hill 1900-1946*; *The Way We Ate: Pacific Northwest Cooking: 1843-1900*; and *Wagon Wheel Kitchens: Food on the Oregon Trail*.

MARY C. WRIGHT served as the editor and project director for *More Voices, New Stories*. She teaches in the American Indian Studies Center and the Department of History at the University of Washington. Wright earned her Ph.D. in 1996 from Rutgers, The State University of New Jersey. Women of the American West, ethnohistory, and cross-cultural relations are the focus of her scholarly work.

# INDEX